E MARIE BELLAMY

SPIRIT-LED

CONSCIENCE

GUIDED

Something is Real

Based on a True Story

Led-by Publishing

Mesa, Arizona
@ledbypublishing.com

Spirit-Led Conscience-Guided: Something is Real
3rd Edition
ISBN: 979-8-234-06243-7
Publisher: Led-by Publishing
@ledbypublishing.com
Mesa, Arizona

Book Cover Design: E.M. Bellamy,
Contributions by: Shannita B. Reid, Lawrence L. Thompkins, Uneka L Reid

INTRODUCTION

Like many people, Crystal is ignorant about the knowledge of God. She believes in God but doesn't know Him personally, and like many others, she believes that God is intangible and sits in heaven on His throne, judging the sins of the world, but nothing could be further from the truth.

God is very much involved in people's lives. Without God, we are nothing. Life can't exist without Him who has given all of us the ability to identify with the world in which we live and to experience its marvelous sensations, but to identify with Him, there has to be a spiritual connection.

The spirit world is different from the physical world you and I live in. It's a mysterious world but just as real as our physical world, which is what you are about to find out when you read that Crystal was able to make a spiritual connection with the creator of the universe in a very profound way. Her true story will enlighten you and, at times, make you laugh. When you aren't laughing, it will move you to tears. As you wipe away the tears from your weeping eyes, Crystal will inspire you with the strength of her character.

As I worked on writing Crystal's story, it was very difficult for her to relive a past that she so much wanted to forget because it was too painful for her to remember. Once she was able to get past the pain,

Crystal understood that her life wasn't any worse because of what she had suffered, and her life is so much better now because of how she chooses to live, and that's by pleasing God in all that she does. She is not perfect, and at times, she does miss the mark of pleasing God, but He is a forgiving God. The truth is she is still growing as a person. We all are.

Crystal doesn't claim the glory for how well her life turned out, which is for the better. She gives God all the glory.

Hanging out at her girlfriend's house, two doors down from where she lives, Crystal and her best friend Bunny are in the living room with both their brothers Ramon and Chad, joking, laughing, and having a good time when in the midst of it all, a thought arises, bringing the hilarity to an end as it dawns on Crystal that she had missed her ten o'clock curfew. Putting all jokes aside, she leaps off the sofa and abruptly says, "I have to go. I'm in trouble."

Leaving her brother Ramon there, Crystal rushes to get home, hoping she wouldn't be.

When she opens the unlocked door, walking into the house at midnight, and on a school night, Maylene is not having it. She yells from her bedroom as she watches Crystal enter through the front door, "Crystal, pack your clothes. I'm sending you to Phoenix to live with your aunt Elleen."

Crystal never saw that coming.

Later in the morning, Maylene enters Crystal's bedroom and calls out her name, "Crystal." She then waits for a response.

Having gone to bed last night with a saddened heart, Crystal groans as she lifts her head off the pillow and says in a low voice, "Yes, Ma'am?"

"I'm leaving for work now. I want you to withdraw from school and pack your things."

While clenching her jaw, Crystal lowers her head onto the bed pillow, instinctively knowing by the firmness of her mother's voice as she gives instructions that she better keep quiet or else.

"Do not put it off until Monday, Crystal, because Sunday at midnight, I am putting you on a plane to Phoenix."

Maylene then walks away, talking as she walks to the front door; "I'll see you when I get home..."

Crystal rolls out of bed, sobbing, "I can't do anything without getting into trouble. Ramon is less than two years older than me—he doesn't have a curfew." She dare not say it too loud.

An eighth grader, Crystal enters the bathroom while calculating on her fingers the number of schools that she has withdrawn from and counts this one as number six.

After washing her face, the sadness quickly turns into anger. Snatching the toothbrush off the shelf, Crystal forcefully brushes her teeth while reflecting on the day, last year, when she was in the backyard of their Phoenix home, swinging a long stick, like it was a sickle, slicing through the tall weeds near the creek and complaining to an unseen presence that is always with her, "I'm tired of moving. I don't want to go to San Diego. I want to stay in Phoenix."

As the scene plays out in her head, the pressure

she uses to brush her teeth is so hard, her gums are on the verge of bleeding but, before it does, she spits the toothpaste out into the bathroom sink.

After leaving the bathroom, still complaining, Crystal slips out of her night gown, “I wish Mama would stop moving us around all the time; and if my sisters and brothers would stay out of those troublesome streets and getting locked up, I wouldn’t be in this situation. I don’t know what she’s trying to save me from. I’m not the problem.”

She then snatches a blouse from the top drawer that matches the skirt she’s wearing and quickly puts them on. After combing her hair into a pigtail, Crystal bursts through the screen door. It slams shut as she stomps down the two steps, leaving the house to go to school.

Walking on an incline alongside the corner store, she then attempts to cross Ocean View, where there’s no traffic light, and when she is safely on the other side of the road, Crystal mimics her mother, repeating the lecture she gave last night, “I’m not going to have you walking in here at all hours of the night, Crystal. I’m not losing you to those streets like I have with your sisters and brothers.”

While envisioning the four siblings in her head, whom her mother referred to, Crystal says to the unseen presence, “It’s not fair. I’m the only one Mama is strict with and enforces her curfew on.”

Spotting a pebble on the sidewalk, she then kicks it into the street.

Approaching the jumping cactus plant growing very close to the sidewalk edge, she sways to the left to avoid being too close. After passing it without getting attacked by its needles, Crystal continues to spew out her frustration, “Yes, the boys are after me for sex, but that doesn’t mean I’m going to give it to them and end up pregnant like my sister Sherry did at sixteen." Crystal glances around at the neighborhood homes. "Shoot, I am only thirteen years old and too scared to get pregnant. Anyway, when I have children, I'm going to be married first."

Sunday night while Crystal sleeps, Maylene rushes into her room yelling, "Crystal, wake up."

Half awake, Crystal quickly gets out of bed fully dressed.

"Get your bag. We have to hurry to the airport. I overslept."

With only minutes to spare before the plane takes off, Maylene stands at the departure gate and hands Crystal a gift wrapped in tin foil. "Here, take this. It's a Christmas gift for the family, and, Crystal, I want you to behave yourself, you hear?"

Frowning and wanting only to please her mother, Crystal takes the gift, mumbling softly, "Yes, Ma'am."

"OK. I'll be writing you, and I'll send money whenever I can."

With her head lowered, Crystal answers, "OK," then lifts it and says softly, "Bye, Mama," as she walks away.

Never flown before, she boards the plane, and is assisted by a jolly stewardess, who leads her to the correct row.

Seated comfortably in the window seat, Crystal gazes out at the dark twinkling sky, and as the plane gained altitude, the view below became an ocean of blankness. Crystal's vivid imagination then conjured up an image of the plane in a nosedive, crashing to the ground. Her head jerks away from the window as she grips the armrest. Skimming the area, she observes the other passenger across the aisle, reading, and he appears to be calm. But, for Crystal, there's not a relaxed muscle in her body. To escape her fear, she lies across all three empty seats in the row, thinking before drifting off to sleep, *If the plane crashes, at least I won't be awake to see it.*

Sleeping the entire flight, Crystal gets off the plane at the Phoenix International Airport and walks into the terminal. Just inside the door, she hears loud voices. Looking in the direction the voices came from, Crystal sees Aunt Elleen and Maylene's other sister, Gayle, standing a short distance away, waving and shouting, "Crystal, we're over here."

On the way to the house, Crystal dozes off in the backseat of the car; and when she's at the house, hours later, sleeping, she opens her eyes, waking up to discover that her cousin Gean, a high school freshman, whom she shares a full-sized bed with, has already left for school.

Out of bed, Crystal crosses the hallway and goes into the bathroom to pee. Afterward, getting back in bed, she lay there thinking about her mother's decision to send her away. The loud TV that's in the living room begins to compete with her thoughts, which are then scattered when she hears Big Mama softly yelling, "Crystal, hun, come turn the TV channel for me. Will you, please?"

As her grandmother sits across the room in a wheelchair, suffering from muscular dystrophy, Crystal switches the TV channels, one by one, until she's told, "That's good. Leave it there. I'll just have to watch that."

"Is there anything else I can do for you, Big Mama?"

"Yes. Make me a Bologna sandwich with tomato and lettuce on it. I am so hungry and make yourself one, too."

Crystal prepares two sandwiches, feeding one to her grandmother, and when she's done eating lunch at the kitchen table, Crystal goes back into the bedroom, where she begins to unpack her small suitcase. While spacing her few clothes apart from Gean's clothes hanging in the closet, Crystal is thinking, *I'm not too keen about this permanent living arrangement.*

She then hangs the last garment and sits on the bed, twiddling her fingers. Looking at the clothes hanging in front of her, Crystal has a thought. Lowering her head, she tells herself, *My life just isn't going to be the same.*

When her cousins, Ervin and Dora, arrive home three hours later from school, their last day until after the holidays, Crystal sits in the doorway of the bedroom. Seeing her there, they blurt out, "Why are you sitting here on the floor?"

Tapping her index fingers together, she smirks and answers, "I'm waiting for you to come home. The last time I was here for the summer, Ervin told me to stay in the room when y'all weren't home."

Dora, the bossy fifth grader who rules the household, glances over her shoulder at her brother and says, "You told her that?"

A seventh grader, Ervin giggles and says, "Crystal, I didn't mean it."

Giving him a serious look, Crystal's voice rises, "Yes, you did."

"Crystal, you've stayed with us many times. We don't have to be home. You're family," says Dora.

They then join Crystal on the floor, rekindling the close bond between them—but for Crystal, it's an awkward feeling, knowing she's not there to visit but to live whether she wants to or not.

After the Christmas holiday, school resumed, and Crystal is now on her way there to enroll.

Trailing behind Ervin and Dora, who are concerned about their mother's tardiness for work, is asking as she walks between them, "Won't the pre-schoolers be standing outside the classroom waiting for you, Momma?"

"My teacher's assistant will be there. She knows I'll be late..."

Their conversation begins to fade from Crystal's consciousness, entering one ear and out the other as her thoughts entertain the uneasiness she's feeling. It's one of the most frustrating and frightening thing to experience for someone who, like herself, is somewhat shy.

Just minutes from the house, they then cross the street and walk onto the school grounds. Crystal again tunes in to the conversation, hearing the end of it as her aunt is saying, "Besides, I only have to walk across the street to my classroom. It's not like I have a long way to go."

Entering the administration office, they walk up to the secretary behind the counter. She asks, "How may I help you?"

"Yes, I am here to enroll my niece."

"Does she have anything from the school where she is transferring from?"

"Yes," says Crystal, handing her the paperwork and then answering questions that only she knows the answers to. Aunt Elleen quickly realizes how well-educated Crystal is about the school enrollment process and, in surprise, says as she hurries to the door, "Crystal, you don't need me; you got this. See you at home, sweetie."

For the next few days, Crystal walks around campus alone, watching all the other kids interact with one another and feeling like the shy weirdo. *Nobody wants to be my friend,* she sobs, dragging her fingers along the length of the chain-linked fence.

Then one day, in the middle of the week, as she's walking behind three female classmates during lunch hour, Crystal begins to think, *Today, somebody is going to be my friend.*

Quickly, conjuring up a plan, she begins walking with a limp. Dragging one foot on the sidewalk it makes a noise, causing the girls to turn and look. Seeing her, they burst out laughing. The four of them become besties.

Within one month, Crystal's natural flair and style for fashion attracts an unrealized popularity among the eighth-graders, which she unknowingly captures the attention of the most popular and attractive boy on campus.

Standing outside her classroom with the girls after lunch, waiting for the school bell to ring, one of Crystal's male classmates runs up to her and blurts, "Crystal. Ward wants to be your boyfriend."

"Oooh," her friends tease.

Not trusting her classmate, she looks around and then asks, "Ward? Who is he?" Then, looking her classmate in the eyes, she says, "You're lying. You're always starting trouble and calling me out of my name. Why should I believe you?"

"When did I call you out of your name?" he asks, pretending to be innocent.

Standing up to him, she says, "Just yesterday, you yelled 'big lips' across the classroom because your feelings were hurt when I ignored you." She then asks snobbishly, "And if this guy likes me, why don't he come tell me himself?"

Crystal's classmate bully points and says, "Look. Here he comes now."

Of a mixed culture, tall with beautiful, dark, wavy hair, he walks toward her, and the moment Crystal's eyes fall upon him, it's love at first sight.

Then, the bell rings.

"I'll see you after school," he says as he hurries to his classroom, two doors down.

Having uncomfortable thoughts, Crystal slides into her seat, sits at her desk with googly eyes, and thinks, *Mama is not going to allow me to have a boyfriend.*

At the end of the school day, Crystal steps outside the classroom and is greeted by Ward, who asks, "Do you mind if I walk you home?"

With those googly eyes, she smiles, "If you want to."

A Saturday afternoon, while sitting on her lower bunk bed in the bedroom that she now shares with both her girl cousins and studying the dress pattern she's going to sew, Crystal overhears Gean softly singing into Aunt Elleen's ears, "Mama, Crystal has a boyfriend."

In surprise, Crystal looks towards the door, questioning herself, *How does she know that?* Her body then tenses up as her aunt's voice rises, "Gean, who?"

"The school librarian's son, Ward. His sister told me," squeals Gean.

Crystal storms out of the room and into the kitchen. Stopping at the door, she shouts, "No, I don't."

Preparing dinner early, Aunt Elleen detects fear in

Crystal's voice and says to calm her, "Crystal, I don't have a problem with you having a boyfriend."

Aunt Elleen's calm voice doesn't help at all. Crystal is still highly upset. Nervously, she answers, "My mama does. She says I'm too young to be courting."

At the stove, Aunt Elleen tries again. "Well, sweetie, you can relax. You live with me now." She then looks over at Crystal. "You can have a boyfriend."

Teasing her, Gean giggles. Crystal looks at her and smiles before turning to leave the kitchen and when she's no longer visible to them, she leaps for joy.

Not sure if she will get away with it, Crystal is in the bathroom, where she sneaks to put on makeup, before school, and is caught in the act as Aunt Elleen pokes her head into the bathroom and says, "Crystal, don't forget it's your turn to come home for lunch to check on Big Mama."

Crystal quickly dips the mascara brush back into its container. Nervously, she asks, "Is it all right if I wear makeup?"

"I don't have a problem with it. You're old enough to."

Standing at the mirror, brushing the black mascara onto her upper eyelashes, smiling, she thinks, *Aunt Elleen isn't strict at all. Mama wouldn't allow it. I'm glad she sent me here.*

At school, Ward rushes out of his classroom, running down the sidewalk toward Crystal's room. Seeing her about to turn the corner, he yells,

"Crystal, wait up." He then says as they begin walking together, "Why do you make me run after you? Every day, for three months, I've been walking you home, right?"

"Yes, but you don't have to."

Ward stops walking and takes her wrist, looking her in the eyes, he says, "I do have to. It's the only time we have together. Why don't you wait for me?"

"When I don't see you at the door, I figure that you're not walking with me, and I have to go straight home to make sure my grandmother is OK." They resume walking. "My grandmother is in a wheelchair. But this month, she'll be leaving to stay with my Aunt Bee in San Diego," Crystal explains.

While holding hands, their arms swing back and forth like a pendulum. "Why didn't you tell me you were one of the speakers at today's school assembly?" asks Crystal.

"I didn't know. The teacher just handed me the speech and had me rehearse it all morning."

"I liked it. You did that very well. In home economics class, I have to model my two sewing projects. It's a graduation requirement, and I have to do it in front of a live audience. I'm scared."

"Why?"

"I'm not good at being in front of people like you are."

"You're talking about the fashion show that's coming up?"

"Yeah."

"Don't worry. I was chosen to be one of the ushers. I'll hold your hand." They smile at each other.

Before leaving her at the door, Ward leans in for a kiss.

Crystal stops him and waves her index finger. "No,

no. No kissing."

As always, he giggles. "See you tomorrow," he says and walks away.

Now inside the house, Crystal says "Hi, Big Mama," and walks past her. Stepping into the hallway, with a big smile, she thinks, *I like that Ward doesn't mention sex.* Then, entering the bedroom, her smile quickly vanishes at the thought: b*ut I know that if I kiss him, sex will be the next thing he wants, and I'll only become his conquest.*

As the teacher's assistant, sewing comes naturally for Crystal, but it isn't as simple for the other girls in the home economics sewing class, who are in an uproar, preparing for the fashion show that's now two days away.

One girl yells, "Crystal, come help us."

Crystal rushes over and stands at the girls' work table. "Y'all are so lucky that I've finished my garments already. Ya'll be in deep trouble without me."

"Girl, you are right, we are lucky. I can't sew to save my life," jokes Cathy, invoking laughter. "I need you to finish this for me."

Crystal looks at her and screams, "Finish it?"

"Please," Cathy begs with praying hands.

"No. You have to. I'll help you."

They worked tenaciously as a team, and on the big night, they all were ready for the show to begin.

Having performed on stage before, Crystal never had to do it alone. She stands behind the closed auditorium curtains with the other girls and is second in line to model while her aunt and cousins are seated in the audience.

Nervously awaiting her turn to walk out on stage,

she begins to coach and encourage herself, *I can do this.*

Then the curtains open. Crystal takes a deep breath. After she quickly reclaims her confidence, the signal is given, and as practiced, she walks to the center stage, making a full circle, and then proceeds to walk the runway, wearing a green and white wrap-around dress with the belt tied in front, strutting as though she's a professional model. The packed auditorium erupts in hysterical cheering.

As she steps off the runway, Ward reaches for her hand and doesn't let go until they are an arm's length apart, causing her to blush as she trots away, excited to model her second garment and looking forward to Friday. The day of graduation.

Dressed in her cap and gown, Crystal is seated in the first chair of the third row, from where she locates Gean and Maylene in the crowd, sitting across the courtyard. Afraid that Gean will squeal on her, Crystal watches them closely, and when she witnesses Gean tapping Maylene on the arm and then pointing to Ward as he marches by, Crystal angrily mumbles, "I knew she was going to tell my mama."

But to Crystal's surprise, Maylene smiles and nods approvingly, which triggers a smile from Crystal. She then watches as Ward approaches her, thinking, *He's so handsome!*

Finally, having time to spend together, Crystal and Ward spent the entire afternoon at the neighborhood park swimming. Nicely tanned, they leave walking under the hot summer sun. Walking side by side, laughing at the silly things he did with friends during the school year, they come to a stop at the street corner, down from where Crystal lives, and Ward suggests as he takes her hand, "Let's talk some more. I'll call you after I get home and take a shower."

He backs up, releasing her hand and winks at her, making her smile.

At the house, Crystal yells into the kitchen phone, "Ward, you didn't shower before calling. I'm still in my bathing suit."

"I did shower. I can't help that you're slow."

"Ha, ha, ha," says Crystal.

He then shares with her, "You know my friends say we're not a couple if we're not having sex."

"What?! They're jealous because they don't have a girlfriend, and your bully friend is jealous because he can't have me."

"We hang out sometimes, but we're not really friends." Getting back on the subject, he asks, "Do you want to have sex?"

"No. Do you?"

"Of course, and I agree with them. That's what couples do."

"So, you're telling me we're not a couple anymore?"

"I'll ask you again. Do you want sex?"

"No," she says, knowing it would end the relationship.

A loud click resonates in her ear. He hung up.

Now, in her bedroom, she flops down on the bed. Cuffing her face with her hands, she says his name, "Ward."

2

Alone, walking home from Yale High School, Crystal glances over her shoulder, looking into Ward's backyard, and has a flashback of this morning when he smiles and says, before passing her as they change classes, "Hi, Crystal," making her smile. Now a sophomore, she still misses him.

Now walking past Percy Elementary and crossing over onto the street that she lives on, Crystal spots a moving van ahead that's parked in front of the house.

Walking alongside it, she steps onto the carport, speculating as she enters the open kitchen door, *I bet Aunt Elleen is going to send me home. I don't want to go.*

"Hi, sweetie," greets her aunt, who approaches her from the empty living room and, surprisingly, in a cheerful mood.

"Hi," says Crystal, expecting her aunt to show

signs of pain from the baseball size knot on her forehead that she received a few nights ago from the fight she had with her husband, who discovered her infidelity but she casually switches by Crystal, walking over to the sink and turns on the water while explaining, "As soon as your cousins get here, I'll be taking you all to stay at your Aunt Gayle's place. I'll be staying at Dillion's for now."

Trying not to sound overjoyed, Crystal watches as her aunt wrings out the wash cloth, responding, "OK," thankful for not being told she was going home to San Diego.

After two weeks, they move out of Aunt Gayle's apartment and into Dillion's house.

Adjusting well to her new schedule, both at school as a sophomore and living with Dillion, Crystal enters the house, expecting to be greeted by her aunt, but, strangely, there's not a sound of her footsteps anywhere or the smell of a savory dinner simmering on the stove. The house is ghostly quiet, disrupting her normal flow of coming home and hearing her favorite aunt's soft, loving voice saying, "Hi, sweetie."

Walking past her aunt's and Dillion's bedroom, Crystal glances inside. Usually, if she isn't anywhere else, she'll be in there, but she's not.

Proceeding down the hallway and into the room she shares with Gean and Dora, Crystal dumps her books on her lower bunk bed and walks out of the room.

Sitting, relaxing, and cooling off from the long walk home, she's watching TV in the family room when the front door opens and closes.

Certain that it's her aunt, Crystal's eyes are fixed

on the doorway, but it's Dillion, whom Aunt Elleen married over the summer while Crystal transitioned into her sophomore year. He comes and stands at the family room door, looking around.

That's strange. Why is he home so early from work?

Dillion then acknowledges her with a nod and walks out. It's when he returns that Crystal learns first-hand how untrustworthy Dillion really is as he stands in the doorway, holding his crouch, staring between her open legs as she's sitting slouched down in the chair, wearing lavender-colored pants and looking like a piece of eye candy.

He licks his lips, and with a lustful desire to have her body, he looks her directly in the eyes, which plainly expresses his intentions. He again walks out of the room.

Immediately, she sits up in the chair and crosses her legs, mumbling, "You better go and *don't come messing with me, either, you sex predator.*"

He's not the first man to lust after her. Sitting and watching TV, her eyes keep switching to the doorway that leads into the kitchen. She then has a flashback of her earlier years, reminding her of the night when she was ten years old, walking to the park to hang out with her brother Ramon and friends.

As she crossed the dirt field and reached the rear section of the hospital, a teenage boy approached her. "Little girl, where are you on your way to?" he asked before grabbing her and wrestling her to the ground. While he lay on top of her, Crystal fought, wiggled, and screamed, "Stop it. Get off of me."

Then, a woman's voice was heard in the distance. The boy quickly stood up and ran off, shouting, "Here I come, Mama."

Crystal's focus quickly shifts back to watching the doorway leading into the kitchen as the flashback fades. Now, in a tight knot, she stares at it, praying, *God, I hope he stays where he's at. I don't want to be raped.*

Then the front entry door opens. Crystal hears her aunt grunt after she releases the heavy paper bags on the kitchen table. Feeling safe, Crystal's tensed muscles relax.

Two weeks go by, and Crystal notices that there's no indication that Dillion is lusting to have her sexually.

With her guard now down, she walks out of the family room, spotting Ervin carrying fishing poles as he and Dillion, now his stepfather, are leaving the house. She takes off running through the living room behind them and yelling, "Wait for me. I'm coming."

Ervin argues as he steps onto the porch, "No, Crystal, you're not dressed, and I'm not waiting on you."

Out of sheer boredom, and wearing a green and white floral housecoat, she gets in the backseat of the car.

From the front, Ervin screams, "Get out, Crystal."

Dillion starts the engine and intervenes, "It's all right, Ervin. Let her come along. We're coming straight home anyway after I drop you off."

Riding across town, Crystal enjoys taking in the scenery, which deflects her attention away from the boredom she had been experiencing earlier.

Arriving at the city park, thirty minutes later, she habitually takes Ervin's place when he gets out of the front seat, totally disregarding that she and

Dillion are now alone, together, and with her naïveté jolted, Crystal feels the touch of Dillion's hand caressing her thigh. *Dang, I forgot about this horny idiot,* she thinks, and then realizes as the vehicle begins to coast, *it's too late now to get in the backseat.*

Crystal quickly removes his hand, screaming, "Stop! Don't touch me. I will tell my aunt about you."

He attempts to touch her again. Crystal moves closer to the door, grabbing the door handle, saying to him, "I'll leap out of this car if I have to."

He draws back his hand and says, "Tell my wife. She is not going to believe you over me. I'm her husband; she'll believe me before she'll believe you. You're just her niece."

The entire ride home is a heated confrontation. As soon as Dillion drives onto the carport and stops, Crystal leaps out of the car, running.

Just before she opens the door to go tell her aunt, her memory is triggered by a childhood incident: swimming at the neighborhood pool, Crystal, at nine years old, hurried out of the pool dripping wet and ran up to the lifeguard, pointing and saying, "That boy is feeling on me."

The lifeguard looked down at her and asked, "Little girl, what do you mean, he's feeling on you?"

His question made her feel foolish. Now, seven years later, facing a similar experience, Crystal enters the house, thinking as she walks past her aunt's bedroom, *she's going to question me if I tell her, so I can't because I'll be the one looking foolish.*

With her mind now changed, Crystal lies across her bed, restrategizing what her next move will be. "Someone will believe me," she mumbles.

The following Saturday morning, Aunt Elleen, dressed up for a special event, yells as she and Dillion walks out of their bedroom, “We’ll be back as soon as it ends.”

Crystal, hiding in the bedroom from Dillion, rushes out of it, down the hallway, and walks into the kitchen, where Dora and Ervin stand around the kitchen table preparing waffles, their Saturday morning favorite. Confiding in them, she stands between them and says, “Ervin, guess what?”

“What?”

“Dillion was feeling my legs after we dropped you off at the park last Saturday.”

Ervin lifts open the hot waffle iron and goes on the defense. “Crystal, you’re just trying to start trouble.

Dillion wouldn’t mess with you like that,” he blurted.

While stirring the waffle mix, Dora is in denial mode and remains silent.

“Don’t believe me then,” Crystal sneers, jerking her body as she turns to walk away. *If anyone was going to believe me, I knew they would,* she thinks, walking into the bedroom and falling onto her bed.

Lying there pondering her thoughts, she decides: *Monday, at school, I’m going to tell my friends. They’ll believe me.*

While changing classrooms, Crystal and Shyla walk together, talking and laughing.

Crystal then tells her, “Girl, my aunt’s husband is after me for sex.”

There’s silence. Absorbing it, Crystal looks over her shoulder at her friend, seeing a blank expression. Their conversation totally ceases.

Just ahead, Crystal turns right, where her

classroom is, and says, confused by Shyla's behavior, "All right. See you at lunch time."

Once she's inside the classroom, Crystal sits at her desk, behind another friend, waiting for the teacher to arrive. Crystal leans forward and tells her, "Girl, my aunt's husband is after me for sex."

After receiving a shocking coldness, Crystal leans back in her chair in disappointment, convinced that Dillion's theory must be right. Hearing the door opening, she looks up and sees the teacher walking into the room, Crystal tells herself, *I'm not telling anybody else.*

Purposely staying out of Dillion's sight, Crystal lies on her bed doing homework when he enters the room in a sneaky manner, acting as though she summoned him, saying loudly, "Hey, did you just call me?"

"No. I didn't call you." She smirks at him as he approaches her. Touching her leg, she screams, "Stop."

In the hallway, there are footsteps. Ervin enters the room, seeing Dillion pretend to tickle her armpits while playful laughing as she hits him and yells, "Aunt Elleen, will you call your husband. He's in here bothering me, and I don't want him messing with me."

Aunt Elleen yells, "Dillion," calling him to her. It becomes her reaction, time after time. Left alone, Crystal wonders, *Why don't she come and ask me what he's doing? My mama would.*

The absence of Aunt Elleen's and her cousin's

support, has pushed her to spend time alone in hiding. The night, she realizes that the house has become too quiet, Crystal comes out of her hiding place. As she walks around the house, discovering that everyone has left without informing her of their departure, she hears keys jiggling in another part of the house.

A tsunami of fear floods her entire body. Crystal silently yells, *Oh my God. It's Dillion,* who often wears his keys on his belt.

Spotting her, he moans out of pleasure.

For protection, Crystal recoils back into her shell. The bedroom. While inside, she fears that he may possibly enter the room, so she climbs off the bed and just as she walks quietly out and into the hallway, he turns the corner, smiling when he sees her. Cautiously walking towards him, she makes a quick escape through the opening doorway into the living room. Crystal continuously eschews him, by moving from one area of the house to the other.

Once again, as she leaves her bedroom, and turns the corner of the hallway, she meets him, faced to face, in the kitchen and combined dining room. And with their eyes connecting, they pass one another.

A muscular man, Crystal shows no fear. At a safe distance, and with his back to her, she turns and says boldly, "I'm not having sex with you, so leave me alone."

He stops and faces her, saying sternly, and with confidence, "I'll get it from you whether you give it to me or not."

His response sends a shock down Crystal's spine, paralyzing her. She can't respond but only stares into his eyes, seeing that he means every word.

For days, she's haunted by the memory of when she was almost raped. Having no one she can trust,

Crystal becomes terrified that Dillion will rape her. Not wanting him to, she surrenders, and at the opportune time, she walks into the family room, where he's alone and says, defeated by fear, "OK. I'll give you sex."

He looks away from the TV with his blood shot eyes smiling and says firmly, "Tonight then. "Don't go to bed. Stay in here, and after everyone is sleep, I'll come."

Crystal nods and walks away. Later that night after giving him sex, Crystal walks down the hallway to her bedroom and while feeling some kind of way that she hasn't felt before, she gets in bed. Pulling the covers over her shoulders, Crystal acknowledges that the happy life she has found living with her aunt has crumbled. Heavy at heart, she rolls over, thinking, *as much as I love my aunt and I want to tell her the truth, I can't now. It will break her heart.*

In the morning, Crystal wakes up and visualizes herself standing in front of Dillion and saying to his face, *I despise you with your no good self, demanding sex from a sixteen-year-old and betraying the love of your wife. How could you do that to her? I hope she finds out and divorces you.*

Now, thinking less about herself and very disappointed with herself, she dreads getting out of bed but does and goes into the bathroom. While getting dressed for school, the anger she woke up with begins to fester inside of her.

Recalling a tactic she overheard older women saying, "When a man is using you for sex, take him for everything you can get out of him," Crystal marches through the hallway and into the kitchen while her aunt has already left for work and demands from Dillion in a low voice so no one can hear her, "I want some boots."

A plumber, he sits at the dining room table having a cup of hot coffee before leaving for work. He looks at her angry face and nods. Sarcastically, he asks, "Anything else you want?"

Crystal rolls her eyes, thinking as she walks away, *I'll think about it. I'm going to make you pay big time.*

But once wasn't enough for him. Finding Crystal lying on the family room floor, watching TV with her three cousins, Dillion stomps into the room. Pointing her out, he says, "You come go with me."

Crystal and her cousins look at each other. Obediently, Crystal stands and does as she's told. "What?" she asks as she follows him out the door.

"Get in the car."

"Where are we going?"

Dillion drives her to the piece of land, where he keeps his cattle, and ejaculates inside of her.

Driving back home, he discusses his plans for them and insists as he turns to look over at Crystal, "I don't want you getting pregnant. You have to get on the pill."

Crystal whines, "I can't get on the pill. I need an adult's permission."

"Ask your aunt. She'll put you on the pill."

Boiling inside with anger, Crystal stares out of the car window and becomes radical in her thinking: He *must be out of his freaking mind if he thinks for one minute that I'm going to ask my aunt to put me on the pill, so he can have sex with me. He's a damn fool.*

She then has an idea and laughs.

He looks over at her leaning against the side window, "What's so funny?"

She shrugs her shoulders, "Nothing."

3

Sick in bed, during the first quarter of her junior year, Crystal lies in bed. *I've been sick through the Christmas break. What's wrong with me?* she wonders while noticing that her breast feels enlarged and tender. To take a look at herself, she gets out of bed, and in the bathroom, she stands in the mirror, exposing her chest. "Could I be pregnant?" Crystal touches one breast. "Ouch," she squeals in pain.

She's lying down when Aunt Elleen returns home from work, walking into the girl's bedroom, and stops just inside the door. She asks, "Crystal, how did it go today? Are you still vomiting?"

"Yes," Crystal groans.

"Tomorrow afternoon you're going to the doctor," she says and continues to talk as she turns to walk out of the room, "So we can find out why you can't hold down your food."

The thought of food affects her physically, and she

sits up in bed now feeling sick to her stomach. *Dang, what if I am pregnant?* She thinks. Salivating, she hops out of bed, running.

At the opposite end of the hallway, bending over the commode, straining to vomit. Her stomach is empty from not eating.

Standing with her hands on her hips after gagging and somewhat out of breath, Crystal listens to the pots and pans rattling in the kitchen, where Aunt Elleen begins to prepare dinner, and not knowing what tomorrow holds, Crystal takes a deep breath while thinking, as she does, *I'm not looking forward to tomorrow at all.*

Driving home from the doctor's office, Aunt Elleen glances over at Crystal and asks, "Crystal, you're not dating anyone, how are you pregnant?"

Feeling shame, Crystal turns her head to look out the side window and to protect her aunt's heart from being broken, she hesitates. Then, blurts out a lie, "I met this new boy at school."

"What is the boy's name?"

Lying, Crystal lowers her head and says the first name that comes to mind, "Robert."

Returning home from school, three days later, Crystal walks into the house, knowing that her school counselor talked to Aunt Elleen and told her the truth, and it's now time for her to face the piper. Turning the living room corner into the hallway, she walks straight down it and into the bedroom. Facing the mirror and the shame that has befallen her, Crystal avoids looking at her reflection.

As she's setting her school books on the dresser,

Aunt Elleen enters the room behind her, closing the door. Walking past Crystal, her voice sounding raspy, she sits on Gean's bed and says, "Crystal, come sit down."

Crystal stalls, wishing she could run and hide, but she does as she's told. Looking at Crystal, across from her, Aunt Elleen says, as her face turns red with anger, "I'm so sorry for what you've had to go through, sweetie, and although he is my husband, I have to say, some men are dogs."

Her words are music to Crystal's ears. She smiles, thinking, *That's right. He's no good. Tell me more.*

She gets a question instead. "How many times did he have sex with you?"

Crystal hesitates. *I can't tell you it was three. It's too shameful to say, and it will break your heart.* So, to protect them both from the pain, Crystal lowers her head. Lying, she answers, "One."

Crystal then begs silently, *Please don't make me tell you that it took place in the family room while you slept.*

That's if it only happened once, but luckily, Aunt Elleen doesn't ask.

The rest of the day, as she remains in her bedroom, lying on her bed, hiding in shame, time ticks away, and when Dillion comes home from work, he and Aunt Elleen go into their bedroom. Shortly after, Crystal is summoned by her aunt, who yells down the hallway, "Crystal, come to my room."

Crystal goes and stands in the door and says to her aunt sitting at the head of the king-size bed, "Yes."

"Come in and close the door."

Crystal sits at the foot of the bed, holding on to the doorknob as Dillion stands against the long dresser, his backside reflected in the mirror. He begins to flip everything, putting all the blame on Crystal, pointing, "You knew I was married to your aunt, didn't you?"

In response, Crystal eyes squint as she's about to shout, *You weren't worried about your wife when you were putting your dick in me,* but she doesn't. She has already lied to protect her aunt's heart, and anything else she has to say will not change that, so Crystal pushes herself backwards with her back against the wall. Losing again to his control, she answers, "Yes."

Now relaxed with his arms crossed, Dillion continues, "Then, if you knew I was —"

Aunt Elleen shushes him, shouting, "Dillion, stop it." She then looks at Crystal and pleasantly asks, "Do you want an abortion? Dillion will pay for it."

Without hesitating, Crystal leans forward and answers "Yes, I want one."

"OK, sweetie, I'll have to make arrangements for it, and after school tomorrow, I'm taking you to your aunt Gayle's to stay there until everything has been confirmed. You can leave the room now."

4

Oblivious as to what's going on with Crystal, Maylene is outside hanging a load of laundry at the side of the house in the late morning hours while Crystal hides out in her bedroom, growing deeper into depression and dropping out of school after three weeks in attendance.

Lying stretched out on her back, Crystal stares out the window at the cloudless blue sky. She likes the blue color, which is supposed to soothe one's mood when feeling down, but it isn't soothing hers. All up in her feelings, Crystal then begins to think, *It's not my fault no one believed me when I told them that Dillion was touching me where he shouldn't be.*

Meanwhile, outside, Maylene pins the last piece of laundry on the clothes line, and just as she walks into the house, the phone begins to ring.

From behind the closed bedroom door, Crystal can hear her mother arguing, "She's been going to school."

No. Crystal pretended to be going to school, but instead, she hid out at the top of the hill, across the street, watching Maylene leave for work, and then she re-entered the house.

"I'll look into it, and thank you for calling," says Maylene, hanging up the phone.

She has been so busy that she didn't see Crystal leave for school this morning and goes to stand outside Crystal's bedroom.

Expecting her mother to come searching for her, Crystal watches intensely as Maylene slowly turns the doorknob. She opens the door midway, exposing Crystal in bed and staring at the ceiling.

"Crystal, why aren't you in school? I just got off the phone talking to the school administrator, who says you haven't been to school all week. What's going on with you?" Maylene probes her but quickly realizes that silence makes no sound—not a single word escapes Crystal's lips. She refuses to talk and is emotionally detached from the world, not fully conscious of the fact that she has been traumatized and is dealing with the outcome of her situation in the best way she knows how—in silence.

Because of Crystal's unwillingness to talk and not wanting to berate her, Maylene quickly closes the door.

Later, while in the living room and ironing,

Maylene expresses her concerns about Crystal to her sister, Bee, who usually visits after work and with the living room wall between her and them, Crystal can't ignore their conversation.

"Crystal will not come out of her room except to go to the bathroom. She isn't going to school but just lies in bed and never says a word."

"Maylene, is she depressed?" Bee, a nurse, asks.

Crystal begins to cry silent tears.

"She must be. I think she wants to be in Phoenix."

"She hasn't been home long enough for you to determine that, Maylene. She just needs more time to adjust."

"She was doing very well after she got here. I don't want her home if it makes her unhappy. Our sister Elleen says she can't come back to live with her. I think I'll call Auntie Val and Uncle Robbie and see if they'll allow her to stay with them and attend school."

Comforted by her mother's words, Crystal wipes away her tears and begins to question her mother's behavior. *Mama hasn't said anything about my pregnancy or abortion. What did Aunt Elleen tell her?*

5

Arriving back in Phoenix just days before her seventeenth birthday, riding in the backseat of her eldest brother Jake's car, Crystal notices, as Jake pulls up in front of Uncle Robbie's and Auntie Val's house, that all the lights are off and both the car and truck are gone.

She murmurs, "Uh oh."

Stopped outside the gate at around seven o'clock in the evening, Jake asks, "Crystal, they knew you were coming today, didn't they?"

"Yeah, I think so."

"Well, I'll have to take you and leave you at Aunt Elleen's. I'm too tired to wait around for them to come home."

Unsure how Jake's idea is going to pan out, Crystal leans back in her seat, and as different scenarios play out in her mind, Jake zigzags his way through the neighborhood, and just two streets behind Auntie Val's and Uncle Robbie's house, he coasts the car onto Aunt Elleen's carport. The beaming headlights expose her and Dillion sitting outside on the porch, hiding in the dark, the truth of what went on there.

Totally unaware that Dillion molested his little sister and got her pregnant, Jake pokes his head out of the window and yells, "I was supposed to drop Crystal off at Uncle Robbie's, but no one's there. Do you mind if I leave her with you until they get home?"

"They know she's coming, Jake. They might be running late. Let me go inside and call over there."

From the backseat, hiding behind Jake's fiancée in the front, Crystal prays, *please be home.*

Aunt Elleen then yells from the partially open screen door, "Jake, Uncle Robbie is home. He said he just got there."

"Thank goodness," Crystal silently rejoices.

After making sure that Crystal is safely inside the house, Uncle Robbie stands at the door with his hand on the knob. "Baby-doll, I'm going now. Your auntie should be here shortly. Just make yourself at home."

"OK, Uncle Robbie," she says as he closes the door.

Crystal sits glancing around the living room that's in dire need of a good dusting and listening to the tick-tock of the wall clock. She grows impatient with waiting for Auntie Val to come home. Tired out by constantly watching the time, she finally slips off her shoes and stretches out on the sofa.

Standing at six-one in height, Auntie Val unlocks and opens the entry door. Seeing Crystal sleeping with the light on, she very quietly closes it and then softly tiptoes across the red living room carpet to where Crystal lies on the sofa and begins to pinch her thigh, causing Crystal to immediately sit up, reflexively slapping Auntie Val's hand, pushing it away and whining, "Stop! That hurts, Auntie Val."

Auntie Val reacts with a loud, boisterous laugh as she always does. "Haha!" She then asks, "Why are you sleeping out here on the sofa? Get yourself up from there and follow me to your room."

At the end of the short hallway, she switches on the bedroom light. "This will be your room. Now go on and get in the bed."

Days after her birthday, Crystal is home alone and inside her bedroom, struggling with feelings of guilt from having had the abortion. It keeps jabbing at her soul, reminding her daily of what she did as it rips her apart spiritually.

Sitting on the full-sized bed, she looks up and starts speaking toward Heaven, "I told you, God. I am sorry about having the abortion. I promised that I wouldn't do it again. What else do you want from me?"

Lowering her head, she closes her eyes. "I can't take this grief anymore."

She hasn't talked to God in a long time. Then remembering back, Crystal opens her eyes with a new perspective. "That's it, God. I stopped communicating with you." Right then and there, she decides, "I'm going back to church and to seek you."

A surprised visitor knocks on the door. Leaving her bedroom, running into the living room, Crystal yells out, "Who is it?"

"It's me, Cathy."

Crystal yanks the door open, shouting cheerfully, "Hi, girl. How did you know where to find me?" She then gestures. “Come on in.”

Now juniors, they were sophomores when Cathy transferred to another high school, and they’ve barely seen each other since then.

Cathy, dark, tall, and slender, enters the house giggling. She then stands facing Crystal and says, “I called over to your Aunt Elleen’s house. She told me.” She looks around the room. “How long have you been living over here?”

“I just got back from San Diego, living with my mom, two weeks ago.”

“Why don’t you live with your aunt and your cousins anymore?”

Crystal shifts her weight. “Well, you know I was pregnant by my aunt’s husband, right?”

Cathy nods. “Yeah, you told me the last time we spoke.”

Crystal then says seriously “Girl, I had to stop him from raping me. He had me terrified, so I gave myself to him more than once. Then he wanted me to get on the pill.”

Cathy’s eyes widen and she yells, “He what?!”

“Yes. That was his plan.” Crystal nods. “But I thought to entrap him so everyone could see for themselves that I wasn’t lying about him molesting me.”

“How did you entrap him?”

“Simple. I didn’t get on the pill.”

Cathy leans forward and softly demands, “Crystal, why didn’t you just tell your aunt?”

Crystal places her hand on her chest and says with a raised voice, “Girl, I tried to tell people and my cousins, but when they didn’t believe me, I was so afraid she wouldn’t believe me, either.” Crystal hunches her shoulders and says with both palms facing out, “Then, when she found out that I was pregnant through the doctor, I made up a name and told her that it was a boy at school."

With curiosity, Cathy stares into Crystal's eyes. "Then how did she find out it was her husband?"

"Mrs. Hinks, remember her?"

"Yeah, the hippest counselor on campus."

Shamefully, Crystal lowers her head. "At school, I stayed off to myself. Mrs. Hinks noticed that I was always sitting alone on my lunch breaks and called me into her office. I confided in her, and with my permission, she told my aunt for me. I was sent back home to my mother and became deeply depressed because I didn't want to be in California and for having had the abortion."

"So, you had an abortion?"

"Yes. Basically, that's it. My roots are in Phoenix. It's where I want to be."

Crystal still doesn't know she's been traumatized and says, "That's enough about me. What have you been into?"

Once the best of friends, they had kept no secrets from each other. "Girl, I'm dating an airman in the USAF."

Crystal screams, "Cathy, are you for real? You're seriously seeing a man in the Air Force?"

"Is the sky blue?"

Cathy's silly jokes always make Crystal laugh. That's what Crystal likes most about her.

Cathy reaches for the phone on the glass-top coffee table and asks, "Crystal, do you mind if I use the phone? I want to call the barracks and see what my baby is up to."

Cathy picks it up and before Crystal can say, "Yeah, go ahead," she's already dialing the number.

An airman whom Cathy is acquainted with tells her that the person she's looking for has left the barracks. Cathy then shouts, “Wait, Travis, don’t hang up yet. I have a friend I want you to meet.”

Crystal quickly realizing that she’s that friend, leaps off the sofa and yanks the phone from Cathy’s hand. Crystal sounds off with an empathetic, “Uh-uh. No!”

She then proceeds to hang up the phone, but Cathy reclaims it, grabbing it from her.

Placing her hand over the receiver so Travis can’t hear them, Cathy whispers, “Crystal, talk to him. He’s a nice guy.”

“So, I don’t want to talk to him.”

“Please, Crystal,” Cathy pleads as she shoves the phone into Crystal’s hand. “Just say hi.”

Crystal reluctantly puts the phone to her ear, and in an overly pleasant tone she says, “Hello.”

“Hi, I’m Travis, and you’re?”

“I’m Crystal,” she says while shaking her index finger at Cathy, who knows revenge is coming. Cathy giggles, and now that she has done what she had come to do, she exits the house while Crystal’s back is turned, yelling just before the screen door slams shut, “I’ll see you later, Crystal.”

Travis takes full control of the conversation, talking for fifteen minutes before saying, “Someone needs to use the phone. Can I have your number so I can call you back later?”

Crystal’s first thought is to give him the wrong number. Hearing a soft voice whispering, “Hang up the phone,” she switches the phone to the other ear, listening to hear it again, but only hears Travis speaking.

Crystal scratches her scalp and is about to give out the wrong number but thinks about her actions. *After lying to Aunt Elleen, I don’t want to practice it.* Deciding against it, she reluctantly gives out the number, telling herself as she hangs up, *Maybe, he won't call back.*

Minutes after hanging up the phone, it rings. Sure that it isn't him, Crystal answers it and listens to Travis saying, "I just called to check if you gave me the correct number."

Crystal's impulse is to hang up, but then considers, *That would be so rude* and says, "I thought you wouldn't call back."

"I'm glad that I did. I'll call you again later," he says and hangs up.

On Sunday, before church, Crystal begins her journey back to God, leaving the house and walking three-quarters of a mile to the neighborhood corner store.

Inside, she goes straight to where the off-black pantyhose are and grabs one package that's her size off the shelf. She pays for it and then hurries out of the store, crossing a vacant lot, thinking as she hurries her steps, *If I had done this yesterday after talking to Travis, I wouldn't be rushing. I hope I won't be late on my first day going back to church.*

Arriving at the house, Crystal increases her pace through the living room and into the bathroom, where she bathes and quickly dresses. Continue to walk fast; she finally walks through the church doors, right on time.

Later, Travis calls. On the phone, laughing infectiously, she calms down and says, "That didn't happen. You're kidding me."

"No. Really, it happened while I was stationed in Alaska."

"Alaska?"

"I was only there nine months. I didn't like it

there. It was always night."

"You didn't like living in igloos, either? Crystal giggles.

"I didn't see one igloo; and I would have slept in one if I could."

"Not me," she says, captivated by him. Wanting to know more, she asks, "Why did you join the military?"

"I used to be in a singing group and, one day, they decided to leave Dayton and go to LA in the pursuit of fame. I didn't want to take the chance, having no money to live there, so I didn't go, I signed up for the military."

"I would have gone, too," Crystal says excitedly. "The group must be good if they took that kind of risk."

"Yeah. We were very popular in Dayton along with 'The Ohio Players', who I know."

"Who are they? I don't think I heard their music."

"I have one of their albums. Maybe, one day, I'll let you listen to it."

After two weeks of getting to know one another, Travis begins to romance her with his sensuous words. "When can I come over to see you?"

Sitting Indian style on the bed, Crystal twists the phone cord around her index finger as *Something* whispers, "Crystal, say no."

Crystal's eyes dart from left to right, unsure if she heard it or thought it, and then thinks, *It's time that I see who I'm talking to, and* tells Travis, "I'll have to ask Auntie Val first. What day do you want to come?"

"Is this Friday too soon?"

"No. Friday is fine, but it's my aunt who has the final say."

"What is she like?"

"She's bossy, loves to talk, childless, but she's real cool when she's not telling me what to do."

"Do you think she'll like me?"

"Yeah, she will, without a doubt."

Working five to sometimes six days a week and doing whatever it is they do when they're not working, Auntie Val and Uncle Robbie are seldom home, which leaves Crystal home alone most of the time. Travis has become someone she depends on to fill those lonely days.

Standing in the bedroom mirror, putting the final touch to her short, thick black hair, she's thinking, *Tonight, I'll finally get to meet Travis in person,* when there's a loud knock at the front door. She quickly drops the comb onto the vanity table and dashes out of the room, running into the hallway, where she is met by Auntie Val, who walks out from the kitchen. "Young lady, don't you dare answer that door. Go back to your room until I call for you to come out."

"Why?"

"Because it's not proper. Now, you go on."

In her bedroom, waiting to lay eyes on him, Crystal anxiously sits on the edge of the mattress, listening.

"Hi, you must be Travis. Come on in. I'm Val. I'm married to Crystal's great-uncle."

Aunt Val then yells into the kitchen, "Robbie, come on in here and meet Travis."

Usually, Uncle Robbie would be fishing on the lake in his large boat or hanging out at one of his favorite bars along Broadway Road, getting drunk. A chubby man of average height, he walks into the living room, shuffling his feet and grumbling, "I'm coming. I'm coming. You don't have to yell. I'm not hard of hearing, you know."

"Robbie, just get on in here."

Taking notice of herself sitting in front of the mirror, Crystal begins to fidget with her hair, and hears Auntie Val saying faintly, "Have a seat, Travis." And almost in the same breath, she hollers, "Crystal, Travis is here."

Now, in the spotlight, which she doesn't like—at all—but despite having the jitters, Crystal leaps off of the bed and walks into the hallway, unsuspecting of the unseen presence that's there with her.

Crystal enters the dim-lit living room, smiling, as Travis, sitting in Uncle Robbie's rocker, looks over his shoulder at her and returns the smile.

Then the weirdest thing occurs that she has never experienced before. Simultaneously, as they look into each other's eyes, time stops, and as Crystal is in a frozen-like state, the veil blocking her insight into another existence is quickly lifted, and her spiritual eyes, like that of a camera lens, zoom in on Travis's caramel skin complexion, capturing his round, strikingly handsome face. A light flashes; and this deceptive spirit posing to be Travis is engraved upon the surface of her memory.

After a split second, Crystal is jolted out of the spirit realm and back into the physical realm. Walking past Travis, in awe of his attractiveness, she takes a seat on the sofa.

Travis rushes over and sits beside her. Affectionately, he takes Crystal's hand and instantly notices the gold band on her finger. He admires it. "That's a man's ring you're wearing."

"Yeah, I know. I found it outside."

"You don't need to be wearing a man's ring. Let me have it."

She quickly jerks her hand away as he tries to remove it from her finger. "No. It's mine, and I'm keeping it." She giggles as they playfully fight over the ring during most of his visit.

After an hour, Travis steps outside onto the well-lit porch to leave, but when he turns to face her standing inside the entrance door, Crystal's immediate reaction is: *What the...?*

Suspecting that her eyes are playing tricks on her, Crystal stares into the night; then, again, she looks Travis in the face, which is now dark, narrow, and framed by a short black afro. A nicely trimmed mustache traces the outer edge of his thin top lip.

His lips part, and he politely says, "I enjoyed being with you tonight. When I get off work tomorrow, I'll give you a call if that's all right with you."

The voice whispers, "Tell him no," causing her to stiffen.

Feeling awkward and uncomfortable, Crystal leans against the door frame. And not knowing how to tell him no, politely, she instead nods and says, "Good night."

Totally confused and spooked, Crystal quickly closes the door and hurries to her bedroom, avoiding Auntie Val and Uncle Robbie, who have been in the kitchen, all the while, conversing with each other. She knows that if she tells them, they will laugh in disbelief.

In bed, Crystal lies beneath the covers, mystified and unsure of what she saw. Meeting Travis wasn't at all what she thought it would be, and as she lay tossing and turning, she wonders which one of Travis's two faces is actually his.

In the late morning, when she awakens, Crystal immediately recalls the remnants of last night's experience and thinks, *That was the weirdest thing. I could have sworn that he was light-skinned and that his face was round. My mind had to be playing tricks on me.*

Deciding to put the ordeal out of her head, Crystal then gets out of bed. All day, she doesn't give it another thought but then Travis calls and before she can properly greet him over the phone, the first words out of his mouth are, "Now that we've seen each other, do you think we can be a couple?"

As she notices his forwardness, *Something* begins to whisper, "Say no." Again, the voice causes her to become stiff.

She stops breathing. She then exhales, answering him, "I don't know."

"You don't know? What? Do you think I'm ugly?"

Crystal likes his sense of humor and giggles. "No, you're not ugly."

"What is it, then?"

Crystal begins to explain everything that she saw last night.

"It sounds like you're disappointed. Are you?" Travis asked.

"No. It was just weird. That's all."

"I don't know what you saw, but I am dark complexioned."

Again, *Something* whispers in Crystal's ear, "Say no."

It has become redundant. Now believing the voice is just her thought, she ignores it. Walking alongside the foot of the bed, she's thinking, *I need to heal so I can feel better about myself again. A relationship with God is the solution and it's what I lack in my life right now.*

She then separates the curtains and peeks out of the window overlooking the backyard.

The voice whispers, "Crystal, just say no."

Crystal answers without realizing that she's doing so, *But I like him. He's intelligent, sensitive, and he makes time to be with me, even though it's by phone.*

"Well, are we a couple or not?" Travis demands in her other ear.

Crystal continues to hesitate.

"Well, I'm waiting."

Crystal gives in to the pressure that she feels right now and hunches her shoulders before answering, "Yes, we can be a couple."

The weekends are the only appointed days Travis is allowed to visit, but he calls each school night.

Sitting and rocking in the rocking chair, Crystal listens to him talk about taking her to an upcoming concert that will be held at Big Surf in Tempe. She likes the idea—but her female intuition tells her that Travis isn't being completely honest with her. Crystal finds it very suspicious that since they've been dating, every weekend, he has taken her to the park or shopping, wanting to buy her expensive clothes and jewelry, which she always refused.

While he rambles on and on about his favorite band that will be performing at the concert, Crystal begins to question his authenticity: *where is he getting all this money?* And when she finally gets the opportunity to speak, she asks, "You always have a lot of money. Does the military pay that well?"

"Not really."

"Then why do you always have so much money to spend on me?"

"I just want to show my girl a good time when we're together, and that takes money. A lower-class airman—such as myself—doesn't earn much, and we only get paid twice a month, and so to get by, I sell drugs."

Crystal suddenly stops rocking. "Wait a minute. Did you say that you sell drugs?"

"I've been meaning to tell you. I just didn't know how you would react."

Crystal shouts angrily, "No. You knew exactly how I would react because you know that drugs are not what church people do." She begins to rock again to calm herself down, asking, "So, are you doing drugs, too? I know you're not just selling them."

"Yeah. I smoke a little marijuana."

Having belonged to the "Don't Do Drugs" club during her sophomore year, Crystal's anger reaches its boiling point. Vehemently, she screams in his ear, "No, uh-uh. We can't be together. If you want to be with me, you can't deal with drugs, period."

"I have to go; other people are in line waiting to use the phone," says Travis as though to avoid the subject.

Crystal slams the phone onto the glass-top coffee table and doesn't hear from Travis again until one day while outside the house, unlocking the front door, she hears the phone ringing. Leaving the key in the door, she rushes inside and breathes out the word, "Hello."

"It took you long enough; I was about to hang up," says Travis.

"I'm just now getting home from school," she says, sounding edgy and wishing she hadn't answered the phone. "What do you want?"

"Crystal, I thought about what you said, and I've decided to give up the drugs. I really like you, and I want us to be together. I've even stopped selling drugs, too."

Crystal rolls her eyes. "I'm not in the mood for your pretentiousness, and I don't believe you, Travis."

Something whispers to her, "Hang up."

As before, assuming it's just a thought, Crystal

ignores it, thinking, *It would be rude.*

"I'm serious," shouts Travis. "Crystal, I don't want to lose you."

"Travis, I haven't heard from you all week. I thought this relationship was over."

"I just needed some time to consider your ultimatum," he says sounding sincere.

Speechless, Crystal flops down in the rocker, and after a brief conversation, she hangs up, slamming the phone down, wishing they had ended the relationship.

Rocking in the rocker, she begins to think of ways to do it and comes up with an idea.

Removing the key from the door, Crystal walks toward her bedroom, mumbling, "I hope his feelings don't get hurt when I tell him that I'd rather we be friends."

Saturday afternoon, Crystal makes the mistake of sitting on the sofa, nestled close to Travis, which gives him the wrong impression. Interrupting the afternoon program they're watching, she nudges him with her elbow and says, "Travis, most everyone at school who wants to be friends wear a friendship ring to symbolize their friendship." Referring to the hint as gently as she can, Crystal specifically raises her right hand and continues to say, "And I want one, too."

Travis quickly jerks his head toward the TV and watches it in silence.

"Well, what do you think?" asks Crystal.

He doesn't comment but ignores her.

Gently nudging him again, Crystal says, "Travis, talk to me." She then leans forward and is moved by compassion when seeing the painful expression on his face.

She then sits back and, together, they silently

watch TV until his ride drives up, tooting the horn.

Travis walks slowly to the door, and despite his despondency, Crystal walks behind him, knowing firsthand how it feels to be rejected. Then, Travis suddenly stops walking. Putting his arms around her waist, he kisses her on the lips, catching her offguard. Caught in a moment of weakness and to refrain from crushing his emotional state any further, Crystal accepts Travis into her arms and kisses him back.

They are two young people holding on to the pain of past relationships that they still have not let go of. Being a father at a young age, Travis yearns for his daughter, whom he is no longer allowed to see. Crystal, still to this day, has not been told why, other than that his ex-girlfriend from high school would not forgive him and broke up with him.

Travis has learned of Dillion through Cathy, but he has no idea the depth of Crystal's pain in losing the loving relationship with Aunt Elleen that has not brought her closure. While holding Travis in her arms, she siphons the love he's offering. She doesn't have the heart to reject him, and so she holds him tight.

Travis finally releases his arms from around her. Whether he knowingly or unknowingly broke through her wall of vulnerability, he looks into her ambiguous, confused eyes and says, "I'll call you later tonight."

Crystal is left standing in the doorway, watching Travis walk with his back to her, and is reminded of how she spent the week planning to dissolve this relationship. She shakes her head in disappointment.

"This is not the outcome I expected," she mumbles, closing the door.

Sitting in the rocker, rocking, she criticizes herself. *Why did I do that? I should have stuck to my plan and ended it, damn.*

Striking the arm of the rocker with the palm of her hands, Crystal stands and leaves the living room. Walking into her bedroom to prepare for church in the morning, she's thinking, *My wounds from having been molested, the rejection by family and friends, and the quilt I carry from the abortion, needs time to heal. I can't love him. I need God's love and acceptance.*

Having taken the first step in God's direction, the Bible scripture—*if you will draw near to God, He will draw near unto you* (James 4:8). Crystal's journey to finding God has begun.

6

In her bedroom, chatting with Travis on the phone, Crystal is pleased with herself for not missing a Sunday service.

"What are you doing?" he asks.

"I'm deciding what dress I'm wearing to church in the morning."

"What time does service start?"

"Ten. Why do you ask?"

"Because I am going with you if you don't mind."

"No. I don't mind."

"Well, I'll see you in the morning."

While they're walking to church, in the middle of the street, Travis expresses his testimony, "Every time I heard of Oral Roberts or Billy Graham coming to Ohio, I made sure I had a ride to their crusades."

"I've never been to anything like that. What is it like?" she asks.

"Girl, people come from all over the place to see

Oral Roberts and Billy Graham. They always have a huge crowd but that's because they're both so well-known. I, myself, enjoyed their teachings," he says.

Arriving just before the sermon begins, the church pews are full, and they have to sit apart. Within the first twenty minutes, Crystal looks over at Travis sitting across the aisle and discovers him sleeping. She then questions if the story he told her is true.

Tapping his leg while tithes are being collected, Crystal says as he opens his eyes and lifts his head, "Let's go."

After changing clothes, Travis suggests, "I brought a Frisbee, let's go outside and throw it."

"Yeah. That was thoughtful of you," says Crystal as they hurry outside.

Auntie Val's dog, Rax, resting nearby, becomes disturbed by the hustle of it all and struggles to stand on all four paws.

Withholding the Frisbee from Travis, Crystal watches as Rax barely makes progress, moving at a snail's pace to a quieter location—the backyard.

Then, *Something* whispers in her ear, "He's dying."

Still thinking it's her own thoughts, she's overcome by feelings of sympathy.

"Crystal, throw the Frisbee," Travis yells.

After he yells a second time, she throws it, watching as he reaches up, catching it in the air.

Disturbed by what she heard, Crystal senses the disruption in her energy flow, missing the Frisbee thrown back to her. She yells, "I don't want to play anymore."

Travis then follows her inside.

When it's nearly dark outside, Crystal, still in a funk, stands in the doorway, waving goodbye to Travis as his airman friend drives away.

In her bedroom, she reaches into the closet and

pulls out a white dress with blue diamond-like designs that she had sewn, as she begins to feel overwhelmed by a strong sense of remorse. And with this heavy cloud of sadness hanging over her, she drops onto the bed. The sadness sprinkles down and begins to pour into her soul. It's the kind of sadness that reminds her of when someone dies—of death. Up until now, Crystal has never known that sadness can hurt so badly and penetrate so deeply that it touches the soul as it is doing at this very moment.

Why do I feel this way? she wonders as she musters up the strength to stand on her feet again, hanging the dress on the closet doorknob and then looking underneath the bed for a pair of shoes to wear with it to school in the morning.

The sadness hovers relentlessly over her, day after day and throughout the week. It's like a gloomy day that never goes away. It begins to freak her out, and on a Saturday morning, while home alone, explosions of thunder, sounding like bombs dropping, one after the other, stir her out of slumber. A loud rumbling sound follows the thunder, and the house seems to shake. The continuous, rapid pounding of rain on the rooftop sounds like machine guns firing in the distance. Horror-struck, Crystal behaves irrationally.

Adrenaline rushes through her bloodstream as she thinks, *I'm under attack.* Hopping out of bed, she takes off running through the living room and into the kitchen, where she grabs a butcher's knife from the cabinet drawer. Running fast, she maneuvers around the glass-top coffee table, through the short hallway, and back to her room.

Placing the knife on the nightstand beside the bed, and at the sound of thunder, Crystal plunges into bed, hiding beneath the covers. The sky then rumbles, and the force of it causes the house to tremble and the front door to shake. Crystal reacts in fear, saying, “Someone is trying to break in.”

Grabbing for the knife, she silently waits for her imagined attacker. Staring down the hallway, she murmurs, “I’m not going down without a fight.”

Then the phone rings. Hoping that help is on the other end, she speedily runs into the living room. With the knife in hand, she quickly spots the white phone, snatches it from the coffee table, and with it to her ear, she dashes out of the dark living room and runs back down the short hallway, screaming, “Hello” as if yelling for help.

Travis says, “Girl, what’s wrong with you?”

Sitting up in bed and rocking with the blankets pulled to her waist, she cries, “Travis, I’m scared. Someone is trying to break in. Auntie Val is at work and I’m here by myself.”

He listens to her carry on frantically about it. Then, it thunders, followed by loud rumbling, and he laughs. “Crystal, it’s only a thunderstorm.”

Cuddling the blankets, she pleads, “No, Travis. I’m scared to be here alone. Will you come over?”

More seriously, he tells her, “I can’t, Crystal. I’m at work. I’ll call you when I get off, and don’t be afraid; you’ll be all right. Nobody is trying to get in.”

He finally calms her down and promises, “I’ll call you later.”

Crystal cries into the phone, “OK.”

Keeping the butcher’s knife close by her side, Crystal lies in bed while keeping her eyes fixed on the entry way into the hallway, looking into the dark, creepy living room and remembering the night Dillion woke her up crying, and she could hear Aunt Elleen pleading with him, “Dillion, put the gun away.”

He replied, "You promise that you won't leave me."

"I'm not going to leave you."

Crystal was sure that night that Dillion was coming for her next. Terrified out of her mind, she rolled out of bed, crawled across the bedroom floor to where her cousin Gean lay in bed, and woke her up, pouting, "Dillion is coming to kill me."

"Why do you think that, Crystal?"

"Because I told on him."

She had no clue as to what Crystal was referring to and assured her, "Girl, you had a bad dream. Go back to sleep."

No longer remembering the night when she was traumatized, Crystal becomes aware of the silence. The storm has finally passed over, and peace has returned to the sky.

Mustering up enough courage, Crystal slides out of bed, mumbling, "I wish that this was a bad dream because then I could understand and move passed it. There's some weird stuff happening that I've never experienced before."

Not connecting this ordeal with the spirit realm, Crystal slowly ambles into the dark living room as it occurs to her, *Shoot, with Dillion living two blocks away, I could be paranoid that he's coming to kill me.*

After drawing open the red drapes in the living room, and seeing the light rush in. Uncertain if Dillion is the source of her fears, she walks away from the window. *At least I'm sure I wasn't dreaming.*

In the kitchen, choosing to have cereal for breakfast, she removes a gallon of milk from the refrigerator. After pouring it over a bowl of cornflakes, Crystal enters the sun-lit living room and with a foreboding awareness of something lurking around outside, she sits on the sofa in an emotional knot.

Eating and watching reruns of Soul Train on TV, she slowly raises the spoon full of cereal and puts it into her mouth. Chewing it and feeling eerie, Crystal glances away from the TV, looking around the living room at each window. Her eyes then stare into the hallway, and straight into her bedroom as she begins to think, *I don't know what's going on, but whatever I am sensing, it's outside of my room.*

Turning her head, to watch TV, she can't stop looking around and thinking, "Whatever is out there, I pray it doesn't come inside."

7

Off-base, at a car dealership, Travis fulfilled all the requirements of a first-time used car buyer, and he now drives his newly purchased vehicle through the guarded gate onto Luke Air Force Base.

As he's parking it, he can't wait to tell Crystal the good news.

Just recently getting home from school, she's in the living room dancing to her favorite songs. Dancing distracts her attention away from her feelings of sadness—plus, it's a pastime she often enjoys—but lately, she'll do anything she can think of to rid herself of the anguish.

When entering the barracks, Travis is so excited that he speeds walk to the end of the long corridor, picks up the phone, and dials Crystal's number.

On the first ring, she quickly turns down the stereo.

"Crystal, guess what I got?" shouts Travis.

Now relaxing in the black leather recliner, she curiously asks, "What?"

"The credit union approved my car loan. I got the car!" I'll be coming over later today and show it to you and take you and Auntie Val for a ride. Then, on Saturday, I'm taking my baby to the drive-in so we can see that new movie that's out."

"That's cool, Travis." Crystal smiles, "Now, you don't have to depend on friends for a ride."

Arriving early at the house, before nightfall, Saturday evening, Travis parks the olive-green Pontiac LeMans with a tan-colored vinyl top, outside the front gate.

Frowning as he approaches the front door, Travis knocks. Walking inside, he blurts, "What is that awful smell?"

Crystal hears him talking and dashes out of her bedroom, stopping at the hallway entrance. She almost laughs when he looks at her with a distorted expression, asking, "Don't y'all smell that?"

Crystal tightens her lips together so she wouldn't laugh and shakes her head. She then says, "I don't smell anything."

All day, as she slowly awakens to the spirit realm, she has sensed a feeling in the atmosphere—a cheerful one. She can't explain it and guesses that it's because she's excited about going to the drive-in.

Auntie Val, sitting in her usual spot on the sofa with her legs spread open and her dress hem sagging between them, looks up and over the top of her cat's eye glasses at Travis and laughs her boisterous laugh. She then says, "We don't smell a thing, Travis. You are such a kidder."

"I'm serious," he responds, and with urgency, he turns around to walk back out of the house.

Crystal quickly runs past Auntie Val and follows

him.

They walk toward the backyard, alongside the house, between it and the chain-linked fence, with Travis leading the way. Suddenly, rushed by a swarm of flies, their arms begin to swing wildly, swatting the flies as they make their way to the backyard. Standing outside Crystal's bedroom window, they stare at a figure lying on the ground near the grapevine not far away.

Crystal hides behind Travis, asking, "What is that?"

"I don't know. Let's go get a closer look."

Crystal tightly holds onto Travis's arm as they approach. The closer they walk upon it, the worse the smell is. Crystal covers her nose and mouth. They stop just a few feet away from what they identify as Rax's dead body, completely covered with a thick blanket of flies. There's no telling how long he's been dead.

Now running away from the nauseous stench, they dash inside the house. Travis shouts, "Auntie Val, that stench I smell, it's Rax. We found him dead in the backyard."

"You did?"

"Yeah."

"Oh, well," she says, standing up. "He was old, Travis." At six-feet-one, she walks into the hallway and removes an old blanket from the closet, saying indirectly, "Come on. Let's go wrap the body and put it out near the street so the Animal Humane Society truck can come get it."

"Don't expect me to help," says Crystal, walking out of the living room, "I can't do it."

In her room, she stands in front of the mirror styling her hair into an Afro. With both hands, she slightly presses her hair into a perfectly round shape, while remembering how disturbed she felt when *Something* spoke of Rax's death. She mutters, "Why do these strange things keep happening?"

Later, in a remorseful mood, Crystal joins Travis in the living room, where he listens to Auntie Val laugh and reminisces about Rax's life. He then stands, interrupting her, "I hate to cut you off, Auntie Val, but we should be leaving if we don't want to miss the beginning of the movie."

And as they slowly drive past his dead body, Crystal, at that very moment, realizes that her unexplained sadness, which showed up and hung around for as long as Rax remained alive, had vanished—*That's why I was so cheerful today,* she silently acknowledges.

Diligently, as Travis travels north, Crystal searches her heart and mind to understand the root cause of the fear and asks herself, *But why was I so scared?*

Travis then comes to a stop and turns left. Now, as they head west on Broadway Road, Crystal's answer to her curiosity reveals that it was the unknown that she was afraid of, while being spiritually aware of Rax's slow, lingering death.

The movie was all they knew it would be, and in the morning, Crystal rolls over in bed onto her back, rejoicing with a big smile. "What a relief," she mutters, stretching both arms and legs. "Thank you, God. I am finally rid of the sadness and the fear that have plagued me every day for more than a month."

Gladly, she gets out of bed, and the entire time that she's preparing for Sunday's worship service, her mind is preoccupied, thinking of last night when Travis held her close as they took turns dipping their hands in and out of the large popcorn container while engrossed in watching an action movie.

Finally, leaving the house on her way to church, and with her mind still preoccupied with thoughts of Travis, she strolls up the street. Faintly, she senses the unseen presence that's there with her and begins to share her feelings of mixed emotions. First, looking around to see if anyone isn't close enough to hear her, she says, "Travis continuously wants me to say, I love him, and it isn't true. He is a good person. I like him a lot, and that's for sure—but I'm not sure if it's love. I don't feel for him the way I felt for Ward, and it isn't easy to tell Travis the truth, especially when it's not what he wants to hear."

With that heaviness now lifted from off her chest, Crystal stands at the side of Broadway road and then scurries across it after a car passes. Entering the church building, her thinking immediately switches. *I like this church.*

Finding a seat in the middle pew, she observes the other believers who are kneeling, praying, and praising God with their hands lifted toward Heaven. She wonders, *I must not have the Holy Ghost because I don't act like that, and it doesn't seem necessary.*

Crystal crosses her legs. *Oh well, I'm just happy that my life is normal again.* For now.

8

After two months of dating, and confident that Crystal would accept his marriage proposal, Travis went and purchased an engagement ring.

Arriving at the house, as he does every Saturday afternoon, overly dressed for the occasion and with the ring carefully tucked away in his back pants pocket, he knocks on the screen door. Peeking inside, he sees Crystal sitting on the sofa, watching TV.

"Come in. It's unlocked." Crystal tells him, having no idea what Travis is up to when he kneels at her feet, take her left hand, and holds it ever so gently.

Not liking his hat, she begins to muse over it while he's down on one knee and says, "You look like a pimp when you wear this kind of hat." And as she usually does, Crystal snatches the black, wide-brim hat off his head, setting it on the back of the sofa against the wall.

She finally realizes that he is down on one knee. “What are you doing?”

Travis, younger than he says he is, looks directly into her dark brown eyes. “I love you, Crystal. Will you marry me?”

She laughs and says, “Stop playing with me.”

“I’m serious.” He reaches into his pocket, pulls out the ring box, and opens it. “Will you marry me?”

Crystal is totally thrown off. Staring at the ring with pop-eyes, her mouth opens wide. She had dreamed of this day but never anticipated being so young. Her mind then silently spurts out the words in her head: *‘I asked for a friendship ring, not an engagement ring.’*

Something whispers faintly in her ear, “Tell him no.”

Crystal’s first impulse is to tell him no, but her thinking fast-forwards, and she sees a bleak future ahead. *Beauty School is just a thought, and because of low grades, College is definitely a no.* But becoming a wife, the very thing that she has always dreamed of, excites her, and, without further ado, Crystal spreads her fingers and says with a smile, “Yes. I’ll marry you.”

Also smiling, Travis slides the ring onto Crystal’s finger. Simultaneously, they lean forward, and at the age of seventeen, Crystal’s fate is sealed with a kiss.

Auntie Val enters the house shortly after Travis leaves, carrying a bag of groceries. Crystal runs and blocks her path, raising her left hand. "Auntie Val, look!"

"And what is this, Crystal? You mean to tell me that you and Travis are engaged to be married?"

"Yep."

While Auntie Val unpacks the groceries, Crystal sits in the living room, and as she admires the half-carat diamond ring on her finger, *Something* whispers. “Don’t do it.”

Still assuming it’s her thoughts, Crystal agrees. *I am not ready for marriage; and I don’t think Mama is going to allow it.* Curious, she yells into the kitchen, “Auntie Val, do you think my mama will give me permission to get married?"

"I don't think she will stop you.”

Crystal can’t believe what she’s hearing, “*What!* You don’t think she will stop me?”

“No. It's your decision."

Crystal sits quietly, repeating in her head, *It’s my decision? But she’s the mother and I’m the child.* Not understanding the logic behind it, Crystal goes to her room.

She walks back out after Auntie Val yells, “Crystal, your mother is on the phone and wants to talk to you.”

My savior has arrived, thinks Crystal as she hurries into the living room and picks up the phone, cheering, “Hi, Mama.”

Certain that Maylene will disapprove, Crystal is quickly thrown for a loop as Maylene sings, “Ooh, Crystal, you’re getting married?”

In a state of confusion, Crystal responds, “Ahh. Yes, Ma’am.”

She then waits for her mother to ask the most important question of all, “Is this really what you want?” but instead, Maylene says proudly, “Well, I’ll have to come to Phoenix and meet Travis before the big day.”

While her mother is talking, Crystal’s mind drifts away from the conversation, and she stares into space, thinking, *This cannot be my mother. The mother I know would tell me,* “Crystal, you are still in school. You don't know anything about marriage.

You first have to finish high school."

Maylene captures Crystal's attention, yelling into the phone, "Crystal, are you listening to me?"

Even though she wasn't, Crystal answers, "Yes, Ma'am."

After talking to her mother, Crystal hangs up the phone, disappointed that Maylene will not be stopping the wedding. Dragging her feet, she walks into her bedroom, now, feeling more confused by both Auntie Val's and her mother's logic, she sits on the bed and asks herself, Dang, h*ow can it be a good thing for me to get married while still in high school, but it's a bad thing when I come home passed my curfew?*

Crystal shakes her head. *None of it makes sense, and if I question their intelligence, I'll risk being disrespectful and I'm in enough trouble as it is.*

On the phone, days later, Travis starts to pressure Crystal, asking, "Crystal, what month do you want us to get married?"

In her room, seated Indian style on the full-size bed, she lowers her head and frowns slightly, saying, "I haven't thought about it."

"Why not? You should be thinking about it."

"Because I haven't," she snaps at him.

The days that follow, Travis does not let up. Annoyed, Crystal avoids him and quits answering the phone. While it sits on the living room coffee table, ringing consistently, she walks past it, wondering, *What is his rush?*

After a week of continuously harassing her, he wears her down, and Crystal becomes tired of him calling. Finally, she picks up the ringing phone and listens as Travis complains about her not answering it, but his complaint is short, and he says in a much calmer manner, "Anyway, I was calling because I was thinking that we should get married in my birthday month. I'll be nineteen."

"Don't you mean you'll be twenty-one?"

"Ooh. I lied about my age."

"But why would you do that, Travis?" she says, becoming upset.

"I thought you liked older men. Cathy told me about Dillion."

"Well, she shouldn't have, and I do not like older men."

"Anyway, answer my question. How does July sound?"

Now, frustrated about everything, Crystal throws up her free hand, thinking, *What in the hell is going on? He's lying, I'm lying.* Then, out of frustration and feeling trapped, Crystal answers half-heartedly, "Yeah, why not?"

"Then July it will be," he cheers.

Word of the engagement travels fast among the rest of the family, and when the gossip ricochets back to Crystal that her Aunt Elleen is insisting the wedding that's to take place in two months be held at her house, Crystal is infuriated.

Coming from the kitchen, she storms into the living room, where Auntie Val sits smoking a cigarette and unleashes her anger. "Auntie Val, since Travis doesn't want to get married in a church, I want to get married here, at your house. Aunt Elleen didn't ask me if I wanted to get married at her place, and I don't want to."

"Crystal," she says, tapping her cigarette ashes into the ashtray. "I am honored that you would want to get married here, but I think if your Aunt Elleen wants the wedding at her house, that's where it should be. You lived with her longer than you have with me. At least that's how I see it."

"That's beside the point. Why should she have what she wants? It's my wedding, and I want to plan it."

Whenever Crystal gives Auntie Val a hard time, she's called a name other than her birth name. "A-hole, I'm not going to fight about it with you."

"Auntie Val, you know that her husband molested me. Why should it be at his house?"

"Dillion is a low-down dog for what he did to you, but Crystal, just this time, let Elleen have her way."

In a tantrum, Crystal rushes out of the house. She shouts through the screen door from outside, "It's my life."

Overheated with emotions, she re-enters asking, "Auntie Val, if you were me, would you do it?"

Now smoking her second cigarette, she answers, "It's not about me, Crystal. Please stop being an A-hole, will you? Let Elleen handle it."

Huffing and puffing, Crystal walks past Auntie Val, yelling as she goes to her bedroom, "I'm leaving."

"And go where?" asks Auntie Val.

Crystal switches on the bedroom light. "Travis moved into the studio apartment, I'm going to go stay with him."

Auntie Val sits quietly, smoking her cigarette while watching Crystal carry her luggage outside, placing it on the front porch.

Uncle Robbie, arriving home, parks his truck outside the gate. Walking into the yard, seeing Crystal, he calmly asks, "Hey, doll-baby, what are you up to?"

"She's leaving Robbie," Auntie Val yells through the screen door.

He looks at Crystal and giggles. “Doll baby, how far do you think you will get, carrying those heavy things?”

“I’ll tell Travis to come get me and move in with him. Auntie Val says that I need to let Aunt Elleen plan my wedding. I don’t want it to be at her house.”

Standing with the door open, Uncle Robbie gives a firm answer. “Doll-baby, you can’t move in with Travis until you two are married. Now get your things and bring them back into the house.”

Crystal addresses her great-uncle softly, “But, Uncle Robbie...”

“Don’t make me tell you again,” he says. “Come on inside, and I want you to apologize to your auntie.”

Having never been corrected by him, Crystal bows her head. She says, “Okay,” and obediently does as she is told.

The night before the wedding, Crystal gathers everything she owns into the corner of her bedroom when there’s a hard knock at the front door.

“I got it,” shouts Auntie Val, allowing Crystal time to prepare for tomorrow. “Crystal, it’s your mama.”

Maylene, who has been shopping, walks into the house, calling Crystal to her. When Crystal walks into the living room, she is handed a large stuffed bag containing two pillows.

“I just thought you and Travis could use them in addition to the wedding gift that I got you.”

“Thank you, Mama. We do need them,” says Crystal, carrying the pillows into the room and placing the bag in the corner with her other packed belongings.

“Crystal, come tell your mother who got you pregnant,” insists Auntie Val. She has been itching to expose the truth about Dillion ever since she snooped inside Crystal's head and found out.

Now having their support, a little too late, Crystal finally tells her mother, "It was Dillion."

In shock, Maylene looks away, slowly shaking her head. She then looks up and says, "I suspected he was up to no good. The last time I visited Crystal at my sister's house, he couldn't stay away from her. He just had to help Crystal wash her hair."

Crystal, expecting all of hell to break loose, eagerly watches her mother, noticing Maylene's fingers that twitch nervously at her side. That's one thing about her mother that hasn't changed, and it means she's highly upset.

Auntie Val begins to calm her down. "Maylene, I suspected it, too. Elleen had to be blind not to see it, herself. But you are going to have to act normal now. Don't ruin this child's wedding. We know how upset and out of control you can get when you're angry."

"No. I should have listened to my intuition. Instead, I listened to Elleen tell me, ""Dillion doesn't mean any harm. He's always teasing the kids.""

"I tried to get the girl over here to talk to her, but she wouldn't come," says Auntie Val puffing a cigarette.

Standing next to the black recliner, Crystal remembers that night. "Auntie Val, if you had told me that you wanted to talk to me about Dillion, I would have came, but you told me that you had a cold and wanted me to come warm you up some soup. I didn't come because I had homework. I was telling people, but no one believed me."

"I would have believed you." Auntie Val looks at Maylene. "You're awfully quiet over there, Maylene, are you OK?"

Crystal then watches the unfamiliar side of her

mother re-emerge. "I'll be okay. I'll have to be. We have a busy day tomorrow." Maylene looks at Crystal and asks, “What about you? Are you OK?”

Not really. I don’t want to get married over there, and you shouldn’t want me to, is what she really wants to say, but reconsiders, knowing it cost her mother a lot to pay for the wedding. Money she didn’t have and most lightly had help paying for it.

Crystal nods her head that she’s OK, approvingly.

After Maylene leaves, Crystal returns to her room and continues packing. Solemnly, she reflects on that time in her life, now a year ago, *I did what I had to do to save myself from the irreversible damage of rape when no one else would.*

9

Wearing a simple self-made, flower-embroidered, floor-length white wedding dress, Crystal walks out of the house, holding onto her father's arm, stepping, in time, to the wedding song "Here Comes the Bride" and onto the patio decorated with pink paper bells hanging from the roof.

Crystal's eyes become fixed on Travis, now nineteen, and handsomely dressed in his Air Force uniform, waiting eagerly as she slowly approaches him.

The ugly masonry walls of Aunt Elleen's and Dillion's unfinished bedroom then initiate the thought in Crystal's head: *Who in their right mind plans a wedding to be held in an unfinished bedroom?*

The music then stops as they stand next to Travis, and she sadly regrets that she didn't fight harder to have a church wedding, where Dillion would not have been invited and Aunt Elleen couldn't use her wedding as a cover up.

Crystal's church pastor, officiating over the ceremony, asks, "Who gives this young lady away in holy matrimony?"

"I do," says her father, whom she hasn't seen in five years. She watches him walk away as Travis takes his place, leaving her not at the altar but at the opening where sliding glass doors will soon stand when Aunt Elleen's and Dillion's newly constructed bedroom is completed.

Immediately after saying their vows, Crystal is rushed inside, where she changes into comfortable attire. She makes her grand entrance back onto the patio, joining the reception when someone yells, "OK, Travis, it's time for you to dance with your bride."

Travis wraps his arms around Crystal, looks her in the eyes, and says, "My pleasure."

He gracefully guides her into a slow dance. Crystal glances over his shoulder, looking into the crowd of thirty that's gazing back at her, and asks, "I don't see my daddy. Where is he?"

"Oh. I'm sorry, baby. I forgot. While you were in the house, he told me to tell you that he apologizes for not staying. An emergency came up, and he had to hurry back home to Palm Springs, California."

It doesn't take Crystal very long to figure out that Maylene must have told her father about the molestation. So, not to spoil Travis's day, Crystal hides her disappointment at her father's sudden departure.

However, deep down in her heart, she wants Maylene to lose her temper and physically attack Dillion. Crystal tells herself, *That's the mother I know who doesn't let anyone mess over her.*

Wrapped in Travis's arms, Crystal lowers her head against his shoulder, and as they slow dance, her thoughts switch to the words to the love song he's singing beautifully in his tenor voice, soothing her frustrations.

"Crystal, that's enough dancing. It's time to cut the cake," her oldest brother, Jake, yells.

Then, the real Maylene appears, asserting her motherly scorn, "OK, Jake, you drunk. You better behave."

"Mama, everybody is dancing. You know I can't dance. So, I'm ready to eat."

Jake would not stop demanding. "Crystal, I said, cut the cake."

Because he's causing such a disturbance, everyone begins to beg, "Crystal and Travis, please cut the cake so he can shut up."

As they walk off the dance floor to cut the cake, Jake begins to sing, "Let's get it on."

He then sits quietly watching, and after a short time, he yells, "It doesn't take all night to cut a cake. Feed me. Y'all can take pictures another time."

Crystal yells, "Jake, you have to wait," and laughs at his drunkenness.

"Crystal, I've waited long enough."

Maylene walks towards him, "Jake, I'm coming to whip your ass. I told you to behave yourself."

Jake puts up his arms in defense. "Alright, Mama, if you put it like that, I'll wait." He then stomps his feet and softly grunts behind her back, "Shoot."

At 2 a.m., Travis and Crystal arrive at their studio apartment after celebrating their marriage at a late-night club in downtown Phoenix with the best man and his wife.

Inebriated. They stagger from the parking lot, holding on to each other and laughing at themselves with every step they take. They finally stand outside the large studio apartment beneath the dim porch light, and when Travis inserts the wrong key, Crystal laughs hilariously at his misjudgment.

Inserting the right one, Travis pushes the door open. Slurring his words, he says, “Wait out here.”

Trusting the strength of the wall to hold him up, he staggers inside, switches on the kitchen light, and comes back outside, saying as he picks her up into his arms, “I have to carry my bride over the threshold.”

They laugh so hard that Travis loses his balance and almost drops her. He quickly regains his stance and carries her into the living room, where he puts her down, but not before kissing her passionately.

Now, having set the tone for romance, heightening the mood, he stumbles over to the stereo and switches it on. In the dark, Travis clumsily stacks more than one album that keeps dropping as he incorrectly positions the arm to balance the albums on the stand, holding them all up.

He finally does it right, and their favorite love song, which he selected yesterday for this very moment, drops and begins to play. Travis draws her close to him, holding Crystal in his hard, firm arms, and as they slow dance, he serenades her with the sultriest tenor voice that she loves to hear.

Then the song ends. Their lips passionately meet again, and with an increasing desire to make love to his wife, Travis’s hands move up her back, unzipping the top garment she’s wearing from the neck until it gets stuck midway down. In the dark, he struggles with the zipper and out of frustration he pulls it off, over her head.

With the two twin sofa beds, joined together the night before are now a full-sized bed, where their youthful naked bodies melt down onto it, and they unite in the flesh as one, consummating the marriage.

While commemorating one week of marriage, Travis romantically carries Crystal around in the swimming pool in a loving embrace. After they've made love all morning, there's no better way to cool off on a hot August day than at the pool, surrounded by two-story apartment units.

Crystal is relishing the moment when unexpectedly—but playfully—Travis throws her from his arms and sends her flying backward into the air and into the water she sinks. She comes up, splashing water, and begins to chase Travis. Catching him, she leaps onto his back, leans backward, and they both go under. They then take turns chasing each other. Sounds of laughter and screams echo loudly within the confines of the gated pool.

But the ambiance inside the apartment the following weekend is not as playful when Travis, planning to leave Crystal home alone, walks into the living room and says, "I have somewhere to be later today."

"I'm going with you." Crystal cheers, just wanting to go for the ride.

"No, Crystal, you can't go."

"Why not?"

"I don't want you to."

This time, Crystal is not playing. She becomes upset and conniving when thinking—*If I can't go, you can't go either.*

As soon as Travis's back is turned, she hides the car keys, and when he looks for them, pouting like a child, he cries, "Crystal, where's the keys?"

Acting innocent, she passes through the living room, walking into the kitchen to reheat the hot comb on the stove. Hunching her shoulders, she says, "I don't know."

Then, on her way back to the bathroom to hot press her hair in the mirror, Crystal walks past Travis lying on one of the green-covered, hard pillow-back twin beds and begins to tease him.

"You spoiled brat."

Travis ignores it as she continues to walk in and out of the living room, repeating the words until she teases him one time too many. Travis leaps from the sofa and chases her into the bathroom, where she locks herself inside and listens as he bangs on the door and yells, "Crystal, unlock this door."

When she doesn't, he begins to force his way, beating his body against the door until the hinges break. Travis then leaps into the bathroom and picks Crystal up by the neck. With her legs dangling in the air, he insists, "Where's my car keys, Crystal?"

Barely able to breathe and her eyeballs about to pop, she immediately points above the medicine cabinet. He releases her.

Landing on her feet, Crystal leans against the bathroom wall, gasping for air, watching as Travis grabs the keys and then hurries out of the apartment. Massaging her neck, Crystal walks into the living room, shocked at his behavior, thinking, *Never could I have thought that the man, who loves me, would treat me this way. If he acts like this over small things, what else is he capable of?* Crystal then asks herself as she goes and stands at the sliding door, looking out to see if the car is gone. After seeing that it's gone, she hears the voice whispering, "Crystal, leave him."

Crystal begins to remove her clothes from the dresser drawer, but has a thought: *If I hadn't done what I did, it wouldn't have happened.* Convincing herself that she instigated it, Crystal takes the blame and mumbles, "It was my fault. I won't leave him."

In the kitchen, she begins cooking dinner. Afterward, she leaves and takes the long walk to Auntie Val's house, where she sits on the living room floor playing one-hand solitaire.

Crystal yells into the kitchen, "Auntie Val, earlier, Travis chased me into the bathroom and kicked down the door. He then choked me."

Now standing in the kitchen doorway with a worried look, she asks, "He did? Why?"

Crystal flips the top card of the deck and places it on top of another one that lined up in a row. "I was teasing him and hid the car keys from him."

Now somewhat relaxed, she asks, "Why did you do that, A-hole?"

"He was going somewhere without me. I just wanted to go with him and he wouldn't let me."

"That's terrible what he did, choking you. Are you leaving him?"

"I was thinking about it, but because it was my fault, I'm not going to."

"I agree." Auntie Val begins to laugh as she checks on the food cooking on the stove. "He shouldn't have done it, but I bet you won't do that again," she yells, still laughing.

"I sure won't." Crystal laughs, covering up the wound she acquired and has to heal, along with the other wounds that haven't quite healed yet.

Returning home two hours later and opening the door, the apartment smells of 'weed'. As Crystal suspected, Travis lied that he had given up drugs. Sitting on the living room floor with the stereo music blasting, he asks, "Where have you been?"

"I walked to Auntie Val's. Did you eat the dinner that I left for you in the oven?"

"Yeah. I'm sorry, Crystal, that I behaved the way I did."

"I'm sorry, too; I was wrong. I shouldn't have teased you."

Crystal sits beside him on the floor. They then kiss. Travis offers her the "joint," and she takes it, trying marijuana for the very first time and, now, saying yes to drugs.

After taking a puff, Crystal passes the 'joint' and then starts a conversation, "I miss church. I haven't been there since we've been married."

As Crystal is talking, Travis quietly puffs on the 'joint'.

"And why did you wait until the day after we were married to confess that you don't believe in Jesus?"

He takes another puff of the 'joint' before passing it to her, asking, "Would you have married me?"

"No," she answers, understanding his reasoning but a deception all the same.

Feeling mellow, Crystal sits in silence but thinking, S*omething told me to tell him, 'no'. I should have listened.*

Her quest to seek God and have a loving relationship with The Most High is the motive behind her asking Travis, as he holds the 'joint' to his lips, "Travis, now that you have me, does that mean you'll no longer go with me to church?"

She then takes the half-smoked 'joint' from him, holding it without taking a puff.

"Crystal, I told you how I feel about church. I don't like it, and it's full of hypocrites."

Crystal then takes a quick puff, hands it to Travis, stands to her feet, and mumbles in disappointment as she walks away, "I've gone to church most of my life. I want to learn of God and know the truth—that *God is real?* And I'm not going to stop because I'm married to you."

Unlike her, Travis is more interested in the Ouija board and witchcraft. He surprises her when he brings out the Ouija board that he kept hidden and shows it to her.

"When did you get that?" she screams at him. Shocked.

"I've had it for a little while."

"But why? It doesn't work."

"Let's try it and see."

"I don't want to see. It's evil," she says firmly, while frowning.

Not giving up, Travis finally convinces her to try it. Sitting with it between them on the table and their hands barely touching a triangle object, Travis asks, "What is Crystal's last boyfriend's name?"

The object begins to move slowly across the board, spelling Dillion. Crystal's first thought is to throw it to the ground and stomp on it. She stops herself, shouting, "That's a damn lie. He was not my boyfriend! And I told you that thing doesn't work."

"How did it spell his name if it doesn't work, Crystal?"

Spilling out anger, she screams, "You did it. That's why."

"Crystal, no, I didn't. Let's ask it a different question."

"No," she says, forcefully pushing the chair away from the table while she's sitting in it. "I'm done.

You're just like everyone else, believing that I liked that man."

That same week, Crystal begins her senior year. After Travis leaves for work and before school, she begins to look for the Ouija board. *Where is it?* she's thinking. *That evil thing has to go.* Searching the closet, she finds it.

Outside, rushing to school, Crystal stops at the trash bin. She looks at the Ouija board in her hand and says, "I might be in trouble for doing this, but in the trash is where you belong."

She then tosses it, watching it flip in the air and then fall. As she walks to school, Crystal worries how Travis will react when he finds out.

It's not a thought or is mentioned again until weeks later when Travis walks into the living room, glancing around, he asks, "Crystal, what happened to my Ouija board?"

She avoids his look and says, "I put it in the trash. I don't like it."

The room is deafly quiet as Crystal becomes stiff from fear. Hunched over with her elbows resting on her thighs, at the edge of the sofa, her eyes move with each step he takes, praying that he doesn't turn around and strike her. But he grabs his keys lying next to the stereo and walks out of the door. Crystal leans backward and breathes relief. *God, I'm glad he didn't come for me.*

On another day, he returns home from having worked the day shift. Walking into the living room, where Crystal sits on the floor, Travis tosses a stack of papers onto the coffee table, informing her as he walks past, "Here are my orders."

He has been teaching her the game of chess, and she's practicing her skills so she can beat him at his own game. With the chessboard in front of her, she immediately puts down the how-to-play chess book she'd been studying, picks up the stapled one-inch-thick stack of military orders, and begins to review the printed information.

While Travis stands nearby in the hallway and combined clothes closet, undressing, Crystal reads: *Spouse is not allowed to accompany you to Thailand nor in the near future while in Thailand serving active duty.*

Highly upset, Crystal yells, "We've only been married three months. They could have waited until after our first anniversary."

"I told you that I would be getting my orders sometime soon."

"Yeah, you did, but I didn't think it would be this soon. No wonder you wanted to get married so fast."

Pulling his T-shirt off and over his head, Travis responds, "Next month, in November, I'll have thirty days of leave time before I report to Thailand. I think it will be a great opportunity for us to travel to Dayton so you can meet my people. But before we go, we'll have to give up this apartment."

"If we do that, where am I supposed to live?"

"Auntie Val. Tomorrow, when we take her out for dinner, we can ask her."

"Why can't I stay here? The school is just down the street, which makes it easier for me to get there every day."

Travis then enters the bathroom. "The allotment check you'll get from the military each month will not be enough," he yells. "And I can't send you money because I have to live too."

Instead of arguing about it, she lets it go. Releasing the stack of orders into the air, Crystal watches it crash onto the coffee table. As the thought of taking a trip somewhere begins to amuse her, she can't begin to imagine what's outside of Arizona, other than California, and is curious to see what's out there.

At the restaurant, while Auntie Val converses with Travis, Crystal eyes a slice of Lemon Meringue pie sitting on the countertop that's nearby. Her attention is drawn back in when hearing Auntie Val saying, "Sure, Travis, you know 'Ahole' is welcome to stay with her uncle and me, while you are away."

The second Friday in November, one day before starting their trip to Ohio, Travis accompanies Crystal to Yale High School. He holds her hand as they walk from one classroom to the next, meeting all six of her teachers and verifying her one-week absence, which begins on Monday.

Late Saturday morning, with his stereo system and music collection in the trunk of the car that he's leaving with his uncle Joel in Dayton until he returns from Thailand, Travis drives across northern Texas as Crystal gazes out of the side window at the countryside, nervously wondering if her in-laws will accept her and vice-versa. Crystal and Grace have been writing to each other before the wedding. At her mother-in-law's request, Crystal has been calling her Mother, which didn't come easy at first because Maylene has been the only mother she's known.

Crystal's attention quickly becomes diverted to watching the immense trees in the not-so-far distance that majestically glorify themselves in brilliant arrays of yellow-orange, reddish-orange, and golden brown.

"Those are some strange-looking trees," she thinks aloud.

"What's wrong with them?" Travis asks.

"I don't know. They look weird."

In disbelief, Travis glances at her and then back at the road. He then jokes, "Oh, I forgot. You're from the desert, and the desert doesn't grow trees. It grows cactus."

They both laugh. More seriously, he says, "Crystal, it's autumn. You know—fall!"

Her jaw drops. "Ooh," she says.

It's elementary, but for her, it's like receiving sight. Crystal admires the beauty of it all, seeing but not seeing in real time that God is subtly revealing himself to her.

After two days of driving, Travis finally pulls off the road and parks the car across the street from his parents' house. His plump five-year-old sister stands inside the house, behind the all-glass storm door, smiling and waving with excitement as Travis and Crystal cross the snow-covered street.

"Hi," she sings while pushing the door open as they step onto the porch, clear of snow.

"I am glad to finally meet you, Crystal," she says, giggling.

Crystal quickly notices her sister-in-law's woman-like maturity and giggles. She then says, "The same here."

In the dining room and ironing, her mother-in-law suddenly leaps away from the ironing board with such wide strides that it feels like she has caused an earthquake. The wooden floor beneath their feet is so shaky it's terrifying to think that it could cave in, plunging them down into the basement at any minute.

As soon as Grace comes to a standstill, the floor stops shaking. Gleefully, she giggles and says, "I'm so happy to see y'all. I was so worried. That was a looong journey y'all made. I prayed for y'all to have a safe trip, and I thank God y'all made it here safely."

"Yeah, we're happy to be here too, Mama," says Travis. "And where's our hug?"

In his mother's company, Crystal quickly notices Travis's discomfort as he expresses his eagerness for Crystal to finally meet his grandparents, who mostly raised him.

"Mama, we'll be back." He says, cutting the visit short. "I'm taking Crystal to Nana's and Papa's house while we still have daylight."

Slightly brushing his arm against Crystal's side, he gestures for her to take the lead. As Grace candidly shares her emotions with her son, Crystal steps outside, off the back porch, and onto the snow-covered ground. And while waiting for Travis, she overhears Grace saying from inside the kitchen, "I like her, Travis. I like her a lot."

The words of approval transfigure into a smile on Crystal's face.

When it's nearly dark, Travis and Crystal walk two short blocks back to his parents' house and with their arms full of wedding gifts, they enter the dining room where Travis's stepfather is sitting and eating dinner. The surprised look on Mr. Ryder's face as he rises to his feet is unexpectedly humorous, making them laugh. He quickly swallows his food and shakes Travis's hand, loudly screaming in his southern dialect, "Well, hi, son."

Extending his hand to Crystal, he politely says, "Good to meet you, Crystal."

"It's good to meet you, too." She grins from cheek to cheek.

"Y'all, put those presents down, and come have dinner with me." He then raises his voice an octave, yelling to his wife. "Mother, fix them a plate."

While sitting around the table after dinner,

Crystal is now aware that Travis isn't as close to his mother and stepfather as he led her to believe. In her eyes, it is obvious that he doesn't favor his stepfather, and even though he's laughing and appears to be having a good time, it's just an act.

In the morning, after eating breakfast, Travis kisses Crystal. "See you later," he says, leaving her studying in the living room so she won't get behind at school.

The mornings and nights are the only times she sees him. He couldn't get her to come with him anyway because of the night in Phoenix before leaving for Ohio, they lay in bed as he told her, "Before I came into the military, people were afraid to go outside because of drive-by shootings. People would be walking down the street, minding their own business, when a car drove up the street and started shooting and killing innocent people for no reason."

"You're scaring me," she responded. "I don't want to live in Dayton."

So, to avoid being one of those unfortunate people, Crystal spends the entire week indoors, where she feels safe.

Then, on their last night in Dayton, her fear of leaving the house, literally, has Travis on his knees begging her to come with him to meet his biological father. "Please, Crystal, come on. He's waiting to meet you."

Shaking her head, she says firmly, "No. I'm not going."

Frustrated, Travis finally turns to his mother, who raises her voice. "You shouldn't have told her that. It happened years ago." Calmly, she then says,

"Crystal, it's safe now; you don't have to be afraid."

Trusting her mother-in-law's word over Travis's, Crystal leaves with him and visits his extended family, who live only two long blocks away.

10

In the waiting area of the Phoenix Sky Harbor International Airport, Travis and Crystal sit quietly, holding hands. It's so hard to say goodbye to the man she has fallen so deeply in love with. The mere thought of being without him evokes feelings of loneliness. She thinks, W*hat am I going to do for a whole year without my husband*?

For four months, they've been almost inseparable. They did just about everything together; they even bathed together. She has clung to him, and now he must leave her to fulfill his airman duties.

Interrupting their last few minutes alone, a female voice announces, "Flight 154 is now boarding at Gate 2."

Together, they rise to their feet. Travis pulls Crystal into his arms and holds her close. He places his finger underneath her chin and lifts it, looking into her already lonely eyes. Disrupting the silence between them, he says, "Promise me that you'll be faithful."

Crystal scans every inch of his handsome face so she wouldn't forget what he looks like and says, "I promise."

"I'll write to you every day. OK?"

Holding back the tears, she nods. "OK."

He presses his lips to hers ever so softly and then reassures her, "I love you, baby."

Crystal becomes emotionally disturbed as a lump swells in her throat. She continues to fight back the tears. Her words are sincere when she can finally say in truth, "I love you, too."

After another kiss, he walks away. Crystal stands at the window, watching as he boards the plane and looks so handsome in his uniform. Before stepping on board, Travis waves a final goodbye. Overcome with emotion, Crystal strolls away from the window.

Once inside the car, the tears flow uncontrollably. Cupping her hands over her face, Crystal leans forward, resting on the steering wheel, and allows herself to feel the pain. She cries until she can't cry anymore, and then she returns to Auntie Val's and Uncle Robbie's house.

While out of school for Christmas break, Crystal sits in the living room rocking chair, moping and looking the same as she feels—lonely. It's been twenty days since Travis left for Thailand. He has kept his promise to write her. Having received a letter, she sits thinking of him and misses him tremendously, and wishes he were with her so that they could celebrate Christmas together, which is less than a week away.

Then Auntie Val, with her inconsiderate self,

walks into the room and sits on the sofa. She begins to verbally attack Crystal. “You need to open your mouth and talk to people. You just sit around and don’t say a word.”

Crystal isn’t in the mood to be badgered. If she misses her husband, she has every right to. She feels insulted and begins to strike back. “Just because you run your mouth all the time doesn’t mean I have to. You talk too much anyway.”

Crystal slaps the arms of the rocker and, with strength in motion, she rises from the chair. “I don’t have to put up with this,” she says and enters the bedroom, immediately packing her belongings.

With everything now loaded into the car, Crystal drives to her and Travis’s friends’ apartment, who are an older couple.

Sitting in the living room, they listen as Crystal describes the situation she is in, and then adds, “I will pay you every month to stay in your second bedroom.”

Ace and Constance look at each other. He then says, “It’s up to you.”

“Yeah, Crystal, no problem. Ace works nights, and now with you here, I won’t be home, scared and alone,” says Constance.

It’s where Crystal spends the holidays.

The following month, she still misses Travis, a vital part of her life that she has depended on for her daily needs and comforts. To lie in his arms, to kiss his lips, to listen to him talk, laugh, and sing to her is what she longs for.

At school, walking to the car, she’s having one of those days when she’s thinking of him and needing intimacy. Slowly dragging her feet, being in a downcast mood, she spots a friend walking ahead of her, whom she has known since the eighth grade, and yells his name, “Darrell.”

Having had a crush on her during their sophomore year, he looks back and waits for her to catch up to him.

Crystal approaches, asking, “You act like you don’t know me anymore?”

Surprised by her question, he looks at her and answers, “You’re married, right?”

Thrown off, Crystal takes a second to think. Not comprehending his reasoning, she replies, “Just because I’m married doesn’t mean you can’t talk to me.”

Adjusting his stance, he apologizes, “You’re right. I’m sorry. How is marriage life working out?”

Missing Travis, Crystal frowns slightly. “It’s all right. Right now, he’s serving overseas.”

Taking a quick glance to look in the direction he was headed, Darrell then faces her and suggests, “I have weight training to go to. I don’t want to be late. Let’s exchange phone numbers.”

“OK,” says Crystal, thinking it’s an innocent request. She writes down the number and hands it to him. “By the way, weight training is looking good on you.”

He smiles and says before going their separate ways, “Thanks. I’ve lost over a hundred pounds.”

Barely eating and due to a decrease in her appetite, she has also lost weight.

Days later, she seeks professional advice. Visiting the free walk-in health clinic, Crystal coasts into the parking lot minutes before it closes, and rushes inside, where she’s attended to right away.

“Why aren’t you eating?” a doctor asks after she states why she’s there.

“I’m missing my husband who’s in Thailand. He writes me every day but it’s not the same as him being here."

"I understand. I can prescribe medication that will increase your appetite. I also suggest that because you're not adjusting well to being separated from your spouse, you go for counseling."

Crystal refuses but takes the prescription he gives her. She soon regains her appetite but she begins to drift—daydreaming.

The day it becomes most noticeable is when she picks Constance up from work, driving up to the intersection without slowing down and causing Constance to scream, "Crystal, don't you see that red light?"

Car horns begin blowing. Quickly, Crystal snaps out of the daydream and presses the gas paddle, safely speeding out of the way.

"Crystal, you scared the living hell out of me."

"I'm sorry, my mind was on Travis."

"It needs to be on the road."

"I know. It won't happen again," says Crystal, and then asks, diverting Constance's attention, "How was your first day on the job?"

With a more relaxed attitude, Constance answers, "It is so easy; I think I'm going to like it."

"I'll turn eighteen next month," says Crystal, keeping her eyes on the road. "I can't wait to find a job and hopefully save some money."

"You will," reassures Constance. "If you don't kill yourself first," they both laugh.

For Crystal, that was a wake-up call. No longer does she allow herself to focus so much on Travis. Accepting that he can't be there with her, she begins to concentrate on her upcoming birthday.

The day of, Crystal sits in first-period American history class, at the edge of her seat, eagerly watching the clock on the wall. As the long hand moves, setting off the school bell, she leaps to her feet, bumping other students as she hurries out the door.

Trotting down the stairs and running to the car, Crystal speeds out of the school parking lot, drives past the apartment complex and pulls into the grocery store lot, where she gets out and goes inside, grabs a newspaper off the counter, pays for it, and then drives one block to Constance's and Ace's apartment.

After jogging up a flight of stairs, she unlocks the door. No one else is home. Inside her rented room, Crystal drops onto a pile of blankets on the floor, her bed, and searches through the want ads. Right away, a sewing position catches her eye. She circles it.

Anxious to be one of the first to arrive at the factory, Crystal grabs her purse, hurries out of the apartment, down the stairs, and drives twenty minutes to the north side of town.

At the factory, she sits at the table completing a job application, occasionally looking up to see the interviewer as he moves from one person to the next. Finally, he approaches her, picks up her application, scans it, and says, "Mrs. Wallace, I see that you're a senior in high school."

"Yes. I have one class in the morning. I can work after class, though."

"Okay. The job is yours. I'll see you tomorrow at nine O'clock."

While on her way to share the good news with Auntie Val, Crystal merges onto the highway and can't contain her joy, singing, "Happy Birthday to me…"

Arriving there, she parks the car outside the gate and enters the house, knocking as she slowly pushes the door open.

Crystal eyes a package sitting just inside the door as she enters.

"Hi, A-hole! That package came in the mail for you," cheers Auntie Val sitting on the sofa in her usual spot.

Crystal picks up the box and carries it to Uncle Robbie's rocker. She rips it open. The note on top reads: "Happy Birthday!"

"A Bible?" she screams. "Out of all the other things in the world to buy, he sends me a Bible for my birthday. I don't believe this. What's wrong with him?"

"A Bible is always a good thing to have around the house. You should be thankful he sent you that. He didn't have to send you anything," grumbles Auntie Val, a Jehovah's Witness, in Travis's defense.

"Yeah, and the day he doesn't get me a gift for my birthday will be the day I'll forget his."

Auntie Val's loud, boisterous laugh fills the room. Crystal laughs, too, and places the Bible on the coffee table. Never having read a Bible, in her life, she begins to rock back and forth in the rocker, saying, "Guess what, Auntie Val?"

"What?"

"I got a job. I just got hired as a seamstress and came right over to tell you."

"That's good, Crystal, but what about school?"

"Well, I flunked American history in the first semester, and this semester, I am repeating it. It's my only class, and the boss is letting me work afterward."

"I like that even better. You should finish high school. I am proud of you, Crystal. You're doing the right thing."

"Oh, yeah, and I also want to apologize for being

disrespectful to you and to say that I'm sorry."

Slightly nodding her head, Auntie Val accepts Crystal's apology.

"So, can I move back in with you? The woman I'm staying with, her cousin, is spreading the lie that I'm enticing her husband Ace. I don't want him."

"Sure, you can. You don't need to be around that mess. I didn't tell you to leave in the first place, you A-hole."

As the echoes of laughter fill the room, the name "A-hole" has become a symbol of her affection.

Without hesitation, that day, Crystal moved back in.

After sitting for one month on the job, Crystal wears two-inch heels to work, only to find out when she is placed on the floor to hang garments for shipment that wearing them was a bad idea.

Kicking them off, rubbing her feet, she moans in pain. Looking around, Crystal sees the supervisor nearby and calls him to her, asking, "Why am I hanging garments? I wasn't told I would have to do this."

"Sorry, but we're out of sewing work right now."

"Well, I didn't take this job to do this," she mumbles softly as he's walking away. "I come to sew."

Limping, she leans on work tables for support as she hangs the garments on the track-line.

At lunch break, and with aching feet, Crystal walks to the car as she usually does, but today, she doesn't sit in the car to eat lunch. She drives away, quitting the job.

The following day, at the Motorola manufacturing plant, Crystal passes all of the tests and sits in the interviewer's office, where she is told, "I'm sorry, young lady, but here at Motorola, we prefer to hire high school graduates. When you graduate in two more months, give me a call. I will put you to work."

He then hands her his business card.

Crystal feels encouraged, and as she walks out of the office, stuffing the card into her shoulder strap purse, she mumbles, "I'll be back."

Saturday afternoon, Auntie Val's and Crystal's usual wash day, they sit in the living room waiting for the final wash cycle to finish when the phone begins to ring. Auntie Val answers it and then hands it off to Crystal. "Here. It's for you," she says before walking out of the room, humming and leaving Crystal alone, talking to Darrell. Crystal had hooked up with him shortly before moving back in with Auntie Val.

He's only calling for one thing. "You want to get together later?" he asks.

Crystal is done with the guilt that she is feeling, telling him, "No, we can't. I'm busy," only to be rid of him.

As she's hanging up the phone, Auntie Val, three minutes later, and still humming, re-enters the living room, sits down, and asks, "Crystal, are you having an affair?"

"If I am, it's my business," Crystal says firmly. The only reason she was with Darrell was that she missed Travis and just wanted to be held. Not allowing Auntie Val to treat her like a child, Crystal argues, "If everyone thinks that I am old enough to be married than I'm old enough to do whatever I damn well please."

Auntie Val grabs her handbag and hurries out of the house. The screen door slams behind her. From the living room window, Crystal watches her get in the car and speed away.

It was the last time Crystal spoke to Darrell.

Deciding not to be there when Auntie returns, she grabs her purse and mumbles, “I’m sick of this.”

Crystal then drives to Cathy’s house, where she is led into Cathy’s parents’ bedroom.

“Ma’dear, Crystal wants to ask you a question,” says Cathy, knocking before entering.

On the bed, relaxing, she looks up and asks, “What is it?”

Fearful that she will get a no for an answer, Crystal timidly steps into the room. “Ma’dear, she says pausing. “I have to move out of my aunt’s house. I don’t have anywhere to go. Can I pay fifty dollars a month to live here? It’s all I can afford.”

“Sure, Crystal, you’re more than welcome to stay here.”

“Thank you, Ma’dear,” smiles Crystal, who then grabs Cathy’s hand, “Come and help me move my things.”

While Auntie Val is away from home, Crystal moves out for the final time.

Determined to get that job at Motorola, Crystal doesn’t miss a day of school, and as graduation draws nearer, she’s holding a conversation with Cathy and Ma’dear, discussing what all needs to be done before the big day. Crystal then remembers, “Someone at Motorola told me to call him when I graduate,” she blurts. “I’m going to call him now.”

Leaving them in the next room, she runs into the kitchen. On the phone with the interviewer, Crystal introduces herself and reminds him, “You promised me a job after graduation. I graduate in two weeks.”

Cathy and her mother slowly enter the kitchen,

watching Crystal's expression—a smile.

"He wants me to come to his office tomorrow for another interview," says Crystal as she hangs up the phone.

"Crystal, that's good," they both cheer.

The minutes can't come quick enough as her excitement bursts like fireworks within her. Finished sewing the dress she's wearing for graduation, Crystal stands ironing it, wishing that Travis could be there to share the excitement. She then begins to reminisce about a particular morning, nine months ago: she lay in bed expecting to have a fun-filled day with her man, as Travis rolled over, put his arm around her, and said, "You're going to be late for school."

Snuggled gently in his arms, she replied, "I'm not going."

With quickness, Travis lifted his head off the pillow, and with his eyes widened, he shouted in her ear, "You're not going?"

With confidence, Crystal uttered, "Nope."

His soft-spoken words became authoritative. Not allowing it to become a pattern with her, Travis screamed loudly, "Take your butt to school, Crystal." Then, violently, he pushed her out of bed.

Irked, she got up from the floor and argued, "I don't want to go. I want to stay home with you."

Travis was not having it; he slung the sheets off himself, and as he got out of bed, he looked into her eyes and demanded, "You're going, and I'm taking you."

Crystal pouted for the entire four minutes it took him to drive her there. He coasted into the circle and stopped in front of the school administration building and said, “Give me a kiss.”

She quickly pecked him on the lips.

“I’ll see you when you get home.”

Crystal didn’t respond. She slammed the door in anger, and as Travis drove away, she could hear him laughing.

The memory of that day is commendable. He should be here, she thinks, resting the hot iron down on the ironing board. Crystal then wondered if Travis had received the letter she sent, stating, “I wish you could be here to see me graduate."

At the start of the graduation ceremony, Crystal stands in line, staring out into the crowd packed into the bleachers, but doesn’t recognize the faces that stare back at her. Wearing a red gown and cap with red, white, and blue tassels, she takes a step forward, following the person in front of her as the theme song, “Pomp and Circumstance”, begins to play.

The long line of students move forward, marching onto the well-illuminated football field toward rows of seats positioned in the center of the field and facing the podium.

Crystal comes to her seat, and the rows of students remain standing until the last row is in position. Then, together, the entire graduating class is motioned to sit. The music stops.

Bored with listening to the valedictorian and the other speakers talk about the past four years, Crystal identifies her friend in the row in front of her, four seats down. Speaking softly, she says, “Shyla. I got the job.”

“Shh,” murmurs everyone, including Shyla, who looks at Crystal and smiles.

Finally—it's time to award the diplomas. Speaking into the microphone, the principal calls, "Crystal M. Wallace."

Crystal walks across the stage to receive her diploma with well-earned self-esteem. Family and friends become wild, clapping, whistling, and screaming, "Yeaaaaa!" She even blushes when she hears them shouting, "Crystal!"

The first of Maylene's ten children to graduate, Crystal walks off the stage smiling and waving her diploma, making her mother proud.

11

At the start of a new work week, working in the testing department at Motorola, Crystal hangs around the house before leaving for work when she hears Cathy yelling from the kitchen, “Crystal, telephone.”

Puzzled as to who it could be, Crystal speaks into the phone, “Hello.”

“Hi, girl, what are you doing?”

Crystal recognizes Gean’s voice. It’s not like they’re close cousins and question the reason for the call. “I’m about to leave for work, why you ask?”

“I know of some two-bedroom apartments that are newly built, and I’m hoping you will be my roommate.”

“Hmm...,” Crystal wonders before she answers, “I’ll think about it.”

“Girl, don’t you want your own place and some privacy? I know you’re not getting it where you’re at."

Gean tends to be two-faced and untrustworthy. Crystal again says, "I'll think about it."

"Crystal, please. It's time I leave my mama's house. She's getting on my nerves, please."

Crystal finally gives in to Gean's begging and, reluctantly, answers, "Dang, OK."

In September, on her way to work, Gean gets into the car. But it doesn't start. She then hurries up the stairs, calling Crystal, waking her up, and says, "Girl, I need a ride to work. My car won't start."

Having worked the second shift, Crystal raises her head off the pillow, mumbling, "What, your car won't start?"

"No."

Crystal sits up in bed. Wiping her hands down her face, she says grumpily, "I was having the best sleep."

"Hurry up and get dressed. I don't want to be late."

Arriving a little early at Gean's place of employment, Crystal parks between two other cars near the curb while Gean is talking, saying, "I know I'll have to hear mama complaining when I call her to come pick me up after work, but I have to hear it, she says. "And I have to stay with them at the house until I get my car fixed."

"I thought Aunt Elleen was getting on your nerves," asks Crystal as she turns off the ignition switch.

Gean laughs. "Now that she has calmed down, considerately, everything is cool. I go there after work anyway. The drive to the apartment is too far, and I don't always feel like making that long drive after work."

"Oh, that's why, all this time, I hadn't seen you?" asks Crystal.

"Yep. That's why."

Crystal grows used to Gean not being at the apartment, and over the next two months, somewhere between October and November, she moves out permanently to live with her parents—behind Crystal's back.

It's while Crystal is busy hanging a large wood-framed painting of a desert sunset on the living room wall when Gean returns to the apartment, and is outside climbing the apartment stairs. Hearing the sound of the door unlocking, Crystal glances over her shoulder and sees her opening the door. "Girl, I like that painting," says Gean. "Where did you find it?"

"I got it from the flea market this morning. I'm just seeing how it looks on the wall," Crystal says, looking surprised to see her. "The last time I saw you, it was before Thanksgiving."

Gean closes the door. "I know, right? Time sure flies. But I decided after we talked about you and Travis sub-leasing from me for two weeks before y'all left for San Antonio, Texas, where he will be stationed, I wouldn't be able to afford my own place on a secretary's salary. I just came to get the rest of my things before he gets here."

"Which is next weekend, December first," Crystal informs her, and with her palms turned up, she hunches her shoulders to say, "Now I don't know where we'll stay."

Gean walks toward the bedrooms, "I don't know what to tell you," she answers, behaving as though she did Crystal a favor instead of the other way around.

"If you had told me that you moved out, I would have had time to find somewhere to go."

"I was wrong. I should have told you," she responded, now walking toward the door to leave, carrying her last few possessions that she left behind when she first moved out. "I'll see later."

When Gean is long gone, Crystal begins to have afterthoughts about the situation, discovering that she's been backstabbed by her cousin. Crystal mumbles, "I knew she was going to do me wrong. I just knew it! She won't get a favor from me ever again."

While contemplating her and Travis's possible homeless predicament, Crystal must act and act fast.

Monday morning, she rushes out of the second-floor apartment, hoping to locate the landlord in the office. Luckily, he's outside walking with his back to her. Crystal trots down the stairs, yelling, "Excuse me!"

He turns in her direction. "Are you talking to me?"

"Can I talk to you for a minute?" she asks.

Walking on the sidewalk alongside busy Thomas Road, they meet halfway. Crystal shouts over the traffic noise. "As you know, I've already given you notice of my intent to vacate at the end of this month, but my husband is in the military and is returning from Thailand. The problem is I don't have anywhere else to go, so I'm hoping you'll allow me to keep the apartment until the fifteenth."

"Well, I've already rented it to someone else." He then pauses to think.

While he's thinking, Crystal worries, *If he says no, I don't know what I'm going to do.*

She then feels relief when he says, "OK, I'll put them in another apartment and prorate your rent, but you will have to be out in two weeks."

"Yes. We will. Thank you so much," says Crystal, shaking his hand.

Now, in an upbeat mood, Crystal is inside her bedroom and busy sewing when she is suddenly spooked by the ringing phone. Jumping in her seat, her heart feels like it's about to leap from her chest. Placing her hand over her heart, she trots out of the room and into the unoccupied bedroom, grabbing the phone off the floor that she assumed Gean disconnected before she left.

The overseas operator says, "You have a collect call from Travis Wallace. Will you accept the charges?"

Surprised and with her upbeat mood now increased, she says cheerfully, "Yes."

"I need you to say 'over' when you are finished talking. Do you understand?"

"I understand."

Travis, sounding very faint, speaks into the phone. "Hi, baby. I just want you to know that I'll be there Saturday. I don't know what time, so you'll have to call the airport to find out. Over."

Crystal talks loudly so she'll be heard. "Hi, baby. I can't wait to see you. Over."

"I sent you a letter with all the information about the airline and flight number. Over."

The operator interrupts, "You have one minute. Over."

They scramble to get their last-minute conversation in and then exchange, "I love you. Over."

Fantasizing about holding him tightly in her arms, she drives to the airport on Saturday morning and is quickly let down when she arrives. It's the wrong flight.

Crystal returns to the airport three times before finally, on the fourth trip, and on the exact date that he left one year ago, Travis walks into the airport terminal with his duffel bag and begins to browse the waiting area, looking past her.

His expression of disappointment is evident when he doesn't recognize her standing far from the door, wearing a shoulder-length, curly black wig and dressed in an all-black pantsuit that perfectly accents her figure. She had purchased it from the sewing factory where she worked and hadn't worn it until now.

At a standstill, Travis continuously looks past her leaning against the wall wearing black suede and leather, four-inch heels—she looks hot. She already contemplated that he wouldn't identify her, and when he finally makes eye contact, she smiles.

Joyfully, he smiles back. His duffel bag crashes to the floor, and like a magnet, they draw near to one another, and while in each other's arms, they kiss a long, passionate hello.

The next two whole days are spent in bed, completely naked. They can't stay off each other, whether having sex or just being affectionate.

The third day as Crystal lies on top of her man, she suggests, "Travis, let's get dressed and get out of here."

"And do what?"

"Let's walk down the street to the Thomas Mall."

Not particularly looking for anything, they stroll through the entire mall, holding hands until finally, Travis asks, "Crystal, do you see anything you want?"

"Nope. Not a thing. What about you?"

"Nothing. Let's just head back to the apartment."

Walking outside, they come upon a pet store they hadn't noticed before, and seeing a four-month-old female cocker spaniel puppy in the window, Crystal says, "Oh, it's so cute."

She quickly releases Travis's hand, squats down, and taps on the window. The puppy begins to scratch it.

Secretly looking for a Christmas gift for her, Travis says, "Do you want it?"

"She is so adorable. Yeah, I want her."

"How much is the puppy in the window?" Travis asks as he walks into the pet store.

"Two hundred," says the sales clerk.

"She's a pedigree?"

"Sure is. She has all her shots and comes with all her pedigree documents."

"We'll take her and throw in a leash and some dog food."

The sun is now setting, as they begin walking the puppy on her leash back to the apartment, where Crystal veers left into the kitchen. She yells into the living room, "Travis, we only have frozen meals to eat for the two weeks we're here. Do you want a pot pie? They're the large ones."

"Yeah, a pot pie will do," he says, while on the floor playing with the puppy. He then asks, "Crystal, have you thought what to name her?"

"Not yet. We just got her."

Crystal places two pot pies in the oven and then joins Travis playing with the puppy. She tosses a toy across the room and watches as the puppy runs after it.

"I know what I'll name her. Goldilocks, because of her golden coat," says Crystal.

"Goldilocks it will be," says Travis as he rises from sitting on the floor. In the kitchen, he opens a bottle of wine and pours them a glass.

Relaxing on the living room floor, Crystal sits straddled atop him while he lies on his back with his head resting in the palm of both hands. She then begins to feel intoxicated and her conscience gets the best of her, spilling the beans about her affair, it flows out, "I have a confession."

Travis's eyes widen as he stares directly into hers. "What confession is that?"

"I'm sorry, baby, that I broke my promise to be faithful. I missed you, and I just wanted to be held. I'm telling you because I don't want to keep secrets."

Travis lay there quietly. Crystal can see his tears forming while staring into his eyes, wondering what his thoughts are. It was his idea that they be open and honest, and not keep secrets.

As she awaits Travis's confession, tears stream down the side of his face but suddenly, he lifts his upper body off the floor, forcefully pushing Crystal off of him, and accidentally pokes her in the left eye. He slowly walks into the bedroom and closes the door. On the floor, in pain, Crystal sits with her hand covering her injury, and when she can no longer bear to listen to him crying, she goes outside and wanders around the parking lot in the dark, fearful of him coming after her and chock her as he did two weeks into the marriage.

Crystal wonders around in the dark, speculating and mumbles, "I know he isn't as innocent as he is letting on. With a sex drive as big as his—no way could he have gone a full year without sex. No way!"

After thirty minutes of hiding outside, Crystal

hears her name. He's calling her.

"What?" she yells.

"Where are you?"

Crystal walks out from the front of the car to the rear.

"What are you doing out here?" he asks.

"I was afraid you would hit me."

Travis meets her halfway. He reaches out for her hand, holding it as they walk back to the apartment. Inside, he looks into her red swollen eye, cups her face with both hands and shouts, "What happened to you?"

"You poked me when you pushed me away."

He kisses her eye. "I'm sorry. I didn't mean to."

Travis then puts his arms around her in a long, warm, loving embrace. He has forgiven her—so she thinks.

12

They're cruising on the highway, gaining mile upon mile and traveling hour by hour while Crystal, feeling exhausted, can't keep her eyes open, so she just sleeps and because she doesn't have experience pulling a trailer, Travis will not trust her to drive.

At past midnight, he crosses into San Antonio, Texas. Leaning against the locked door, resting her head on a pillow, Crystal opens her eyes and glances out the window. As she repositions herself in the passenger seat, sitting upright, she asks, "Travis, where are we?"

"We're here in San Antonio."

"How far are we from the base? I need a bed to lie down in."

"At this next exit," he says, taking the off-ramp from the highway. "I don't know why you're the tired one. I'm doing all the driving."

Merging into traffic, Travis turns onto Military

Drive, and they cruise the well-lit street that divides Lackland Air Force Base, which is to the left and right of them. He then makes a left turn at the green light. Approaching the guard's station, he rolls down the car window to ask, "Which direction is guest housing?"

Pointing, the guard says, "Continue straight ahead. At the stop sign, turn right." He then permits them to enter the base.

At the guest housing, Travis unlocks the door of their assigned kitchenette. He switches on the light and leaves it on long enough to locate the bed. In the dark, they walk over and flop down on it. Exhausted, they sleep all day Sunday.

Monday morning, they're up early, locating the housing authority office. Around noon, they stand opposite the male assistant, assisting them in locating a place to live. Impatient with the assistant, who slowly flips and scans the pages of the huge, thick, green hardback book on the countertop between them, Travis says, "I tell you what. Just look for a furnished one-bedroom apartment listed in the one or two-hundred dollar range and not too far from base."

The guy flips another page. "Here's one for two hundred that's only seven minutes away."

Not expecting to find anything in that low price range, Travis and Crystal rush out of the building with the address written down on paper.

After leaving the rental office, they then cruise up the street, turning into the apartment complex, and quickly locate their unit. While relishing herself in the mild warmth of the sun, Crystal stands at the rear of the U-haul, directing Travis as he slowly backs up the trailer.

"OK. Stop!" she yells.

Together, they begin to unload the U-haul trailer. Beginning with the heavy wooden four-leg cabinet and the sewing machine inside that Maylene bought for Crystal and sent it to her while she and Gean were roommates, they carried it ten feet and through the open apartment door. After fifteen minutes of unloading, Crystal walks beside Travis and agrees with him, "That was quick. We would still be unloading if I hadn't left my stereo system and my album collection in Ohio with my uncle Joel."

"Yeah. I know. Those are a lot of albums."

Travis then suggests as he closes and locks the trailer doors, "Crystal, I'm hungry. It's getting late. Instead of us holding the trailer until tomorrow, let's turn it in now and use the refund money to get groceries and a Christmas tree."

"Ok. That sounds good to me."

On base, sitting in the car, after they've finished shopping, Travis stuffs liverwurst into his mouth and says with it full, "Well, we spent more than we should have. We're broke until payday. So there goes our Christmas tree."

With Christmas only eight days away, Crystal answers, "Yep, and it won't feel like Christmas without one."

Travis starts the engine. "I don't see why not, Crystal. It's just a tree. Christmas is all a scam to get people's money, anyway. We're going to make the best of it, regardless."

Crystal quietly looks out of the window wondering if she should tell him about the five hundred dollars she saved while he was away. She then decides against it. *He'll only spend it carelessly buying things we don't need. I'll just keep it to myself. I might need it in case I have to escape.*

Early Christmas morning, they're up cooking. The glazed ham bakes in the oven as its pleasant smell begins to fill their nostrils and stimulate their appetite.

"Girl, that ham smells good," comments Travis.

Feeling hungrier by the minute, they gather around the kitchen island with a bowl between them.

"Okay, what do we mix first, Crystal?" asks Travis.

"I never made a sweet potato pie. I don't know."

"Well, I think I remember some of the ingredients from watching my grandmother, Nana."

"The sweet potatoes are all I know about," Crystal says as she peels them and places them in the bowl.

Using the spices that Travis recalls, they sprinkle nutmeg, allspice, and a lot of cinnamon into the bowl of cooked sweet potatoes.

Crystal stirs as Travis adds eggs, sugar, and melted butter, and pours in some Carnation milk. After mixing it well, they dip their finger into the bowl to taste. "Needs more sugar," they concurrently agree, then dump more in.

They continue adding more ingredients until they taste it and moan, "Mmmm."

Taking in the luscious aroma from the pie and ham baking, Travis asks, "Crystal, where are the dominoes? I want to try and beat you at a game."

"I don't think so," she says, accepting the challenge. "But first, Travis, open your Christmas present in the bedroom walk-in closet."

"I have a present?"

"Yes. It's that unopened box."

Travis carries the box into the living room and

sets it in the middle of the floor. He becomes childlike as he digs into the box, pulling out, one by one, a camcorder, a movie screen, and, lastly, a projector.

"I love it," he says and kisses her. "Thank you, Baby." He points at Goldilocks sleeping on the floor near the sofa. "That's your gift."

"Yeah. I already know. Now, are you ready to get your spanking at playing dominoes?"

In the bedroom, Travis dumps the dominoes onto the bed and shuffles them around and around in a circle.

"OK, I warned you." Crystal giggles as they reach into the pile, each withdrawing nine.

Throughout the day, they alternate between playing dominoes, eating, and playing cards.

Losing at rummy five hundred, Crystal mixes the cards as she scatters them around on the living room floor and whines, "Travis, I quit. You cheat. I'm going to play with Goldilocks." She claps her hands. "Come here, girl."

"Crystal, I didn't act like a sore loser when you beat me in dominoes."

Now ready for bed, Crystal slips out of the room as the bedroom light illuminates her pathway into the kitchen, where she opens the refrigerator and takes out the last slice of pie. Crystal then goes and stands at the bedroom door and teases, "Mmm, Travis, this pie tastes soooo good."

From the bed, Travis watches with his eyes fixed on the piece of pie and begs, "Crystal, are you going to eat the last piece and not give me some?"

"Yep."

She delicately takes tiny bites, enticing him until she has eaten half of it. Then, pretending to be angry, she walks over to him. "Here!" She hands him the leftover half.

After switching off the light, she lies in bed, giggling at him in the dark, smacking his lips.

Her wounded eye from the poke has now healed, but before she falls asleep, Crystal stares into the dark, asking herself the same question that she asks each and every day, even when they're apart: *has he truly forgiven me for having had an affair?*

13

In the New Year, as Crystal lies in bed unable to fall back to sleep after Travis has left for work, she feels sick to her stomach, caused by the lingering smell of bacon and eggs that she cooked for his breakfast earlier this morning.

Leaping out of bed, she runs into the bathroom, bends over the commode, and violently empties her gut.

When Travis first arrived home from Thailand in December, they agreed to begin having a child and have been trying to conceive one.

I must be pregnant, thinks Crystal as she leaves the bathroom.

It happens again during dinner. Leaving the bathroom, Crystal comes and sits beside Travis at the kitchen island. “I’m pregnant. I haven’t had my period, and it’s the third time today I vomited.”

As though in doubt, Travis mumbles, “That was

quick."

As the past creeps back into their life, Crystal quickly eliminates any misconceptions of Darrell being the father and calmly looks at Travis to reassure him, "Travis, I know what you're thinking and, yes, it's your child. It had to have happened before we left Phoenix."

Travis continues to eat his lunch in silence. His sudden coldness insults her. *I regret that I told him,* thinks Crystal as she walks away, leaving him alone at the island.

As the warm air moves in, pushing away the cold of winter, but it's not yet spring—it's February, Travis and Crystal venture out far from home and drive to one of the city parks.

Inside its immaculate garden are beautiful varieties of roses enclosed by stone walls. Ponds full of large koi fish are scattered throughout.

With the video camera filming their walk along the garden's colorful pathways, they stop to admire an arrangement of red roses, and after noticing one type of koi fish that looks like carp swimming in the pond, they move further along the path, adoring white, pink, and yellow roses before approaching the waterfall that ends their walk.

Stopping the camcorder, Travis and Crystal stand holding hands, admiring how the transparent water rolls thinly over the garden's back wall as if it were a clear window, illuminating the free-climbing ivy behind it as it pours into the pond below.

Travis nudges her and takes a step. Following the pathway leading them out of the garden to the adjacent zoo, it isn't their plan to visit it, but Travis pays their way inside since they're outside its gate, and the day is still young.

It's a small zoo, and with only an hour before it closes, they walk the entire length of it, stopping at times so Travis can share his peanuts with the free-roaming squirrels. After scattering all that he has left of the peanuts on the ground, he takes Crystal's hand. "Let's go."

Surprisingly, on the road going home, there are only a few vehicles compared to earlier traffic. As they slowly approach the red light, Crystal gazes out of the side window, watching an elderly black man sweeping the pavement of the corner gas station. While the car is halted at the light, the man stops sweeping and looks in her direction. He waves. Thinking it's a kind gesture and perhaps, maybe, they're the only black people he's seen all day, she waves back just when the traffic light turns green.

"Crystal, you're flirting with him?" Travis howls as he speeds into the intersection.

She can't believe his accusations and looks over her shoulder at him, screaming, "Flirting? I was not flirting with that man, Travis. I was only waving because he waved at us."

He quickly glances at her, yelling, "Yes, you were."

"I was not." Crystal snarls at him. Turning up her nose, frowning, she's not pleased with his jealous behavior, which leaves her baffled and tensed. Trying to control the argument, she shuts her mouth and allows the absence of words and pent-up emotions to de-escalate the long ride home.

Before leaving the apartment, they forgot to confine Goldilocks in the bathroom and when Travis unlocks the door, he sees his sculptured incense holder, made of coconut shells and carved into monkeys, lying on the living room floor.

"What the hell!" he yells.

Travis picks up the mauled and disfigured sculpture, "Crystal, look what your dog did."

He then shakes his head. Crystal's heart begins to beat fast as she watches Travis violently hurl the sculpture to the floor, crushing and dismantling it even more. He then walks out of the room with his head tilted back, acting as though he's about to scream.

No longer sensing danger, she looks down at the pieces on the floor and at Goldilocks and says, "See what you've done."

Travis walks into the living room, "That was my favorite souvenir from Thailand," he says calmly, bending down to begin picking up the pieces.

Sympathetically, Crystal replies, "I know it was. It's very unlikely you'll find another one just like it. I would be mad, too."

Each of the four monkeys had been carved in a different manner and represents the saying "hear no evil; speak no evil; see no evil." The monkey receiving the most attention sits with its legs spread open while its hands cover its private parts. The words below it read: "Do no evil."

Crystal then confines Goldilocks in the bathroom, and together they clean up the big mess.

When done, Travis walks out of the apartment without saying a word, slamming the door.

A short time later, he comes back inside, tossing a rolled marijuana cigarette onto Crystal's lap as she sits watching re-runs on the thirteen-inch-screen TV that she bought while working at Motorola, Inc.

"I don't want this," she says, placing the rolled joint on the lamp table, assuming Travis will smoke it later.

Travis proceeds to the bedroom. He walks inside it

and, right away, turns around and walks back out. Being argumentative, he says, "I was cleaning out the car, and I found that joint beneath the seat on the passenger's side. You've been riding men around in my car, Crystal!"

"The only male I've had in that car is my cousin, Ervin, and he's still in high school," she says, feeling as though she's a target being hit with false accusations but forgetting that she gave Cathy's older brother a ride somewhere. But Travis isn't in the mood to hear the truth.

Feeling insulted and irritated by his attitude, she enters the bedroom and lies on the bed. Thoughts rush in and begin to jam her mind. Needing to express what she's thinking and to sort out her feelings, Crystal takes the writing tablet and a pen off the dresser, and, while sitting on the bed with her back against the wall, she writes:

My husband doesn't listen to me.
He doesn't understand me.
I feel that he doesn't love me.

Looking for a fight, Travis walks into the room and grabs the tablet from Crystal's lap. He reads it and reacts with foolish anger, throwing the tablet to the floor. His facial muscles—tight and tense—begin to harden into a monstrous form as he rushes toward her, grabbing her legs and dragging her until she lies flat on her back. Furiously, he rips off her clothes.

As Crystal lies naked, watching him undress and unsure of how to respond, she remains silent, hoping not to feed his anger. Completely disrobed, he stares into her eyes and says with a touch of maliciousness, "You don't think I love you?"

The look in his eyes is cold and says: *Fear me.*

At the moment, she does fear him—the other him or the deceptive spirit she saw the night when she first met him and is now showing his hidden but true self.

With her heart pounding, Crystal lies on her back, clinging to the bed sheets for dear life. Travis, like a ravenous beast, separates her legs and forces his erect penis into her vagina, satisfying his appetite for dominance. Then, he suddenly stops. On his knees, he says with his voice deepened, "Turn over," and slaps her thigh.

At his command, she tries to remain calm and very much in submission, but as she rolls over onto her stomach, she begins to tremble. Travis proceeds to penetrate her from behind, but his aim seems to be purposely set for the route that the creator, God, did not intend to be used for sex—the anal route. Crystal begins to wiggle wildly, yelling at the top of her voice, "Travis, no."

Travis can't control her movements, so he punches her, hitting her anywhere that he possibly can as she moves from side to side, afraid that if she screams, the situation will become even worse.

He then pushes her off the bed and onto the floor.

He looks down at her and says in that strange, deep voice, "Put on your clothes. I want you to get the hell out—and take your dog with you."

Reacting quickly, Crystal picks up her pants from off the floor and pulls them up to her waist. While trying to remain calm, cool, and collected to make good judgments in her time of crisis, she opens the door. Not knowing where to go and with Goldilocks on the leash, Crystal is afraid to walk out into the night—it's too risky, being that she's pregnant, so she sits outside the door on the two-foot-high concrete wall facing the apartment. Images of what has just happened keep popping up in her head.

Suddenly, the door opens. Out of his mind and enraged, Travis pushes her large blue travel chest outside and slams the door shut. He reopens it and violently throws out all her clothes and everything else she owns, except the sewing machine.

He closes the door for the last time. Crystal hops down from the wall, gathers all her things, and neatly piles them on the travel chest. She walks away, thinking she'll return to get them.

Walking alongside the wall with Goldilocks at her feet, Crystal suddenly feels a piercing pain in her heart—God, it hurts!

She reaches the front of the apartment complex and sees an empty parking space away from the lights. There, she won't be noticed.

She sits on the concrete parking block as her pain bursts out of her wounded heart and bleeds tears. Her thoughts spin around as she tries to make sense of Travis's behavior.

Quietly, as tears flood into her mouth, she murmurs, "God, why are these bad things happening to me? What am I doing wrong? He didn't have to treat me like that."

She then sobs even harder. Staring into the darkness with blurry vision, the black of night becomes the screen that Travis is projected upon and holding her in the air by the neck as she points to the keys above the medicine cabinet.

The memory of Travis's past abusiveness then slowly dissipates and now her attention becomes focused on Goldilocks, lying on her lap, sleeping.

With a bleeding heart, Crystal's tears stop flowing. Gently rubbing Goldilocks' head, she plays with her golden, curly, long, large ears—tugging at them slightly. Crystal could have never imagined when Travis purchased Goldilocks that she would, one day, be her comforter in her darkest hour.

Breaking through the night silence, she hears her name. Crystal then turns her head in the direction of Travis's voice and sees him walking toward the front, stopping and standing not too far from where she sits, but he doesn't see her.

He calls her name again, "Crystal."

She reluctantly answers, "What?" and then leaps to stand on her feet as he walks closer.

Noticing her fear, Travis doesn't come any closer. "Crystal," he says with a calm voice. "I'm sorry. I hate what I did. I don't know why I acted like that. I love you."

Crystal grunts. "How you treat me isn't what I call love."

"I know, and I'm asking you for forgiveness. It won't happen again. Will you please come back inside?"

"Why? So you can beat me some more, or do you want to beat the dog too?"

"No, Crystal, I won't beat the dog. It was my fault that I left the souvenir out. I'll get over that. It's you that I love and care about. Come inside, please."

Crystal finally gives in and allows Travis to hold her in his arms and kiss her, plugging the hole in her pierced heart that he inflicted, easing her pain.

On an off day, Travis realizes that the bedroom is missing a vital part of any room. He yells, "Crystal, come here."

She runs into the room. "What?"

"Look around and tell me what's missing."

Crystal glances around the room without looking

at the walls. "I don't notice anything."

"We don't have a window in here."

Crystal is just as surprised as Travis and says as she turns, making a three-hundred and sixty degree circle, "Wow, why didn't we notice it before now?"

"That's why we're sleeping past two in the afternoon every weekend. No light was coming in, and because the room was dark, we thought it was still night."

"We rented it without seeing it, also," says Crystal.

A week later, Travis comes home for lunch, and he's excited, saying as he enters the apartment, "Crystal, the people next door have moved, and that apartment has a window. I'm going to the office and get it for us tomorrow before someone else takes it."

"How do you know they moved?"

He sits down to begin eating his lunch. "I looked through the window before coming inside."

Over the next two weeks, as they wait to move into the one-bedroom, furnished apartment next door, the unit is cleaned and painted.

Days after moving, they lay cozy side by side across the width of the bed and browsing in a Spiegel's catalog. "Ooh, Travis, look at these curtains and matching bedspread set," says Crystal after flipping the page, and pointing. "I like its lilac color and design. What do you think?"

"Yeah. That's nice. Let's get it."

Travis observes Crystal filling out the order form, and when she finishes, she rolls off the bed, onto her feet, and tosses the catalog onto the dresser.

Walking away, she leaves Travis lying on the bed, from which he demands, "Crystal, make me a sandwich."

"You get up from there and make it yourself," she says with the same tone he uses with her.

Travis comes into the living room with a slow gait, walking past her sitting on the sofa and with a far-away look in his eyes, he goes into the kitchen, where he opens the pantry door, yanking food out of it and allowing the boxed and canned items to plummet to the ground. As she watches the all-purpose flour falling, an alarm goes off in her head. Crystal's body jerks in her seat as the flour crashes onto the floor and spills out of its package.

Engorged with fear, she looks into Travis's masked face of anger and thinks, *Oh my God, he has lost his freaking mind once again.* Reacting quickly, Crystal tells herself, *It's time to get the hell out.* Leaping from the sofa, she runs to the door and out of the apartment.

Dark outside, she walks alongside the building and with her heart beating fast, she then sits on the concrete block below their bedroom window, realizing, *He's coming to get me.* She takes off running farther alongside the apartment building. Crystal hides outside at the apartment directly behind theirs.

When she decides to come back inside, twenty minutes later, Travis is calmly cleaning up the mess he made. T*hat's a relief.*

Sitting and watching TV, she occasionally glances over at him sweeping the flour into a pile and into the dustpan.

Usually, Crystal doesn't ask God for anything but silently prays, *God, I don't know him anymore. Please protect me from harm.*

"I'm sorry, Crystal. You don't have to be afraid. I won't hurt you," says Travis who then walks over and kisses her. "I love you."

Crystal doesn't respond but stares at the TV and thinks, *You can't possibly love me.*

She now knows that getting involved with Travis was a big mistake, and one she regrets.

Beginning tonight, as she lies in bed, Travis cuddling her, Crystal stares blankly into the dark, saying to herself, *He always says he loves me, but he doesn't.* Then slowly, the love she once felt for him, little by little, oozes out of her now unplugged, pierced, and broken heart.

In the morning, as she gets out of bed at six O'clock, Crystal enters the kitchen, removes the bacon and eggs from the refrigerator, and then cooks Travis's breakfast before he goes to work. Each day, he insist that she does, and she dreads it, purposely withholding the main ingredient—love as she sits next to him at the island, and while he's eating, she rests her elbow on top of the island, placing the side of her head in the palm of her hand. Closing her eyes, she listens to the sounds of the fork tapping against the plate, wishing he would hurry up and finish eating, which he does, kissing her at the door.

Crystal lies down in bed, and by noon, she's up preparing him a sandwich and a bowl of mushroom soup, which he had requested. When Travis opens the door and enters the apartment, his lunch sits on the island.

As he sits eating and yelling, "Damn, every time that I turn on this TV, the news is talking about Mexicans killing each other." while he watches the twelve O'clock news.

He's there, but to Crystal, she has no one to whom she can relate; she's lonely.

After lunch, she follows Travis out the door, and as he drives away, she walks to the front of the complex where she unlocks the mailbox. Reaching inside, she pulls out a handwritten letter from her mother. Crystal smiles and skips back to the apartment, where she sits on the sofa, ripping open the envelope. The loneliness she feels, in that moment is then expressed in words: "I want to go home to Phoenix."

She begins to reinsert the letter into the envelope and hears the voice whispering, "Crystal, leave."

Now used to hearing it, she still thinks it's just a thought and ignores it.

The nights are the worst. When Travis climbs into bed, cuddling her, he asks, "Where's my kiss."

Hiding her displeasure from him, while her back is turned, Crystal squints her eyes shut. Forming a frown, she thinks before turning her head, *I hate this.* She then obediently gives him a peck on the lips.

In the spirit realm, Crystal is not alone. She hears a whisper, again, "Crystal, leave him."

The next day, while Travis is at work and she's busy making the bed, the thought of leaving is predominantly on her mind. Because she doesn't yet know the voice, which has no significance to her, Crystal spreads the flat bed sheet into the air, allowing it to float down, slowly covering the full bed. While smoothing the sheet and believing the voice that tells her to leave is her own, she then circles the bed, tucking the sheet underneath the mattress. Crystal grabs the two pillows and, while fluffing them, begins to recall growing up in a single-parent household since the age of five and witnessing first-hand, her mother's struggle as a single parent. Crystal mumbles, "I don't want that life for myself or my child."

Placing the pillows at the head of the bed, Crystal switches off the bedroom light, and while understanding that Travis disguises control as love, she then goes into the kitchen and begins to prepare his lunch. While it sits on the island until he comes home to eat it, she starts the process of cooking beef stew for dinner. Chopping the meat into cubes, Crystal searches her heart, concentrating on making the right decision for her unborn child.

After washing the beef and placing it into a pot of water on low heat, she then walks out of the kitchen.

In the living room, sitting in deep thought about leaving Travis, she tunes out the TV that's on in the background.

And after much thought and consideration, Crystal then, at eighteen, selflessly sacrifices her own need to feel love and tells herself, "My child is not going to grow up without its father in the home. I'll just have to stay in this marriage."

Crystal becomes Travis's obedient wife.

14

Now showing her baby bump, Crystal and Travis stand at the living room window of their lower-level dwelling, watching their new friends living across from them, getting out of the car. Travis invited the couple over yesterday, and last night, while playing cards, they learned that the couple, with a son and a toddler, is from New Jersey and has been stationed at Lackland Air Force Base for two years now. As they both continue to be nosy, Rome places his three-years-old son on his shoulders and then carries him upstairs to their second-floor apartment while his wife, Nikki, follows close behind with bags of groceries.

"Look at her acting all innocent," says Travis, standing with his arms crossed. "After Rome left for work the other night, I saw her sneaking another man into their apartment." He turns and gives

Crystal a stern look, saying, "I don't want you hanging out with her."

Crystal raises her eyebrows. "She's not interested in becoming friends like that anyway. I summed her up already."

After befriending two other couples who moved into the small apartment complex, they instantly became like family, and every weekend, they alternated to gather at each other's residences to play cards.

Across the way, at Rome's and Nikki's place, Travis gets up from the table after losing and says jokingly, "Well, it's time for Crystal and I have to be going. If we're not winning, I don't see any reason to hang around. I have work in the morning."

"Poor losers," yells Rome as Nikki and the other two couples agree.

After crossing the parking lot and unlocking the apartment door, they both are shocked at what they see. Travis yells, "Damn!"

There's a party going on inside the Roach Hotel. Roaches that are in the kitchen quickly scatter to their hiding places, but before they get away, Travis squeals, "Crystal, don't just stand there. Help me kill their asses."

Overwhelmed by their large numbers, Crystal stands in amazement watching them scatter, and replies helplessly, "Kill them with what?"

"Take off your shoe and get to smacking them," he says with one shoe in hand.

As Crystal is stomping and crushing the roaches, it becomes a moment when all of her pent-up frustrations begin to pour out of her.

Pumped up, she tells herself, *This feels good.*

Smashing one and then two more roaches, she blurts out, "Take this," and looks around for more.

When there's no more to kill, they then clean up the mess.

Travis, the hopeless romantic, cuddles close to Crystal in bed, and having seen her come alive while playing cards, he asks, "Did you enjoy yourself tonight?"

Thankful for the other ladies, a Godsend, Crystal is happy again. Not having many words to say to Travis before now, she answers, "Yeah, I did. It was lots of fun. I think we all enjoyed ourselves."

"I know I did. And did you see the looks on their face when you made that Boston?"

"They were as shocked as I was. I didn't think I could do it, being that it was my first time playing, but I did."

"You sho-nuff did, but, you know, I didn't like unlocking the door and seeing all those roaches. I never killed so many of them in my life. So, on Monday, when I get home from work, we're going to start looking for another place to live. I don't want roaches around my baby and crawling in his ears."

He very much wants the baby to be a boy, and so does she.

In one week, they located a large, roomy, one-bedroom, fully furnished apartment on the south side of the base. The disappointment is: NO PETS ALLOWED.

At the end of thirty days, with their belongings packed inside their car and that of friends, a line of three cars coast out of the gravel-covered lot. Goldilocks barks frantically at Travis and Crystal from behind the fenced yard of a neighbor, who agreed to care for her, as they slowly coast past her. Consumed with deep sadness, Crystal waves while almost in tears, saying, “I will miss you.”

Without Goldilocks' companionship, Crystal does miss her. And over the span of four months, being cooped up inside their new roach-free apartment home, she is lonely. Walking out of the bedroom, passing through the dining room, and into the living room, she sits down in the chair next to the large family Bible that Travis sent her from Thailand for her birthday. Trying to pass the time, she picks up the Bible from the lamp table, places it on her lap, opens it, and begins to scan through it, observing the many pictures of Jesus and his disciples. It all looks unreal—fabricated. Uninterested, she slams the book closed and sets it back on the lamp table.

Crystal then turns on the TV. Searching the channels and not finding anything of interest, she turns it off. Switching on the cheap stereo system that had been purchased with the five hundred dollars she had saved, she sat down on the floor and browsed through Travis’s new album collection, wishing it were Friday when the other couples, including the newest couple to the group, came to play cards and catch up on all the current hit songs.

The remainder of the week is no different. Unwilling to deal with the boredom that she’s experiencing, Crystal, each morning, decides not to get out of bed but to lie there and sleep away the hours. At nine, she begins to feel slight cramping pain and hesitates to get out of bed, but thinks as she slings back the covers, *I have to pee.*

Crystal goes to the bathroom and empties her bladder, but when she gets in bed, lying on her back, the abdominal pressure becomes too intense. Already one week past her delivery date, Crystal rolls over onto her side, and suddenly, she feels a warm, wet fluid gushing out from her vagina, traveling down her thighs and wetting the bed.

Crystal touches her vaginal area, expecting to see bloody fingers, but it's clear like water. Immediately, she calls Travis at work, who, after hearing her say, "My water just broke," rushes home.

He burst through the door. "Crystal, come on. Let's go," he's shouting.

Rubbing her abdomen, she points and says, "First, get my suitcase."

In the car, she can't stop laughing at Travis speeding in traffic with the emergency blinkers flashing.

Amused by it, she pauses from laughing to say, "Travis, we just live across the street from the base. You don't have to speed."

"I know. I always wanted to do this, and now it's my chance."

Crystal laughs harder—all the way to the hospital.

Within hours of giving birth to a girl, Crystal and Travis are given the bad news that their baby girl has yellow jaundice and she'll need a complete blood transfusion.

Full of sadness, Crystal's heart can't bear to see her baby girl's small body hooked up to the transfusion machine, and she returns to her hospital room, shared with seven other women. She lies on the bed closest to the entrance, crying.

Crystal hears footsteps and looks toward the door and with eyes wet with tears, she sees Travis walk through it.

"What's wrong with you?" he asks compassionately, sitting beside her on the bed and gently rubbing her back.

"Seeing my baby hooked up to that machine is

more than I can bear, Travis. She lies there so helpless. I'm scared for her life. I want my baby. I don't want her to die," Crystal says, sobbing.

"She is not going to die. It's just a serious case of Yellow Jaundice. She'll be all right, Crystal."

Now resting on both elbows, she wipes her tears. "I hope so. I feel responsible because it's my blood that's doing this to her."

"Come here," he says, taking her into his arms. "Let's go see how our baby girl is doing."

They're wrapped in each other's arms as they step inside the elevator and arrive at the intensive care unit, one floor down. As soon as they walk into the care unit, they're met by Kimberly's bubbly male nurse. "Your daughter is doing just fine. She's handling the transfusion very well."

Now filled with joy, they hurry over to Kimberly's incubator and are careful not to touch any of the equipment, afraid they'll damage the light hanging over her that contributes to her treatment. They begin to caress and gently massage Kimberly's stomach.

"Hello, Mr. and Mrs. Wallace," greets the attending physician, who walks over to them with one hand extended, shaking their hand. "I'm Dr. K. Davis. I've been treating your daughter. It appears that she has made it through the worst of it, and her progress is improving by the hour, but she is not out of the woods yet. I would like to keep her for further observation and to ensure that she has a good recovery. However, when she grows older, her true blood type, of the four that were infused into her, will take over. Do you have any questions?"

"No." Travis and Crystal answer, relieved to know Kimberly's progress report, but disappointed when they leave the hospital without her.

15

It's Saturday afternoon. In a cheerful mood, Travis, lying on the sofa and reminiscing, yells loudly to Crystal in another part of the apartment, "Crystal, you know what?"

He then leaps off the sofa, talking as he goes, "I haven't talked to Weston since he was best man at our wedding." He sits at the dining room table. "Come to think about it, I have a two week vacation coming up. Let me give him a call. It's time we visit him and Kay for a week."

Growing more out of love with Travis, Crystal walks out of the bedroom, where she's cleaning, and into the dining room, having little to no interest in what he's saying.

Holding the phone to his ear and waiting for someone to answer, he continues to speak his mind, "Then, in June, we'll travel to Dayton and spend the other week there. I want to get my stereo and album collection from my uncle Joel. Mama keeps complaining because Kim is four months old, and she hasn't seen her grandchild yet."

Travis then shouts into the phone. "Weston, hey man. It's me, Travis."

Returning to clean the bathroom, Crystal wipes the mirror, wondering, *What is he up to now? All of a sudden, he wants to see his military friend.*

She then overhears Travis's loud voice bursting through the walls of the bathroom, "I'll call you next week before we leave, so you'll know we're on our way. It's going to be good to see you and Kay again, man."

Saturday evening, driving on the highway, Travis and Crystal take turns speeding behind truckers, following them at eighty-five miles per hour, rushing to get as close as possible to the Arizona border by midnight on Sunday.

Passing a sixteen-wheeler, Crystal is thinking: *This beats being bored at home. I don't even care if we're breaking the law. It's not every weekend that I get to have fun on my way home to Phoenix.*

They drive into Phoenix, Monday afternoon, and visit the Greyhound flea market, where Crystal often shopped when she lived there. Making it a lunch stop, they walk around looking at what vendors are selling, and biting into foot-long hot dogs.

After Weston and Kay arrived home from work, they all sat around the dinner table, eating, conversing and laughing. Later, gathering in a circle on the living room floor, they engage in a game of Scrabble while drinking wine like they did in the good old days. Back then, Crystal didn't have to pretend like she was doing tonight. Sipping the wine, she pauses between sips to fake a giggle or to fight with Travis about a word not being a word.

Halfway into the game, Weston and Kay lift their glass and call for a toast.

Mellowed out, Crystal lifts her glass in remembrance of a time long gone, cheering, "To the good ole days."

Travis then brings up an intimate moment from the past: "Weston, remember that summer day, in the swimming pool, when I carried Crystal on my shoulder and you carried Kay, and they had to pull the other one off our shoulder and the first one to fall in the water, lost?"

"Yeah, I remember. That was fun. No one lost that day."

"I miss those days," says Travis.

So, this is what he's been up to, thinks Crystal, recalling that day, over two years ago, but the memory of it isn't enough to revamp the love she once felt for him. Crystal just looks at Travis with nothing to say. What she felt then is lost amongst the damage he inflicted on her, and can't be found—forever gone.

Pulled off to the side of the road, in the middle of the week, the steering wheel received a hard smack as Travis complained, "This is a bad time to have car trouble. I have to be back in San Antonio on Sunday, so I can report to work on Monday. That leaves us two days to get it fixed and no money for repairs."

Crystal begins to worry about what's about to happen next, not that he would blame her; it was his idea to come to Phoenix.

"Well, what are you going to do?" she asks.

Their fear is quickly relieved when Travis turns the key and starts the engine. "Oh wow," he now cheers. Shifting the car into drive, he speeds into traffic. "We're going to Weston's place before it stops on us again."

In the morning, he goes outside to start the car again, and with it idling, Travis rushes inside, "Come on Crystal, let's go look for a new car."

"A new car? You're still paying for this one."

"Come on. Don't worry about it," he says, getting frustrated with her.

Having advanced in military ranking and higher pay, Travis is approved for another car loan, and Friday night, to impress Weston, Travis treats him and Kay to dinner, driving them to a Mexican restaurant in their new car.

Seated around the table, waiting to be served, Travis then says to Weston, "I admire you, man. You and Kay have a good thing going on. I am truly happy for you."

"Thank you, Travis. We work at it," he says, looking over at his wife. "I love this woman."

Again, Travis begins to recap the days long gone, "I remember when Crystal and I got married. I couldn't go to the bathroom without her wanting to be in there with me. Man, I couldn't take a dump without her watching me do it."

They laugh, but Crystal only smiles, wanting to speak her mind but holds on to her thought, *It's not going to work*, she thinks.

Travis takes a sip from his glass of wine and sets it down. "She doesn't do that anymore. Nowadays, I have to beg her for a kiss."

Crystal sits across from him with a stern stare,

unmoved by his words. To speak up and say how she feels wouldn't change a thing about him, and to say she loves him would be a lie.

Kay then taps her fingers on the table, drawing Crystal's attention. She responds, "The honeymoon period doesn't last very long when children come into the picture."

"You're right about that," says Travis. Kim is still a baby, and so I shouldn't complain."

"But, when she turns two, you'll be complaining for sure," laughs Weston.

16

Crystal bathes Kimberly and then puts her to bed for the night while Travis relaxes in the living room. It's been a long day, and wanting to elude Travis, she turns off the bedroom light and lies down in bed, hoping to fall asleep before he notices. He's been after her for sex, and lately, she's been avoiding him. That stunt he pulled in Phoenix to romanticize her with the help of Weston and Kay didn't work.

While trying hard to win her back, it still isn't evident to him that the love is dead, and not even sex can resurrect it.

"Crystal, have you gone to bed?" Travis calls out to her.

Crystal grumbles, "Yes."

"I was waiting for you to come watch TV with me," he yells.

He then switches it off and slides into bed beside her. Softly, he kisses her on the back of the neck while massaging her breast. She does not want him touching her and tenses up at the feel of his caress; shrugging her shoulder, she rolls over onto her stomach—it's what she's been doing since they returned from Phoenix, a week ago.

Just as before, she becomes nervous, crunching up her face. Her body stiffens as she waits to receive the blow that doesn't come. To her surprise, Travis quietly rolls over like he's been doing this past week, and, with his back to her, he begins to snore.

Crystal relaxes and smiles slyly; she just knew she was going to get a beat down for refusing him—not that he has done so when she refuses him sex, but just because the threat is there, and when he's upset, there is no telling what he will do. But ever since Kimberly's birth, he refrains from his abusive tendencies, which he promised he would.

In the early morning, Travis presses his erection against her warm, soft body, and again, she denies him. Highly disturbed, Travis flings back the blanket and gets out of bed. Without saying a word, he dresses and then leaves the room. Crystal then hears the apartment door slam shut and mumbles from the bed, "Bye. I hope you stay gone."

She enjoys antagonizing him. She's forgiven him for beating her and throwing her out of the apartment a year ago, but she has not forgotten. If not for Kimberly, a delight and the giver of unconditional love in their gloomy and loveless marriage, they would surely be divorced by now.

An hour later, Travis returns home, unlocks the door, and, with a cigarette between his lips, pushes it open. Seeing Crystal sitting in the dining room, feeding Kimberly Cream of Wheat, he quickly closes the door. Travis snatches the cigarette from his mouth and explodes. "I'm not taking this mess from you any longer, Crystal. I'm sending your black butt back to Phoenix. The sooner you can leave the better."

From the tone in his voice, Crystal suddenly senses his mental state. Like a frightened child about to get spanked, she watches closely as he approaches, bracing herself to feel his fist, but he walks on past, exhaling the cigarette smoke.

In the bedroom, he flops down on the bed. Lying on his back, he takes a long drag from his cigarette and gazes at the ceiling.

Crystal puts the last spoon of cereal into Kimberly's mouth and murmurs under her breath, "That's fine with me—the sooner, the better."

To tame his temper, she then goes and stands in the bedroom doorway and asks, "Travis, are you hungry?"

"Yeah," he says halfheartedly.

Crystal knows that if she's going to raise her child with an abusive father in the home, she has to protect the child by humbling herself to obtain a peaceful and loving environment.

Travis becomes cold toward her and doesn't speak to Crystal for the rest of the day. On Sunday, when she and Kimberly returns home from church, where they had gone with a new couple who had become friends and joined the group, Crystal walks past him, lying on the sofa, flipping through a magazine with the stereo blasting—neither one of them speaks to the other.

Then Monday morning, he calls home, which he very seldom does, singing words of joy, "Baby, guess what? We're going to Germany!"

"When?" she asks in total astonishment.

"I have to be there by the fifth of February."

Crystal calculates that it's seven months away.

She then reminds him, “But you said you were getting rid of me and sending me to Phoenix.”

“I’ve been thinking.” Travis, eating his words, now has a sudden change of heart. “Next month, in August, I’ll send you and Kim there to visit family before we leave. How does that sound?”

Crystal rolls her eyes while thinking, *Here he goes again. It has to be his way or no way.*

Now married three years, she already knows—even though he’s asking for her opinion, it’s not really what he wants.

“It’s all right with me,” Crystal agrees reluctantly.

Handling it in such a way, she’ll get to spend time with family whom she hasn’t seen since their last trip to Phoenix.

17

Now, in the middle of January, of a New Year, and with all of their belongings in storage, they arrive in Dayton, Ohio. Having visited Travis's parents back in June of last year, it was a busy year of traveling.

As the streets in Dayton are wet and slippery from freezing rain, Travis slowly drives, at night, through the neighborhood that looks like a magical winter wonderland. Everything is coated by ice, which completely mimicks trees in their exact form.

Crystal is amazed as she watches, in passing, the scenery while, at the same time, being distracted by feelings of uncertainty. The life they've left behind, she has grown accustomed to it during the two years they lived in San Antonio. The closeness that she had developed with the wives was as genuine as friendships get. They all had become like family, and having to say goodbye wasn't easy, although they all vowed to stay in touch.

Her thoughts shift to the moment at hand as Travis finally parks the car across from his parent's home.

Crystal steps onto the salted sidewalk leading up to it and stops along the way to admire the ice-coated tree growing in the front yard.

Travis taps her shoulder. "Come on, Crystal, it's cold out here."

"I never seen anything like it," she says, walking up the porch steps.

The ice and snow linger over the next few days, making it difficult to drive. Therefore, keeping Travis at home, where he and Crystal are inside his seven-year-old sister's bedroom, which once belonged to him, they're making plans for how he wants their lives to progress as they face their inevitable future.

Lying across the bed, next to each other, Crystal is in disagreement with his plans for her and Kimberly to stay in Dayton. Having enjoyed the one week visit she and Kimberly had in Phoenix and the one in San Diego back in August, it makes more sense that she be with family for the short duration that she and Travis will be apart. So, she seizes the opportunity to convince him to send her back there.

Quickly she sits up and begins by sounding pitiful. "Travis, I don't want to be in Dayton. I want to go and be with my family." The emphasis is on 'her family'.

Travis is pissed. "No, Crystal! I want you and Kim to stay here until I send for you." He quickly leaps off the bed and leaves the room.

Because he's not around for her to say it to his face, she somberly and quietly mumbles, "You always have to have things your way with your selfish self."

She then begins to reflect on how she stands in

comparison to her in-laws. *It's not that I don't love them. It's just that they're too religious—I'm not, and not knowing how long Kim and I will be here, it makes me feel uncomfortable.*

And when the day does come for Travis to go away, it affects Crystal even more, especially when she hears Grace yell from the dining room, "Travis, you better hurry. You don't want to miss your flight to Germany."

Crystal and Kimberly, one year old, follow Travis as he rushes out of the bedroom with his duffel bag draped over his shoulder.

"Here we are, Mama. Let's go," he says as they hurry out the back kitchen door.

Outside, everyone piles into the station wagon. The tension level inside the car elevates as the vibe between Travis and Crystal is not a good one. She grows more upset with each accumulated mile about having to stay in Ohio. Avoiding a scene in front of his parents, Crystal sits in silence.

At the airport, standing and watching the plane take off, she now has no love or tears to cry, unlike when Travis left her for Thailand three years ago.

Holding on to pent-up anger, she now rides in the backseat of the car, staring out of the side window, vaguely listening to her in-laws talking. While observing the snow-covered views, Crystal thinks, *The only reason Travis wants me here with his parents is so he'll be secure in knowing where Kimberly and I are at all times. But he isn't as slick as he thinks he is.* Her anger increases.

At the house, she immediately goes directly to the bedroom and closes the door, just wanting to be alone. She then develops a bad headache and dozes off. After sleeping for two hours, Crystal opens her eyes, noticing that the headache is gone. Rolling over onto her back, as though looking into heaven, not praying, she silently grumbles, *I don't want to be here.*

She then hears Kimberly's laughter through the wall, and it warms her heart. Crystal gets out of bed and joins Kimberly and her in-laws in the living room. From that day forward, every moment of each day that she spends in her in-laws' home, Crystal feels dirty, and unworthy.

Crystal may not want to be with her in-laws, but it's where she will learn and grow in the knowledge of God.

While in the kitchen, pouring herself a glass of water, Crystal reminds herself, *The last time I went to Church was that one Sunday in Texas when Kim and I went with friends.* Crystal then lifts the glass of water to her mouth and, after drinking it all, she walks out with one thought in mind: *It's time I go to church, and Travis isn't here to stop me.*

Attending Mr. Ryder's church, where he's a deacon, after three weeks, Crystal joins the church, and, at a sister church, the following Sunday, she's baptized. Stepping out of the baptismal pool dripping wet, she's assured in her thinking, N*ow, I can live with my in-laws without feeling unworthy.*

Because there is neither a remission of sin nor repentance on her part to live according to biblical teachings, she was baptized for the wrong reasons. Therefore, she walks away from, and not towards, the creator, God. Crystal has no idea what she is doing.

Supporting Crystal's interest in learning about

God, Grace, and Mr. Ryder, devoted Christians, sneak up behind her as she sits watching TV on her birthday, and they begin to sing, "Happy twenty-first birthday to you..."

Crystal turns her body and sees them enter the living room. She reaches for the Bible that Grace is handing her. Smiling, Crystal says, "Thank you."

"Now, you don't have to ask to borrow ours," Grace giggles, jokingly.

As Crystal acquires a liking for the word of God, one morning of the following week, she's up early, at 5:00 a.m., and is greeted by her in-laws with a warm welcome. "Good morning, what got you up so early?" asks Grace, seated at the table, eating, and looking flabbergasted.

"I'm joining you for Bible study."

"You are?" blurts Mr. Ryder. "Well, bless your heart. Have a seat. We are glad to have you join us. Aren't we, Mama?" he says.

"We sure are, Daddy," Grace responds to her husband.

The third day, Crysal is a no-show for Bible study. Later when she opens the bedroom door, she is confronted by her in-laws, who question, "What happened to you this morning? We missed you."

"I tried to get up," smiles Crystal. "But I stayed up too late reading the Bible."

Understanding, they giggle and say, "Sometimes that happens."

Again, late at night, while reading the book of Matthew, Crystal has a spiritual moment. Compelled to fall to the floor, she drops down on her knees, crying, her heart filled with sorrow, and begins to ask for and to seek forgiveness for living a life that she now consciously realizes is one of lies and deception. Her intent isn't to hurt anyone, but the one person she's hurting is herself—a self-revelation!

As she's down on her knees having a good cry, the pain slowly subsides, and the weight of her burden is temporarily lifted. Exhausted, she wipes her tears and goes to sleep.

In the morning, while still in bed, Crystal reflects on last night's experience and concludes: *I cannot deny the truth that I no longer love Travis and that—regardless of my real feelings—I just can't walk away either. Kimberly's happiness and growth are more important. Travis loves his daughter, and that's what my sacrifice is all about—that Kim knows her father and knows that he loves her.*

18

Finally, in April, the travel documents that Crystal has been waiting for arrives in the mail. Sitting at the dining room table, she rips open the yellow envelope and reads the letter inside. Then, in a sudden outburst of anger, she runs into the kitchen, shouting, "Mama, Travis says that I have to drive the car to New Jersey and have it shipped from there to Germany."

Grace, standing at the stove preparing dinner, stirs whatever is in the pot and begins to shake her head, saying, "That son of mine. Why did he change his mind about leaving the car with us? You have a child to care for."

"It upsets me when he does stuff like this. He should have driven the car there to be shipped to Germany before he left. I am afraid to drive that far by myself. What if I get lost?"

With concern about Crystal's safety and being

members of Triple-A, Grace and Mr. Ryder secretly drive there. After obtaining a map of the route to McGuire Air Force Base, drawn out in red, they walk into the house, acting as if they never left.

Mr. Ryder calls Crystal into the dining room and hands her the map.

"What is this?" she asks in surprise.

"Open it and see."

Crystal unfolds the map and examines it. Her fear begins to lose its power as she expresses, "This is so easy; I couldn't get lost if I wanted to. Thank you."

Highly respectful of her in-laws, she then hugs both of them.

Having spent the night at McGuire Air Force Base, Crystal and Kimberly enter the small, crowded sitting area inside the airport, holding hands, and are fortunate to get the last available seat.

Kimberly climbs in her mother's lap, resting her head against Crystal's chest and immediately she's asleep. Crystal curiously looks around the room. It has been a long, busy day. She just wants to lie down and sleep, and it's also obvious on the many faces that she looks into that they, too, have had a long day.

Crystal then begins to think about the trip from Dayton that she made alone. Resting her cheek against the crown of Kimberly's head and recalling how scared she had been after Travis told her, in his letter, that she had to drive to New Jersey, she doesn't know why she doubted herself. Proud that she had also drove the car to the shipping port without getting lost, Crystal smiles an invisible smile—telling herself, *I did it.*

Stepping outside to board the military plane, they're met with strong, gusty winds, which made it difficult for everyone to move forward without the powerful wind forcing them backward.

Finally, on board the plane, and in their seat, the pilot announces during take-off, "If you look to your left, you can see the Statue of Liberty. Seated by the window, Crystal looks out but can not identify where it stands. She leans back in the seat and looks over at Kimberly, sound asleep again. Crystal closes her eyes and sleeps.

Stepping off the airplane at 2 p.m. and walking toward the crowd of people lined up at the terminal door of the Frankfurt, Germany Airport, Crystal looks into one face after another, expecting to see Travis among the crowd, but it is evident as she walks past that he's not there.

After walking the entire length of the airport, Kimberly begins to whine, "Mommy, I sit down."

Crystal feels somewhat irritated, which is obvious in her tone. "There's nowhere to sit, Kim. All the seats are taken. I'm tired, too. Let's go outside to see if Daddy is out there."

Stepping outdoors onto the sidewalk, Crystal searches both directions. Still, he's nowhere to be seen, and as they turn to go back inside, Crystal hears Travis calling her. She turns to see him getting out of a beige vehicle parked alongside the curb.

Kimberly jerks her hand from Crystal's grasp, screaming as she's running, "Daddy!"

Travis picks her up and carries her in his arms. "How's my baby girl?" he asks after kissing her on the cheek.

"Fine," she says and smiles.

"Travis, I had hoped you would be here when the plane landed," Crystal says angrily before he kisses her.

"I had a hard time finding somebody to bring me all the way out here. Let's get your luggage. I don't want to keep our ride waiting."

Inside the car, Crystal begins to quarrel with him,

"I don't want to sit on your leg, Travis, it's hard. I would rather sit on the seat."

"Crystal, I want you and Kim sitting on my lap. I missed you."

"Travis, your leg is uncomfortable," she says and tries to remove herself from his grip, but he holds her tight.

Having to ride the long ride into the small town of Rodenbach, sitting on Travis's lap, Crystal finally gets out of the car, rubbing her backside and complaining, "That was painful, Travis. You didn't have to treat me that way."

He giggles. "I enjoyed it if you didn't."

Turning her back to him, frowning, she walks away. "I'm sure you did."

Inside their large three-bedroom off-base apartment, Crystal does a walk-through.

Travis sets up his camera and tripod in the living room and yells, "Crystal come on so we can take pictures."

"Take some with Kim. I don't want to," says Crystal entering the living room.

"Come on Crystal; and why not?" Travis pleads while on his knees adjusting the camera.

After twenty minutes of posing, Crystal begins to feel famished and is sure Kimberly does, too. A pancake, eggs, and bacon breakfast on the plane is the only meal they've had all day.

Walking away from the photo shoot, she asks,

"Travis, what do you have for us to eat?"

"I took out some pork chops. They're in the refrigerator."

Crystal stops in the foyer, standing outside the kitchen entrance, watching him sprint from the tripod on which the camera is mounted and then sit in the nearby stuffed chair. Travis quickly places Kimberly on his lap, and with his cheek touching hers, they look straight into the camera. Just before the bulb flashes, Travis tells her, "Smile, baby girl."

Crystal turns into the kitchen, giggling and liking what she sees—a father's love.

While the pork chops are frying on the stove, Crystal returns to the living room, where she observes Travis removing the camera from the tripod.

Controlling his spending habits, she asks, "How much money did you spend on that?"

"I didn't spend anything. Someone left it for me to find."

Crystal laughs.

"I'm serious. When I got to Germany, and I was waiting at the airport for my ride, I noticed that brown camera case on the floor." He points to it. "And when no one came back to get it, I took it for myself. I did buy more lenses for it and the tripod."

"Travis, you stole that camera?!"

"I told you how I got it. I didn't steal it."

"But, Travis, it wasn't yours to take," she says as she rushes out of the room to turn over the pork chops.

Done with cooking, Crystal sets the dinner table and they sit down to eat. Travis cuts into his pork chop and says, "Crystal, there's an army couple living in the basement apartment. They have a little girl who is Kimberly's age, and when we finish eating, I'll take y'all down there to meet them."

Within two months, Crystal begins to feel fainthearted in her faith.

Downstairs, visiting Winnie, they sit in the living room, sharing their beliefs.

"So you and Cuz don't believe in God or go to church?" asks Crystal.

"We believe in God. We just don't practice any religion."

"Travis doesn't either."

Winnie then snaps her fingers. "Come to think about it, I have an album that you might like by Aretha Franklin."

As Winnie goes for it, Crystal excitedly yells, "Oh yeah, I didn't know she sings gospel, too?"

Crystal takes it from Winnie's hand. "Thank you."

"I don't listen to it. You can keep it."

Leaving Kimberly there, Crystal trots upstairs to begin dinner. The album plays on the stereo when Travis arrives home, unlocking the door.

"What is that? That's not one of my albums," he says with a harsh tone.

"It's mine," says Crystal from inside the kitchen. "Winnie gave it to me."

While she's rejoicing and singing along with the song, the music stops. Upset, Crystal rushes down the hallway. Stepping into the music room, she yells, "Travis, I am listening to that."

"It's not what I want to hear right now," he says, exchanging the album with another one.

Rolling her eyes, Crystal walks away, "You make me sick. I don't do that to you."

To avoid feeling the way she does, like the "oddball" of the group, Crystal begins to separate herself, which is what she's doing when Travis leaves the apartment downstairs and enters theirs. Finding her sitting on the living room sofa, and reading the Bible, he asks, "I thought you were coming downstairs?"

Crystal looks up from the Bible, "Why? What's going on down there?"

"Nothing. I thought you would join me." Seeing the Bible in her lap, he then sits beside her. He pauses before saying, "I have a confession to make, and I think now is the best time to get it off my chest."

Wishful thinking, she asks, "What is it? You want a divorce?"

"No, but you might want one after this. I haven't been truthful. While in Thailand, I had a Thai woman."

Staring into his deceitful eyes, she says unaffected, "I knew it all along."

"So, you're not mad?"

"Should I be, and why did you wait until now to tell me?"

He grabs both her hands, pulling her off the sofa. "Come on. Let's go downstairs. I told Gus that I would be back."

"You won't answer my question," she blurts out as he pulls her by her arm to the door. "You think, as a Christian, I have to forgive you." Stating it just so he'll know that she knows what he will not admit.

After that night, if they are not downstairs being entertained, they're home entertaining.

Seated inside the third bedroom that Travis converted into a music room, Crystal faces the doorway, and with the bass stereo speaker system blasting, she watches Travis walk down the long, wide foyer and straight into the kitchen, where he pours himself a short glass of gin on ice. He then comes back into the room, sitting on the floor between Crystal's legs, and yells across the room, "Fire it up, man."

Gus flicks the cigarette lighter once, setting the hash-filled pipe to blaze. He takes a puff of it and passes it to Travis, who inhales deeply. Travis then raises the pipe above his head and hands it off to Crystal. She doesn't want to do drugs, but because Travis pushes them on her, and in her time of weakness, she surrenders to the temptation, taking the pipe.

Five months, Gus and Winnie have watched her reject alcohol and drugs that's offered to her since she arrived there, and now whisper amongst themselves, "Is she really going to do it?"

Shocking everyone, and for the first time in her life, Crystal inhales the smoke from the hash pipe, and boy—does it burn.

She quickly grabs her throat, coughing. Shaking her head, she quickly hands the pipe back to Travis, who inhales twice before passing it to Winnie, and when it comes back around, Crystal refuses it, never to do it again.

And now that I have sinned, why not have a drink? she thinks, swinging her left leg over Travis's head as he sits on the floor. She goes into the kitchen, pouring herself a rum and Coke, which soothes her burning throat. Crystal pours herself another one, having two and then three rum and Cokes before turning in for the night.

When she awakens in the morning, she suffers from a sore throat, shame, and feelings of condemnation.

As though she's a rope being pulled back and forth, in a tug-of-war between two worlds—the holy and the unholy, the desire to go to church grows with intensity that it begins to filter through the clutter and confusion of her mind. All week it becomes a constant thought. Then, on Saturday afternoon, Crystal approaches Travis, lying and relaxing on the living room sofa, listening to music, and says, "Travis, now that we have the car, I want to go to church service tomorrow."

"Tomorrow?" he repeats.

"Yes."

"No, but we can go to church next Sunday. Gus and I have already made plans for tomorrow."

Rolling her eyes, she turns and walks out of the room. "Travis, don't say it if you don't intend to," she yells, knowing that he is prone to make promises he doesn't keep.

Sunday, at the start of worship service, Kimberly sits between her parents in the middle pews as the organ music plays.

"It's not a lot of people here," Crystal says as she glances around the enormous sanctuary. Then, there's silence, and the pastor begins to speak.

People enter and sit in the pews throughout the sermon until the building becomes full. The spoken words don't stir the souls of the congregation; not even a "Hallelujah" is heard during the forty-five-minute service.

Outside, walking to the car after church, Travis lights up a cigarette and exhales the smoke into the air before saying to Crystal, walking alongside him, "This is one place we won't be coming back to."

"Why not?"

He takes another puff of the cigarette. Allowing the smoke to flow out of his mouth, saying, "It's too damn boring."

Sulking, Crystal sits in the passenger seat, absorbing the simple view of the landscape during the ride home. Her inner thoughts are distracted by cars that occasionally speed past them on the Autobahn, and although she wishes for somewhere else they could go to worship, she agrees—the sermon was boring.

Sundays are boring anyway. There's nothing on TV because it's the one day the U.S. television station is off.

At home, with Kimberly between them on the sofa, Crystal and Travis quiz her, asking her to name the animals in the picture book when they hear a vehicle drive onto the property, and the horn blowing.

"Who's that?" Travis asks as he rushes over to the living room window. Peeping out, he doesn't see anyone. He then dashes out of the room, yelling from the kitchen, "It's Willis. He wants us to meet his family, who just arrived in Germany."

Travis rushes out of the building ahead of Crystal and Kimberly, shouting, "Hey, man. I see you made it."

"I told you. I will come, today. I wasn't lying to you." Willis yells back while still seated in the driver's seat.

Travis, being himself, oversteps his rightful place. "Hi, Barb. Welcome to Germany. I'm Travis."

Willis quickly sets him straight, roaring, "Man, it's not for you to make the introduction. It's mine."

"Sorry, man," Travis laughs. "I thought you needed some help. You have an army inside this van."

"Four children are not quite close to being an army."

Travis puts all joking aside and finally introduces Crystal and Kimberly. He then offers, "Come on inside and have some dinner with us."

"We didn't come to stay. We have a lot to do. How about next weekend?"

"That will do. We look forward to it." says Travis.

As promised, the following Saturday afternoon, they arrive. While Travis shows off his stereo system and his album collection, Crystal and Barb are seated in the living room, where Crystal watches Barb reach into her purse and says as she pulls out a small hardcover book, handing it to Crystal and saying, "I'm a Jehovah's Witness. I brought this for you to read."

"Oh. Thank you," says Crystal, scanning through it. "And I'm going to read it. I'm so glad you're here. Now, I don't feel like the 'oddball'. I haven't met anyone who's of the faith.

Barb rolls her eyes, and frowns. "That's not hard to believe," she says.

19

Inside the building, trotting up the four steps, Travis, arriving home from work, enters the apartment and yells, “Hey, Crystal, guess what?”

Closing the door, he habitually listens for her response.

Accustomed to playing his guessing game, she yells, “What?”

Following the sound of her voice, he crosses the wide foyer into the living room, where she sits hand-stitching patches of fabrics together, and he leans down to kiss her before giving her the news.

“I found out today that we got base housing. We can move in next month.”

“How is that possible? Don’t we have to be on a waiting list first?”

“We have been. I put our names on it, seven months ago, when I first got here in February.”

“Travis, it’s September. You should have told me

when I got here in April."

"It didn't occur to me to tell you, but you know now," he says, leaving the room.

Continuing to stitch the fabric, Crystal doesn't agree and thinks, *It would have helped me to know so I wouldn't have gotten comfortable living in Rodenbach and thinking it's our home for the duration of our overseas tour.* And because she did get comfortable, Crystal isn't ready to move—neither is Kimberly.

Standing in the living room window, Crystal watches as the moving truck follows Travis onto the paved road, taking them to the new apartment.

Hours later, as the night begins to overtake the daylight, Travis drives with Crystal and Kimberly in the car, cruising up the winding road, on base, in Kaiserslautern. As they slowly approach a row of four-story white buildings with white picket fences lining both sides of the street, the moving van blocks the road.

"I thought they would be finished by now," says Crystal, not happy with the move, but at the same time, she's glad that living on base will save them money.

Climbing the apartment building stairwell to the second floor, Crystal listens to Kimberly's whining and encourages her. "Come on, Kim. We're almost there."

Reaching the third-floor top landing, they walk through the open door, stepping into the huge foyer. Crystal glances up at the high ceiling and suddenly feels as though her five-foot-one frame, compared to the apartment's massiveness, seems noticeably small.

In the combined living room and dining room, Crystal glides her hand over the shiny table surface; she admires the beauty of the enormous dark-brown German hutch, matching table, and six chairs just outside the extremely large kitchen. It's the only furnishings inside this colossal apartment that look as though it belongs. Crystal looks around at the living room furniture, which is the same as the other apartment furnishings.

Turning her nose up and still disappointed in Travis for not buying furniture when she asked him to back in Texas, but instead, he purchased a new updated stereo system for himself and for her, the TV, still on its pedestal that the two men carry into the living room, setting it on floor and saying, "This is the last of everything. Do you need for us to unpack?"

"No. I'll do it. Thank you," says Crystal, walking them to the door.

After the third day, it begins to snow. Sitting in the kitchen nook looking out the window at how the heavy white, fluffy snowflakes float down to cover the top of the small forest of trees and nestle upon the playground below, Crystal and Kimberly snuggle close.

"Oooh. Look, mommy," Kimberly points.

"I see it. It's snow."

"It's snow?"

"Yep."

All night, it snowed, and the polar effects of the snowstorm linger long after the holidays.

Now, two, Kimberly doesn't have children, at her age, living in the building to play with. She walks around the living room, dragging her fingers along the length of the sofa.

Crystal lay across from her, stretched out on the loveseat, watching and asks, “Kim, are you bored?” Standing, Crystal goes and gets the camera, and after capturing a few poses of Kimberly, she then suggests, “Let’s go outside and take pictures in the snow.”

She really doesn’t want to go out, but posing for the camera is one of Kimberly’s favorite activities, and if it allows her a chance to have fun, a little bit of cold won’t hurt. No one wants to be indoors all day, every day, anyway.

Outside the entry door, Kimberly sits down on the wooden snow-free bench and strikes a pose.

“That’s going to be a good one, Kim. Now, do you want to swing?”

“Yeah,” Kimberly screams, running in the five inches of snow and falling forward, stopping the fall with her hands. Dusting the snow off her knitted mittens, she begins to walk, dragging her feet and creating a path to the back of the building.

Sitting in the swing, she yells, “Come push me, Mommy.”

Kimberly swings back and forth while Crystal glances around the area, but there’s no one out and about—just the two of them. She’s startled by the noise behind her and turns to look. It’s two squirrels, one chasing the other from tree to tree.

“Push me again, Mommy.”

Feeling cold, Crystal gives Kimberly several more pushes and then complains, “Kim, it’s freezing out here. This is the last push. Then we’re going inside.”

Crystal’s push sends Kimberly high into the air. Gradually, the swing finally stops. Kimberly hops down, pouting.

Having walked a short distance, Crystal turns to see her making a snowball and laughs when Kimberly throws it, only for it to land at her feet. Crystal then yells, "Come on, Kim."

Once inside, Kimberly dashes through the foyer into the living room and grabs one of the boxes from under the Christmas tree. "Mommy, let's play this one."

"Three Men in a Tub?"

"Yes, that one."

"First, go take off your coat."

Just to satisfy her, Crystal sits on the floor and plays the stupid game that she and Travis chose because it was the only toy left on the store shelf, but when you have a father who waits until Christmas Eve to shop, that's what happens.

Less than ten minutes—the game is boring, and Crystal can't pretend like she's having fun when she's not. She gets up from the floor and switches on the TV. The U.S. station doesn't air until noon and is now on.

"No, Mommy," Kimberly screams. "Play with me."

"I don't like that game, Kim. Play it by yourself."

Kimberly starts to throw a tantrum.

"OK. It's nap time."

"No. I don't want to take a nap."

"Girl, get up off of that floor and go lie down. I mean, now."

Kimberly crosses the foyer, screaming and crying. Crystal shakes her head. It's that kind of behavior from the terrible-two stage that she's not looking forward to and decides, right then and there, *One child is enough for me.*

Although she keeps sex on lockdown, Travis does get lucky sometimes, and it's one of those lucky days that she now worries about. Having been on the pill after giving birth, she had stopped taking it because of the headaches and now hopes that this time, as she retries to take them, she won't have to deal with the pain.

Throughout the marriage, they've never spoken of having more children, but when she was pregnant, they had wanted a boy, and now that their union has deteriorated along with her patience, it wouldn't be wise to have more babies.

As he usually does after he's home and has eaten dinner, Travis lies in the living room, watching TV, and doesn't expect Crystal to come and sit at his feet. "Travis, your daughter has really tried my patience today, and it has me thinking. I don't want any more children. I want to get on birth control, so in the morning, when you go to work, will you please schedule me a doctor's appointment?"

Travis doesn't respond. Crystal begins to wonder if he's listening to her or tuning her out, but then he says, "Yeah."

For the entire week, he doesn't mention the appointment until the night Crystal walks into the living room, "Travis, I need to know. Have you made my appointment yet?"

He's quiet, which causes her to question the words he's about to speak. "I forgot. I'll do it first thing in the morning."

She knows he's lying and storms out of the living room. In the kitchen, Crystal slams the dishes into the sink as it fills with water, mumbling, "Since you won't do it, I'll do it myself."

Crystal has no idea of how to ride the buses on base but soon finds out the following day from their neighbor Clora; and then rides it to the on-base clinic.

After sitting and waiting for a half-hour, they

finally call her name.

"I'm Crystal Wallace," she says to the female behind the desk.

"I see you listed that your husband is in the Air Force. Is that correct?"

"Yes, he is."

"In that case, I'm sorry. We're unable to treat you here. You'll have to be seen by one of their doctors."

"You are telling me that I can live on an Army base, but I can't see a doctor here? That doesn't make sense to me."

"Sorry, it's regulations."

"Damn," says Crystal. Out of pure frustration, she walks away.

There is a special bus that travels to Ramstein Air Force Base—but she doesn't learn how to ride it before the inevitable happens. Bent over the toilet on a Saturday morning, Crystal vomits. While trying not to become pregnant, she already is.

On her knees, she flushes the toilet, mumbling, "Oh, my God—no!"

Crystal can't hold back the tears, and while Kimberly is still asleep, she goes into the bedroom and flops onto the bed, blaming Travis for creating this unwanted pregnancy.

Right now, he's in Munich, Germany, where he will be competing, later tonight, in a talent show with the singing group he joined soon after they moved to Kaiserslautern.

For most of the day on Sunday, Crystal lounges around the house in disappointment. Stretched out on the sofa, she observes Kimberly, who—as usual—is bored. It seems preposterous to Crystal because Kimberly has plenty of toys to play with but then Crystal realizes that she's lonely.

You know, love is something. When it has a

stronghold on you, it drives you; there is nothing you won't do. You will do anything when under its spell. Crystal then unselfishly accepts the life growing inside of her womb and looks forward to having another child for Kimberly's sake.

That evening, Travis returns from Munich, yelling as he walks through the door, "I'm home!"

Crystal is sick to her stomach when he walks into the living room with Kimberly in his arms and doesn't let on that she's pregnant—not yet, anyway. "Who won?" she asks.

"It was some other group. They deserved to win. Girl, they were damn good."

"Your group is good, too."

"Not as good as those guys. They had some hell of some voices. You had to be there to hear them for yourself."

"So, where did your group place at?"

"We didn't."

After tucking Kimberly in bed for the night and is no longer angry with Travis for not making the doctor's appointment, Crystal walks into the living room, where he's relaxing on the sofa, and sits down at his feet. She confesses, "I'm pregnant."

As though in shock, he glances away from the TV and stares straight into her eyes. "You're pregnant?"

"Yeah."

Now, with his eyes staring into the TV, he tries to hide his smile, but Crystal sees that little smirk on his face—a son is what he truly wants. Crystal feels betrayed and cannot trust Travis, never thinking he could be so deceptive as to keep her from having things in life that she desire or doesn't desire.

The pregnancy could not have come at the worst time. Two weeks after finding out about it, Travis enters the apartment after he's home from work and walks into the kitchen, finds Crystal busy cooking dinner, and says, "Crystal, I have bad news."

"Oh—oh. What is it?"

Holding Kimberly in his arms, he puts her down on the floor and begins to refresh her memory. "I told you about when I first got here in Germany last year, and my superior officer showed me my desk, which was overloaded with paperwork, and he told me that I had to complete all that work before inspection, right?"

"Yeah, I remember."

"Well, I couldn't get it all done in time, so our division failed the inspection. Now, he blames me and wants to have me court-martialed."

"Court-martialed! What's that?"

"It's when—"

"Is that when they kick you out of the military?" Crystal blurts out.

"Yeah, but I got a lawyer. I'm going to fight it. The hearing is next month in March."

Having served five years in the USAF already and reenlisted for five more, his dream to retire in the military now may never be a reality.

"But what about the money they paid you when you reenlisted more than a year ago? If you're discharged, do you have to pay it back?"

"No. I don't."

The situation is a serious one. Crystal sets aside her feelings and the problems they're having within their marriage and begins to emotionally support her husband. As his wife, it's what she's supposed to do. She begins to think, *This affects the three of us.*

As she merges with Travis for support, it becomes mind-boggling for Crystal to figure out how Travis ended up in this situation. As she begins to recall a time, months ago, when he came home with stacks of paperwork, placing them on the dining table, and asking her, "Will you help me arrange these documents into alphabetical order? We have an inspection on the way and my assignment is to get the department caught up before then."

She told him, "Yeah," and together, they worked until the last pile was finished.

Travis did his very best to accomplish the task that was unfairly put upon him, but still it wasn't good enough.

Days before the court date, Crystal sits at the sewing machine making a dress to wear to the hearing, while keeping in mind the words that Travis has often told her, "Your appearance is a reflection of me."

Having never been inside a courtroom, the morning of the hearing, Crystal walks into the courtroom and sits in the front row, dressed in a royal blue, simple dress that doesn't tarnish his military image.

Turning her head, looking in the direction of Travis's lawyer standing to start the proceeding, he presents his opening statement. "Your Honor, I want to present to the court that Staff-Sergeant Wallace and his wife is expecting their second child."

Crystal holds a calm composer and isn't distracted as others look her way. The lawyer then continues, "I ask the court that throughout these proceedings, as I present my case that it show mercy and consider the implications involved during this critical time in the life of Staff-Sergeant Wallace and his family."

After that introduction, Crystal expects the worst. One after another, she had to endure the testimonies of Travis's coworkers, who sat on the witness stand stating, "I watched Staff-Sergeant Wallace not perform his office duties..."

Because she's not allowed to in court, Crystal repels herself from shouting out loud, *You're lying. He brought his work home.*

She looks over at Travis. He appears nervous as he leans over and whispers to his lawyer.

No one offered to assist him, and Travis's lawyer uncovers it with his interrogation.

Sadly, bowing her head, Crystal concludes that it was obviously the lack of teamwork from Travis's high-ranking officer, who expected Travis to do it on his own, and she blames them as the real reason their unit failed inspection.

Convinced they have failed Travis—big time, Crystal shakes her head, thinking, *That's the military for you.*

After two days of testimonies from Travis's defense team, arguing that he was not properly trained to do the job, Travis appears before the judge. Crystal, not allowed inside the courtroom to hear the verdict, waits anxiously outside. The longer she sits thinking about their livelihood at stake, the more nervous she becomes, and she begins to rock in her seat until Travis finally walks out. Crystal doesn't have to ask about the outcome; the crushed demeanor and the look on his face says it all.

He reaches into his shirt pocket for his pack of cigarettes and commands her, "Let's go."

Outside, he lights a cigarette. "They're throwing me out of the military with an honorable discharge. I'd rather have that than a dishonorable one."

"I agree. At least you can hold your head up."

Putting his arm around her waist, Travis brings her closer to him. "Let's go get Kim from our neighbors, Marcus and Clora, and I told Willis that after we leave the courtroom, we'll be coming over to his place."

Barb and Willis have moved on base, also, and have been very supportive of Travis. When the Wallace family enters the third-floor apartment, Willis sits at the head of the oblong dinner table. "Y'all, come grab a chair and join us."

"They got me, man," says Travis as he sits down to eat with Crystal and Kimberly at his side. "We have to be out of Germany in two weeks."

"I'm sorry to hear that, Travis. You guys are the only true friends we have here. We're going to miss y'all."

"Well, we're going to miss y'all, too."

Chewing with her mouth full, Crystal nods in agreement.

"We'll be taking a cab to the airport," Travis continues.

"What! A cab? No. I won't hear of it. Barb and I will take y'all in the van."

"We sure will," agrees Barb from the other end of the table. She has been a big help in keeping Crystal grounded in the things of God without pushing her religion onto Crystal.

Neither Willis nor Barb relents, regardless of how hard Travis tries to fight the issue, and what was supposed to be a three-year tour in Germany turns out to be only one.

At home, Travis and Crystal go their separate ways. He goes into the master bedroom and hasn't said a word since leaving Willis's and Barb's place.

Sometimes, he gets in his moods, and this is one of those times. Usually, Crystal just lets him be until he feels like himself again.

Sitting in the living room contemplating the

circumstances surrounding Travis's discharge from the military, Crystal hears sniffling sounds. Travis is crying, which begins to affect her empathetically. She gets up from the sofa, walks into the colossal bedroom, and sees him on his knees, bent over the full-size bed. She sits down next to him and gently rubs his back. *My God, what are we going to do? Help us,* is her silent prayer.

Wiping his tears, Travis finally lifts his head. "I'm crying because I heard *something* say, 'Everything is going to be all right.' Has that ever happened to you?"

"Yeah, it has."

Rising from his knees, Travis sits next to her. He regains his composure and says, "Tomorrow, I have to finish the discharge process on base. I need you to write Mama and tell her what happened. Let her know we'll be staying with them until we can afford our own place."

"I'll do it first thing in the morning, but remember, you promised that Phoenix will be our home."

"I haven't forgotten. We'll get there."

In the morning, the alarm clock goes off at the usual time.

Travis quickly silences it as Crystal grudgingly drags herself out of bed at 6:00 a.m. If she doesn't get up five days a week to cook his breakfast before he goes to work, he will have a hissy fit.

While waiting for him to finish eating, Crystal contemplates all that she has to do before their move-out date.

As always, after Travis is done eating, Crystal walks him to the door. They kiss.

Usually, she goes back to bed but this morning, Crystal goes and sits at the table and begins to write Grace a letter, feeling apprehensive about returning to live with her in-laws. As she's writing, Crystal wishes she didn't have to face them, knowing they are going to be so disappointed.

But her life is what it is—one big lie. She can't serve God, living in sin. To her, it's just best not to, and being married to an ungodly man doesn't make life any easier. Reading the Bible since arriving in Germany hasn't been her top priority, but Crystal still has hope.

Done with writing the short letter, she places the sealed envelope onto the German hutch, leaving it so Travis can take it to the on-base post office tomorrow morning.

20

Left standing at the curbside, in front of the airport hotel in Frankfurt, Germany, Travis and Crystal wave goodbye as their friends drive away, and the yellow Chevy van quickly disappears into the night fog.

"I really like Willis and Barb," says Travis as they walk into the lobby of the hotel, where they stay the night.

Rising early, they hurried out of the hotel, later catching their flight.

Traveling into America's time zone, and in the morning, they finally land at McGuire Air Force Base.

As they are walking through the terminal, Crystal notices how quickly Travis's behavior changed. On the plane, he laughed and smiled while they played the card game Rummy 500. Now, he frightens her, reminding her of what happened in Phoenix and in

San Antonio. Before those two abuses occurred, he was a quiet and strange person.

As they now step outside the terminal, he lights up a cigarette and says, “Let’s find a place to eat breakfast.”

Taking the lead, Travis walked aimlessly, having no idea where he was going or where to go. Finally stopping at the street corner, he stands there looking around.

“Do you see anything?” asked Crystal as she and Kimberly caught up to him.

Puffing his cigarette, Travis turns around and walks away from the curb, saying lowly, “No.”

They then hear a sound. A military bus is turning the corner. Travis waves, getting the driver to stop, and asking, “Where can we get something to eat?”

“Get in. I can’t drop you off in front of it, but I know a place. You will have to walk to the other side of the street to where it is,” he informs them.

“That will work,” answers Travis before they get on board.

By noon, they travel from New Jersey to New York. They then board another bus line in Springfield, Ohio.

“Two more hours to go before we get to Dayton,” Travis rejoices as he sits beside Crystal, who rejoices with him, feeling more at ease now that he’s himself again.

Arriving at the Dayton bus station, it’s a modest seventy-five degrees. “Good. An early spring,” sings Crystal, stepping off the bus. They are then driven to Travis’s parents’ house. A perfect day to be out,

Travis takes to the streets, leaving Crystal and Kimberly with his parents. He stays out late, entering the bedroom, switching on the light, waking Crystal. Seeing Travis with a small, brown paper bag, she asks, "What is that?"

"Just some herbs," he says, setting the bag on the vintage dresser.

"When have you been interested in herbs?"

"A friend owns a herbal shop and gave it to me."

Crystal rolls over, suspiciously thinking, *He's interested in another woman and is f**king around.*

Every day, Travis leaves and doesn't come home until after everyone has gone to bed.

On a Saturday, changing his ploy, he comes home, walking through the front door, and says to Crystal, sitting in the living room watching TV, "You and Kim come with me. I want you to meet my friend from my youth and his wife. Hurry up, he's outside in the car waiting for us."

Feeling somewhat rushed, Crystal grabs her purse and follows him out the door. It's late at night when they're returning to his parents' house that she begins to believe that the reason Travis stays out late is to avoid his parents.

Sunday, they had already been to church and back home when Travis climbs out of bed around noon. Quietly, he slips into his jeans, leaving Crystal and Kimberly cuddling in bed.

Kimberly is asleep, but Crystal isn't. She's watching as he opens and closes the bedroom door and then listens as Travis greets his stepfather, who, sitting in the living room, responds with that very pronounced southern dialect, "Good afternoon, son, it's been weeks since I picked you all up at the bus terminal. I haven't seen you."

"I've been busy searching for a job. You're asleep

by the time I get home. When I get out of bed in the mornings, you've gone to work."

The conversation is loud. Crystal detects a quick change in Mr. Ryder's attitude, which is evident in his voice. Seemingly disappointed in Travis, he asks, "While I have you here, Travis, would you mind if I say a few words?"

Crystal listens attentively for Travis's reply. He answers, "Sure. Go ahead, Mr. Ryder."

"Travis, you have to be the man of your house, son. Lead your wife and that there, child. Take them to church. You have to show them the way! Be that example—they're not going to church because you're not going, but I bet they'll go if you go."

Knowing this moment would come, Crystal slightly grins, thinking, *I'm glad it isn't me on the other side of that door.*

She then hears Travis agreeing, "I know. You're right, Mr. Ryder. Thank you. I'll do that."

Cuddled up next to Kimberly, Crystal shakes her head. *He just stood there and lied.*

She then begins to watch Kimberly sleeping. "You're tired, aren't you?" Crystal whispers while stroking Kimberly's soft cheek. She then has a thought: *We're out so late Saturday nights that on Sundays, Mama is too tired to go to church without Daddy. Besides, you and I are bored with being in the house all week, so when Daddy says, "Come on. Let's go," we're happy to go wherever he takes us, uh?*

Without disturbing Kimberly's rest, Crystal turns onto her back and as she listens to the birds chirping outside the bedroom window, Travis's deceptive answer that he gave Mr. Ryder resurfaces to the forefront of her mind. She responds silently, *I am for darn sure of one thing: Travis is not a faithful churchgoer, nor will he confess to others that he's a nonbeliever, not an atheist, but one who does not believe that Jesus is the Son of God.*

On their way to church the following Sunday, Crystal and Kimberly walk alongside Travis, holding hands. As they walk, Crystal already knows that inside Travis's head, he is working out a plan to not waste his day inside of a church if he doesn't have to.

After taking his precious time walking six short blocks that are in the opposite direction of Mr. Ryder's and Crystal's place of worship, they stand across from a church building, and just before they're about to cross the street, the double wooden church doors fling wide open, and a crowd of people rush outside.

Travis and Crystal suddenly come to a halt, looking at each other.

"Oh well. I tried," says Travis, playing it off as though it wasn't his fault.

They then turn and begin walking in the same direction that they came from.

"I'm not ready to go back to the house. Let's walk down to my aunt's house. She lives a few blocks that way," suggest Travis, pointing.

Looking in the direction, Crystal tells him, "Travis, they may not want us popping over there unannounced on a Sunday morning."

About to light a cigarette, he jerks it from his lips. "I know my aunt and uncle. I'm her favorite nephew. She'll be glad I came; and she'll even cook breakfast for us. Come on. Let's go." He then lights the cigarette.

In disappointment, Crystal walks quietly up the

street beside him, aware that Travis has deceived her. Deeply immersed in his world, there's no other attempt to attend church again.

After waiting two months for the car to reach the United States port, Travis checks the morning mail on the dining room table. Seeing a white envelope with his name on it, he rips it open and reads the letter, then stuffs it into his pants' back pocket and quickly sprints toward the front door.

"The car is here," he says as he passes Crystal, sitting and combing Kimberly's hair. "Don't wait up for me. I'm on my way to go get it."

"Where is it at?"

"I'll call you when I get to Philly," he yells from the front porch.

How in the heck is he getting to Philadelphia? Crystal wonders but then answers her question; *He'll find someone to drive him.*

The next day, she's in the bedroom trying on a quick and easy blouse she just finished sewing, while Travis leaves the shipping port in Philly, smoking. He walks to the nearest motel, where he pays for a room and immediately calls her on the phone.

Shouting from the other side of the closed door, Grace yells, "Crystal, Travis wants to talk to you."

Wearing the perfectly fitting maternity blouse, she rushes out of the room, and with the phone pressed against her ear, Travis tells her with some anxiety, "I came all the way to the Philadelphia storage port, and I can't get the car."

"And why not?"

"I left without the shipping orders, and I need you to bring them to me because I'm not coming back to

Dayton, so you need to come to Philly."

"Travis, how could you forget that?" Crystal yells.

"Crystal, I was excited and didn't think to, and when you come, bring Kim with you. We're staying the night."

She begins to resist him, arguing, "But that's a long ride, Travis, and I don't want to ride the bus pregnant."

"We can't afford for you to fly. So, get on the bus and come on."

Nastily, she responds, "OK! We'll be there as soon as I can get on the next bus."

She then yells into the kitchen. "Mama, Travis needs me to bring paperwork to Philadelphia. Can you take me and Kim to the bus terminal?"

"Sure. I can take you," Grace yelled back.

Gathering clothing to wear for an overnight stay, Crystal complains, "I have to ride a bus all the way to Philly, and be uncomfortable."

As she packs the suitcase, realizing as she thinks, i*t's been days since Kim and I have been anywhere.* Her attitude quickly changes. Crystal closes and locks the small case, grabs the handle, and walks out the door into the living room, telling her mother-in-law with gladness, "Kim and I are ready to go."

Now, with the car back in his possession, the following week, Travis rushes into the house with such urgency that he charges past Crystal sitting in the living room. Watching a soap opera, she quickly responds, "My goodness, Travis, why are you in such a hurry?"

He enters the bedroom. "Crystal, come here."

Travis removes a suitcase from the clothes closet and places it on the bed as she enters the room.

"What do you want, and what are you doing with that?"

"Help me pack. I volunteered to house-sit my Uncle Joel's house for two weeks while they vacation in California."

Seeing another opportunity to get away and not have to constantly tell Kimberly to move from in front of the TV, blocking Mr. Ryder's view of it, Crystal doesn't argue but begins to help him pack.

They then drive two miles from his mother's house. With the house key, Travis unlocks the door. Stepping inside the living room that looks like it was hit by a tornado; they mutter simultaneously, "Dang!"

They walk over clothes and toys that are scattered on the floor. Crystal shakes her head and says, "Before I stay here, this house will have to be cleaned."

"I'll go get some cleaning supplies, and I'll take Kim with me," says Travis, reaching for Kimberly's hand. "We'll be right back."

In the kitchen, Crystal begins to unload the sink of dirty dishes and then fills it with hot, soapy water, pouring in some bleach that she found underneath the sink.

It's not until the night is drawing near when Travis and Kimberly walk in carrying bags of carry-out.

"Hi, Mommy," says Kimberly.

"Don't y'all say anything to me; I am so mad right now," says Crystal, lying on the sofa and watching TV. She then sits up as Travis places the bags of food on the dining room table behind her.

"Travis, you told me that you would be right back, and that was six hours ago. It's not fair that I had to clean up this place all by myself. You did this on purpose."

"Baby, I'm sorry. I went to get some cleaning supplies, but then I stopped by Nana's place and got held up over there. You know how she is; she'll talk you to death. Anyway, I got us dinner. Come on. Let's eat."

Crystal calms down and reaches into the bucket of chicken. "You better be glad that you bought dinner because I am so tired and hungry right now. You would have had to cook dinner because I wasn't going to."

Travis then tells on himself. "I ran into my step-brother Leon. He invited us to his graduation tomorrow."

"I thought you said that you were at Nana's all day?"

"Well, I had to go ask him why I wasn't invited to the ceremony. It turned out that our father didn't give me my invitation like he was supposed to a week ago."

"You still lied that you were coming right back," says Crystal, feeling angry all over again.

With only one day left before Joel and his family are due to return home from their summer vacation, Travis and Crystal, after they've been awarded emergency housing for low-income families, walk out of the Dayton Metropolitan Housing Authority building, excited.

Once they're inside the car and have fastened their seat belts, Crystal cheers, "It's about time we have our own place."

"It sure is," says Travis, turning the ignition. "Let's ride over there to see if we want to live in that area."

As expected, early Saturday morning, Uncle Joel drives the family van into the driveway with the horn blaring a long, loud, continuous honk.

Travis quickly runs out of the house ahead of Crystal, who walks out of the door just in time to overhear him bragging. “When we leave here, we’re moving into our two-bedroom townhouse apartment.”

“Y’all have any furniture?” Lilly, Joel’s wife, asks.

Concurrently, they answer, “Nope.”

“We have a dresser set that you all can have.”

“Thanks. We’ll take it,” Travis quickly says as if it were up for bids.

Crystal begins to feel agitated, remembering when he re-enlisted and she tried to convince him while they were in San Antonio to invest in buying furniture, but as always, he didn’t listen. He thought that having a larger TV and a new stereo sound system was a better choice.

Not wanting to accept hand-me-downs, Crystal walks away from the conversation and quickly avoids being knocked down by Kimberly and her cousins running about and playing in the yard.

Grabbing the smaller suitcase from inside the house, she makes her way safely to the car and puts it in the backseat, yelling, “Travis, get the other suitcase, and let’s go. Kim, say goodbye to your cousins.”

Arriving at his parents’ house on the other side of the bridge, the three of them walk into the house. Hearing the door open, Grace walks out of the kitchen and sees them, saying, “Y’all made it back, I see.”

“Mama, we got our own place now. We’re moving in today,” says Travis’s self-pride.

"That is good news, Travis. I'm so happy for y'all. You need your own home.

"What do you have that you can donate to us? We don't even have a bed to sleep on."

"Not having a bed to sleep on is not good." Grace giggles.

She walks from the dining room into the living room and stops at a chair, leaning against the back of it. "Well, let me see," she says while surveying the room. Propping one bare foot on top of the other, she points out the old sofa that she has wanted to get rid of, a set of outdated end tables, a coffee table stacked in the corner, and a blue, floral vintage lamp.

"That's all I can give."

"We'll take it all," says Travis. "Beggars can't be choosers."

And why does he have to say that? It infuriates Crystal. Her lips tighten, fighting hard to remain silent so as not to embarrass anyone. Boiling inside, she silently screams, *I told him that we needed furniture. 'A-hole',* she secretly calls him.

Travis then locates a friend with a pickup truck, and after acquiring more handouts from his grandmother, including aged mattresses, a brown wooden dining table with four white chairs is loaded onto it.

The following Saturday, as Crystal stands at the kitchen back door, watching as the military moving van arrives with their household items, shipped from Germany, the excitement of being in her own place gently expels any anger she has experienced thus far.

After a week of unpacking everything, she relaxes on the sofa, watching soap operas, when the phone rings, and is greeted by Grace, who asks, "Hi, Crystal, where's that son of mine? Is he there?"

"Hi, Mama; Travis isn't here right now."

"When he gets home, tell him that GM wants him to come for an interview. Make sure he calls me."

"I sure will."

After talking with his mother, Travis hangs up the phone. Ecstatic, he enters the living room, where Crystal sits and says, "Crystal, tomorrow I'm going for an interview at GM."

"It's what you've been waiting for and talking about." She smiles.

"Yeah. It's going to make a big difference in our lives."

Not seeing Crystal when he returns home from the interview, Travis strolls over to the living room stairs, stopping at the bottom of them, yelling, "Crystal, I got the job."

Now, in her second trimester, she descends the steps while cheering, "Really?!"

"Yeah. No more living on unemployment. Let's go get Kim from next door and go celebrate," he says, taking Crystal's hand as she steps off the stairs.

21

January whirls up a blizzard and dumps twelve inches of snow on Dayton, closing down the entire city.

Earlier this morning, Travis removed the snow from the porch and the steps, creating a clear path from the door all the way down to the parking lot. Their silver Cougar is the only car in the lot that can be identified as Crystal stands looking out of the kitchen storm door at the amazingly beautiful pure-white snow. Under the bright sunlight, the snowflakes sparkle like diamonds while her favorite artist's music plays softly on the stereo.

In the distance, a yellow bulldozer is busy clearing the street, pushing the snow to the curb as it moves in her direction, and while singing the lyrics, *Our Love is as...*, of the song playing in the background, Crystal glances away from watching the bulldozer. Her eyes move down the row of houses, watching as the chimneys release clouds of grayish smoke into the air, evidence that people are inside using their fireplaces.

Curiously, Crystal observes the small heaps of snow that collected where the tree limbs branch out from the trunk of a young tree growing in the churchyard next to the townhomes, and as the song begins to taper off, she faintly hears a sound that gets louder and louder, interrupting the song and her observation of God's beautiful and marvelous creation—snow.

Recognizing the male voice, Crystal quickly looks down into the parking lot and sees Travis standing on a huge, trampled-on pile of snow. Enjoying his day off work, he simultaneously gestures and yells, "Come on out here."

Having given birth two months ago, Crystal shakes her head no. She is not leaving her baby girl along, even though she's asleep.

"Oh, come and have some fun with us."

Kimberly's small voice yells, "Come on, Mommy."

Again, Crystal shakes her head, and while feeling cold, she notices Travis and Felicia having a snowball fight a short distance from Kimberly and Felicia's two young cousins, who, Felicia, nineteen, is their live-in babysitter.

Crystal begins to laugh as the children interrupt them, throwing snowball after snowball and then running with forceful strides in the deep snow as fast as they can to avoid getting hit when Travis and Felicia retaliate. Snowballs are flying through the air, and Crystal can hear bursts of laughter and screams as she closes the door.

Walking into the living room, Crystal quickly hugs herself, rubbing both arms with her hands to feel the warmth from the friction, and goes over to where

Sheena, the new family member, lies sleeping on the sofa. Crystal very slowly pulls the blanket up to Sheena's shoulders, using it to gently wipe away the pool of milk from the corner of her mouth. Sheena doesn't feel a thing.

Gazing down at Sheena's small facial features, Crystal is suddenly taken back to the night she had a weird dream while pregnant and in the dream, an infant girl sat crying in a walker at the bottom of the stairs. She had fat cheeks that sagged, giving her a false appearance of melancholy. She had dark, bright eyes, a full head of black curly hair, and wore a pink dress. Watching the baby cry from the top of the stairs, Crystal wondered, *Why is she crying?* Then the dream ended. Crystal mumbles to her sleeping angel, "That was you in my dream," and softly kisses her chubby cheek.

The snow and the very cold temperatures are persistent in keeping Crystal and the girls indoors. Now February, she begins to feel too confined as the apartment walls seem to slowly close in on her, squeezing the life out of her. To escape this illusion, she pauses from doing laundry, strolls out of the kitchen into the living room, and sits on the arm of the sofa. "Travis, let me keep the car, and I'll drop you off at work."

He was bumped from the third to the second shift, which interferes with Crystal's no longer having the freedom to come and go as she pleases. Seated across from her and lacing up the combat boots he kept after his discharge from the Air Force, Travis disapprovingly says, "No."

"I am tired of sitting in this apartment, Travis. I need to get out of here and go somewhere."

"I don't want to be waiting outside in the cold, Crystal, if you're late picking me up," he says as he walks over to the sofa. "Give me a kiss. I have to go."

It would have been the right time to take the girls to visit Grace, their grandmother, Crystal is thinking as she watches him walk out of the kitchen door, leaving her feeling denied the same right to come and go as she allows him.

Yesterday's incident begins to replay in her mind of when Travis didn't hesitate when Felicia walked right in, without knocking first, and asked him to drive her someplace nearby. He instantly put aside whatever he was doing, and the two of them nearly ran out of the apartment and stayed gone for at least thirty minutes.

Crystal's reflection causes an ignition within her, setting off an explosion of anger. Yesterday, she didn't think anything about their behavior and just saw it as a marijuana run but, today, she's not having it. Remembering that two hundred dollars are on the bedroom dresser upstairs, her plan to escape the four walls is suddenly set into motion.

"What time is the next bus to Phoenix, Arizona?" she asks the person on the other end of the phone line and is told that it is leaving at five.

Dragging the phone cord, Crystal peeps around the corner into the living room at the wall clock. She exhales a sigh of relief. *Good, I have enough time.*

She quickly trots upstairs, locates the luggage set in the clothes closet and begins to pack the largest and smallest of the three.

Then downstairs, she writes Travis a note:

Travis,

I will not stay here and watch you put Felicia

before me and the girls. We will be at my sister Sissy's house. I don't know when or if I'll return.

Ten minutes later, the cab driver pulls into the parking lot and after putting the luggage in the trunk, the driver gets in the cab and asks, "Where to, Miss?"

"Downtown to the Greyhound Bus Station."

22

While talking to Travis on the phone, Crystal enters Sissy's bedroom to have privacy and lies across the king-size bed. "I've been waiting for you to call me. Were you planning to?" asks Travis.

As if you care, thinks Crystal. She and the girls have been in Phoenix for nearly a month, and he's just now calling. Agitated, Crystal then sits up. "No. For what?"

"Crystal, it was really hurtful that I had to come home from work to find only a note."

Silently, she micmics him, and then runs a finger across the bed cover, outlining the floral design.

"I thought it was best that I left. It's apparent that you care more about Felicia than you do for me and the girls, and you should be glad I left that," she tells him.

"Crystal, I don't know what you're talking about, but anyway, I'm calling to let you know that I sent you the tax return check by certified mail. You should be getting it any day now."

Enjoying that they're miles apart, Crystal lies her back. "Thanks for thinking of us. It will arrive just in time. I'm almost broke."

"Yeah, I thought you might be. But before I hang up, I want to say that I think you need to be sure it's me and our marriage that you want before coming back to Dayton."

Without disclosing to him what she plans to do, she quickly says, "Alright, bye." But all the while, thinking as she hangs up the phone, *I don't have intentions of coming back.*

Within days of their conversation, Sheena, out of nowhere, develops a condition that causes her to choke when spooned or bottle-fed.

In a panic, Crystal boards the first bus back to Dayton. Traveling on the highways and byways, driven by fear, she sits with Sheena across her lap and feeds her small portions at a time. Each time, holding her breath as she places the spoon into her five-month-old baby's mouth, then breathing again when Sheena survives the choking and crying episodes.

An older woman, seated across from them, sits watching her. Crystal glances over at the woman, whose face expresses sympathy for what Crystal is going through, and holds a Granny apple in her hand. She extends her arm and offers it to Crystal, who says kindly, "No, thank you."

Traveling for two days, and terribly worried about Sheena, Crystal hasn't eaten. While holding her baby close, she prays, *I hope Travis or one of his old-fashioned remedies, which I am trusting and relying on, will work because the Jell-O water solution that Sissy recommended didn't.*

However, Crystal's moment of comfort comes when they cross over into Ohio. Looking down at her baby sleeping, she has a thought, *and if Travis doesn't know anything, at least the insurance will cover the total cost of medical treatment. It hadn't dawned on me that I would need health insurance when I left Dayton in such a hurry.*

Unlike when she left in late February, the streets are now free of snow. As the cab driver coasts into the dark parking lot, Crystal notices their car.

Right away, she speculates, *Hmm. Travis must have taken the night off.*

Feeling dirty, tired, and hungry, Crystal unlocks the back door, expecting to see him with a surprised look on his face. Instead, Travis is not there. Yet, the kitchen light is on, the stereo in the living room is on, but nothing is playing, and the front door is wide open, which is odd—that door always remains closed.

Crystal looks out of it and into the night, yelling for Travis, but he doesn't respond, so she closes the door and goes upstairs, where both bedrooms are dark. She switches on the bathroom light, runs the bath water, and goes back downstairs.

She's searching in the suitcase for the girls' night clothes when she hears keys jingling. The kitchen door opens, and while she's bent over the suitcase on the floor, Travis, seeing her, pushes the person behind him backward—out the door—and quickly closes it before Crystal can see who it is.

"When did y'all get back?" he asks, trying to act surprised.

"We just got here."

"Hi, Daddy," says Kimberly, who no longer runs into her father's arms because he thinks she's now too big.

While holding the girls' nightgowns, Crystal trots upstairs and turns off the running water. On her way back down, she asks, "Who was that with you at the door?"

Travis plays dumb. "Who was that with me at the door? Nobody. It was just me."

Crystal steps off the bottom step, looking into his lying eyes. The word, liar, sounds off in her head. "Anyway, Travis," she says, sure that she heard Felicia's voice, "While me and the girls bath, will you drive down the street to Mickey D's?"

"Sure. What do you want to eat?"

Crystal has both girls with her when she yells from the top of the stairs, "Just two hamburgers, fries, and drinks."

After eating, Crystal struggles to feed Sheena the half jar of strained carrots. Across from her on the other side of the room, Travis stops strumming his electric bass guitar.

"What's wrong with fat face?" He nicknamed her because of her fat cheeks.

"She suddenly started to hyper-salivate while we were in Phoenix."

"Oh, yeah? Let me take a look."

He places Sheena across his lap. "Yep, that's the problem. We'll take her to the doctor first thing in the morning."

After putting the girls to bed, Crystal steps off the staircase and into Travis's arms as he pulls her close, embracing her with a long, intense kiss. With their lips pressed together, he slowly guides her, one step at a time, to the corner of the living room and turns off the new gold-trimmed, white ceramic lamp. They melt down to the floor and lie on the dingy-white shag carpet. Travis disrobes her, and as their sexual desire mounts in intensity, Crystal pleads, "Travis, go get a condom." He doesn't listen. He never listens.

Sexually satisfied, he lies beside her naked and smoking a cigarette.

"Travis, you should have used a condom. We don't need any more children."

"I don't have any."

Crystal's memory is jolted, and she has a flashback of the day she left: sitting on the bedroom dresser was a brand new box of condoms beside the two hundred dollars that she took with her to Phoenix.

She then asks, "Why don't you have any? There was a new box upstairs. What happened to it?" Now she's playing dumb, realizing he's having an extra-marital affair.

"No. I didn't see a box or any box," he says, exhaling smoke.

She turns her head to look at him and sees that he's in deep thought. Usually, he'll tell her how happy he is to have her home. This time, his eyes tell her—he's disappointed.

What he said on the phone that day when he called her in Phoenix now makes perfect sense—*that's OK,* she thinks. *As soon as Sheena gets well and I can get my hands on his money, the girls and I are out of here. A father or no father, I'm not putting up with his lies and selfishness any longer.*

Crystal gets up off the floor, and on her way to bed, she has an idea, thinking as she climbs the stairs, *I'll find a job and use that money to leave him sooner.*

In bed, she further plans her strategy. *I can't reveal my intentions to him. I have to act as I normally would.*

Saturdays are usually her busiest day of the week, and while she's in the kitchen washing dishes, all the apartment windows are open on both levels, as the curtains dance in the morning breeze, hinting that it will be an early spring.

Sheena then begins to cry as though she's in distress. Running, Crystal rushes from the kitchen and into the living room, fearing the worst has happened, but thank God, as usual, it's just Sheena's way of communicating that she's uncomfortable. Relieved, Crystal removes her from the rocker swing, taking Sheena into her arms and saying, "Mommy's baby girl sleepy? Come on. Let's go lie down in your crib and take a nap."

While Sheena is upstairs napping, Crystal finishes the dishes and then yells from inside the kitchen screen door, "Travis and Kim, if y'all have to use the bathroom, you better come before I start mopping."

Neither one of them respond. Mopping backward, she steps outside onto the back porch, and after dumping the bucket of dirty water in the grass, she sits down on the concrete steps. While waiting for the floor to dry, Crystal watches Travis, who, down in the parking lot, is applying wax on the car. She then hears Kimberly's voice coming through the neighbor's open door, alerting her to Kimberly's whereabouts.

The floor dries quickly. Upstairs, Crystal goes into the master bedroom, and just as she sits down at the sewing machine and begins to alter a pants outfit, Sheena wakes up from her nap and begins to whine.

"Dog-gone-it," Crystal murmurs as she stops

sewing.

Downstairs, she fetches a bottle of milk from the refrigerator and then carries Sheena into her room, placing her on the full-size bed, thankful that Sheena is now eating and drinking without choking. While Sheena holds her bottle, Crystal continues to sew.

After dinner and long after the girls are in bed for the night, Crystal stands in front of the full-length mirror, dressed in the cream-colored pants outfit she altered earlier to create a tighter fit. Adjusting the vest at the waistline, she turns slightly to view her backside—it's a perfect fit.

Travis loves her curvy figure, and this outfit is sure to get his attention off Felicia and onto her, at least for one night.

Now downstairs, the living room corner lamp provides dim lighting as the radio is on low volume. Passing through the living room and into the well-lit kitchen, she stands at the open back door, looking toward Modena Street, where the streetlight offers visibility in the darkness, but still no Travis in sight.

Where is he? she wonders.

Seductively dressed and horny, Crystal steps outside onto the porch to further investigate his whereabouts. She hears a male's and a female's voice in the distance and steps down one more step. Bending forward to see past the pantry wall, she sees Travis and Felicia turning the corner of the single structure, five townhome units.

It seems that while she was in Phoenix, those two have become closer.

When he's in speaking range, Crystal asks, "Travis, I've been looking for you. Why didn't you tell me you were coming outside?"

"I didn't intend to be gone long, so there was no

need to."

Travis stands a few feet away, ignoring her and entertaining Felicia, who laughs at his every word. Crystal stands there watching them and has no problem spotting their newfound closeness. Anger builds up, and her first impulse is to give Travis a few choice words of her own, but she looks away, deciding, *The last thing I want is for him to think that I'm jealous.*

Then the phone begins to ring. Crystal takes off running inside, picking it up on the fourth ring, and is greeted by Leon's girlfriend.

"Hi, Penny," says Crystal, dragging the extra-long phone cord into the living room, where she sits in the corner chair and then insists on knowing, asking, "Girl, why haven't you and that brother-in-law of mine been over here to visit us?"

"Leon and I haven't been anywhere. I can't do anything until after the twins are born."

"Twins?!" Crystal shouts.

"Yes, I'm having twins."

Unexpectedly, Crystal once again experiences an overwhelming sense of sadness. It's as though Penny had just told her someone died.

Crystal then hears *Something* saying, "She's not going to have the twins. You are!"

Crystal is stunned into silence, but this time, the whispering voice that she hasn't heard in four years is more explicit and a little bit louder than before. No longer can Crystal deny the voice, claiming it to be her own thoughts, and while she's still in disbelief, there comes another whisper telling Crystal to prophesy it, saying, "Tell her."

It doesn't feel right to say that to anyone—it seems cruel. So, she doesn't talk at all.

"What's wrong? You got so quiet," says Penny.

"Nothing."

"Yes, it is. What?"

Crystal remains silent.

"Well, I'll call you some other time." Penny hangs up.

Crystal's plan to seduce Travis has come to naught. Sitting in the corner of the living room, thinking about what she heard, she asks herself, *Why would I tell Penny that I'm going to have the twins and she's not?*

Crystal then recalls when she was a little girl, she used to tell her friends that when she grew up, she was going to have twins. It all seems surreal.

While Crystal feels guilty as if she did a bad thing, Leon walks into the room. Walking past her, he says, "Hi, Crystal."

Upon recognizing him, Crystal jerks her head and looks over her shoulder. "Hey, Leon, I just hung up the phone, talking to Penny. She told me she's carrying twins, and she's really upset that she's confined to the bed until she delivers."

"Yeah. She's mad, but it's for the best."

Travis, their father's firstborn, enters the room with a bag of weed and sits next to Leon on the sofa. "What's wrong, bro?" he asks, dipping his fingers into the bag, and he rolls a joint.

While Leon updates Travis about Penny's situation, Crystal goes to the kitchen and reaches for the bottle of red wine on the table, pouring herself a glass.

Seated again in the chair, slowly sipping it, Crystal begins to fade away in thought, thinking, *That sure was weird for something to prophesy that I'm going to give birth to twins.*

Travis then yells across the room, "Crystal, you're awfully quiet over there. You, OK?"

"Yeah. I'm all right. Just thinking," she says, now contemplating whether she has a gift or not.

23

Travis rushes inside the townhome apartment after getting his hair cut, yelling, “Crystal!”

He passes through the kitchen into the living room, where she and the girls are playing on the floor with Kimberly’s toy tree house.

“What?” she asks, standing on her feet in response to the urgency in his tone.

“Get ready. We’re going to the hospital.” Travis walks past her and begins to climb the stairs.

“We’re going to the hospital for what?”

“Penny miscarried.”

“What! She miscarried? When?”

“Yesterday, I guess,” he yells from the top of the stairs. “And hurry up. Felicia said she’ll keep the kids.”

Because she has already sensed Penny’s unhappiness about the pregnancy, Crystal walks slowly up the stairs, null of emotions, unsure if she should feel sorrow or worry that she's next. Finding a job, so she can finally leave Travis, keeps her too busy to think about having twins.

Days later, after returning from job hunting, Crystal, home an hour, has a sudden urge to throw up. She takes off, trotting upstairs, covering her mouth with her hand until she makes it to the bathroom, and then forcibly expels it into the toilet.

That night, back in late March, when she and Travis had sex on the living room floor without the use of protection, is the reason Crystal's plan to leave him, can never become a reality. Her mind begins to violently rip and shred her plans into pieces as Travis drives out of the parking lot, leaving for work.

While the girls are still next door, where she left them this morning, Crystal bitterly walks down the stairs, and the phone begins to ring.

In the kitchen, picking it up, her mood quickly changes. Excited that it's a potential employer calling about the phone operator position that she applied for and has been hoping to fill, Crystal cheers, "Yes, I am Crystal."

Crystal's excitement plummets when asked, "Can you come in for an interview?"

With the taste of vomit still on her tongue, she remembers, *Dang! I'm pregnant.* Hoping it wouldn't matter and out of curiosity, Crystal asks, "I just learned I'm pregnant. Will it hurt my chances of being hired?"

"I'm sorry. We can't hire you if you are pregnant."

Crushed, Crystal hangs up the phone and goes upstairs. Lying across the bed, she begins to cry, mumbling in tears, "Every time I try to better my life, there is always an opposition." Then in anger, she shouts, "God, you know I don't want any more children. How can I love this child if I don't want it? Tell me, God, how?"

Crystal doesn't wait for God's answer and in the days ahead, she searches her heart for her own outcome, and in doing so, her mind rejects that mistakes do happen. Not accepting her condition, the answer then comes to her in the form of resentment. Crystal drifts into a state of depression. She barely eats as hate increases and consumes her.

Sunday evening, as Crystal stands over the stove, stirring the gravy to serve over mashed potatoes for dinner, Travis sits at the table behind her, playing one-hand solitaire. He realizes the state of mind that she's in and breaks the silence. "Crystal, I will understand if you don't want this baby. I don't want any more children either, so do you want an abortion?"

Crystal's first response is to say yes, but hearing that word only reminds her of the past. The guilt of having had an abortion five years ago was worse than the pain of childbirth itself. Crystal's conscience condemns her, and she says, "No."

Travis is unaware that she's not eating when he's not home. Her body has become weaker as it's deprived of nourishment, but Crystal does attempt to eat around Travis, who watches her run to the stairs, rushing to the bathroom to regurgitate. Her inability to hold down food makes it a lot easier to starve herself.

Monday, after Travis leaves for work, Crystal locks the front and back doors and then closes all the curtains.

Upstairs, in the master bedroom, she has the thirteen-inch-screen TV on. Kimberly is not allowed to go outside, and no one is allowed in. There's nothing outside of the apartment walls or the life growing inside of her that matters. The only things that are significant to her are her two girls. They're now the only part of her that she loves.

Lying in bed in a daze, Crystal stares at the TV, but she isn't watching it. She can hear the girls playing nearby and feels their love and loveliness even in her despair, but to play with them, hold them, and smile at them is beyond her capability.

As Crystal avoids the coldness of her heart, her mind drifts, and the white bedroom wall becomes the screen on which her imagination creates false images. They are images that offer no sorrow and no regrets. Alone, inside her head, Crystal visualizes herself running in a field of purple, yellow, and white wildflowers, laughing and twirling around. She imagines herself living a life without Travis—without this pregnancy. She's happy. It's a faraway place but a better place, and she wants to go there and never return to this unhappy life she is now forced to live.

But just as she's about to enter that world of no return, Kimberly reaches out her small, caring hand and touches Crystal on the shoulder.

Kimberly, very concerned, looks her mother in the eyes. "Mommy, you don't feel good?"

Blankly, she stares into Kimberly's beautiful, deep, dark irises as the answer comes in tears.

Kimberly pats Crystal's shoulder. "You'll be OK, so don't cry. I'll help you get better. All right, Mommy?"

Then Sheena starts to cry. Kimberly runs to her rescue and is now playing house. Sheena and Crystal are her babies.

"What is it, baby girl? Are you hungry?" Kimberly

asks Sheena.

Kimberly goes over to the dresser, takes the already prepared bottle, hands it to Sheena, her imagined child, and then returns to Crystal, her other child.

“Are you hungry, Mommy?”

Crystal doesn’t say a word as the tears continue to flow.

“I’ll get you some food to eat.” Kimberly runs toward the door.

Crystal listens to her footsteps as she trots down the single flight of stairs.

Sheena climbs over her mother and rests her head against Crystal’s abdomen while sucking her bottle. Sheena looks over at her, takes the bottle from her own mouth, and offers it to Crystal, trying to force the nipple into Crystal’s mouth, but she’s unable to and gives up. Sheena then drinks the milk from the bottle until it’s empty.

When Kimberly returns with a plate of bologna and saltine crackers and sets it at the foot of the bed, Sheena quickly climbs over Crystal, takes a cracker from the plate, and eats.

At nearly four years old, Kimberly demands from the foot of the bed, “Here, Mommy, eat!”

Because of Crystal’s love for her girls, she knows that not eating the fruit of Kimberly’s labor would be to reject her love offering. It’s for them that she chooses to live in a loveless marriage. Therefore, she begins to consider that what she’s doing will affect her girls. Crystal suddenly snaps out of her temporary insanity, and with all the remaining strength in her and for the happiness of her girls, she sits up in bed, takes a bite of a cracker, and allows it to soften on her tongue.

The taste of it makes her sick. Nauseated, she

swallows. Her stomach trembles as she continues to eat. The food stays down at first; then, she suddenly springs off the bed onto her feet. Being very weak, her legs wobble as she hurries to the bathroom, but she vomits before she can make it out of the room.

With trembling hands, Crystal uses an old rag from the hallway closet to clean up the mess. She then tries to eat again, and this time, the food stays down.

Crystal realizes the danger of starving herself and begins eating regularly, but her thoughts are unhealthy and every day, in the midst of spiritual warfare—between love and hate, she tenaciously struggles with her heart not to succumb to the hateful feelings that she harbors for her unborn child.

24

On a hot and humid day in July, the small oscillating fan stands in front of the open living room window, circulating air around the room as Crystal lies stretched out on the sofa, holding Sheena tightly with one arm against her growing abdomen.

Feeling exhausted from the heat, Crystal quickly falls asleep and wakes up just in time to witness Kimberly walking away from the stairs with Sheena dangling from her arms, kicking and whining.

"No, no, Sheena, you can't go upstairs. Daddy is sleeping," Kimberly says.

"Sheena, you weren't supposed to get away from Mommy," says Crystal as she struggles to sit up.

The fan is no relief for her and the girls, so she wiggles her big self off the sofa and goes into the kitchen, where she removes the box of popsicles from the freezer.

In the living room, she and Kimberly take turns

sharing their popsicle with Sheena, who sucks it and bites it, rolling the pieces around in her mouth as the contents dribble down her naked belly and onto her pamper, staining its white color to red and orange.

Feeling much cooler and rejuvenated, Crystal and the girls begin to stir up a racket, disturbing Travis, who usually doesn't gets out of bed until five o'clock, and it's now a little past three. As his footsteps are heard coming down the steps, Kimberly rushes over to greet him, with Sheena crawling fast behind her. Travis lifts Kimberly into his arms, kissing her on the cheek. After putting her down, he reaches for Sheena and carries her over to the corner of the room where Crystal sits.

"Daddy, do you want to play with Sheena and me?"

"Not now, baby girl; we're going somewhere in a few minutes."

“Going where?” Crystal asks before he kisses her and then Sheena, setting her down on the floor.

"I've been thinking,” he says. “With another child on the way, we're going to need more room, and they're going to need a backyard to play in. So, we're going to ride around and look at houses up for sale."

“That sounds good to me,” she says, totally forgetting Travis's promise that Phoenix will be their home and is not thinking of it as a permanent move but seeing it as an opportunity to get out of the apartment, to have a change of scenery, a distraction from the negative thoughts surrounding this unwanted pregnancy.

Now at five months, Crystal appears to be six, and tonight, as she lies in bed, wide awake, her mind is busy. *The one time I have sex without protection, I become pregnant. I could be in Phoenix but now I'm stuck here. Why me?* She brews in anger that then spills over into what she's thinking; *I hope I miscarry like Penny did.*

Spiritually weak and hollow inside, wanting her womb to be as empty as she feels, Crystal, soaking in self-pity, begins to sense a presence—that sense of knowing when someone is nearby.

Lying on her side, facing the door, she listens for any sounds different from those of traffic but hears nothing. She focuses on the space before her—she sees nothing, only the white wall. To avoid being noticed, Crystal slowly turns her head, inch by inch, until she can finally see behind her, which is the box fan in the window, contributing very little relief from the heat.

Crystal decides to disregard what she is sensing, and just as she's about to close her eyes, there appears to be a shadow—black as night, standing and leaning against the door frame. Having the form of a man, it's looking directly at her.

Motionless, Crystal stares into its face, looking for the white of the eyes, but she doesn't see any facial features. The shadow begins to move toward her as though floating in midair. Crystal tries to scream, but she's unable to utter a sound. She tries to shake Travis, who is asleep next to her, but she can't move. She's scared stiff.

In the form of a man, this shadow reaches the bedside and looks down at her. Again, Crystal searches for the white of the eyes, but it doesn't have a face. Then, the shadow reaches out its hand and rests it on her abdomen. Crystal quickly closes her eyes, the only moveable part of her body, and then reopens them—it's gone.

Crystal, bewildered and now having freedom of movement, glances around the room, trying to see if it's still there. It isn't. In relief, she rolls over onto her opposite side, and finally, in the hot, noise-filled room, she falls asleep.

In the morning, Kimberly stands in the doorway, dressed in a T-shirt and panties. Quietly, she whines, "Mommy."

When Crystal doesn't answer her, Kimberly whines even louder, "Mommy."

"OK, Kim, I heard you the first time. Go downstairs and turn on the TV," Crystal mumbles from her pillow.

She then looks over at the clock on the nightstand. It's nine o'clock and time for *Uncle Al's Show*—Kimberly's morning favorite.

Crystal isn't ready to get out of bed and snoozes for five more minutes. She then forces herself to sit up at the edge of the bed and looks back at Travis, who has suddenly stopped breathing. She shakes him, and he starts to snore again. She hates it when he does that.

Now, out of bed, she dresses into a long, brown, zip-up robe with yellow diamond-like designs. Stepping into her slippers, she exits the room, and just as she walks into the box-like hallway, looking straight into the girl's bedroom, she observes Sheena, nine months old, sitting in her crib and sucking an empty bottle.

Upon seeing Crystal, she drops it, grabs the side of the crib, stands up, and begins to whimper.

"Mommy will be in to get you," Crystal says as she turns into the bathroom, where she listens to Sheena cry and hurries out.

Crystal lifts her from the crib. "Here I am. Is Mama's baby hungry?" She kisses Sheena's fat cheek and sucks it into her mouth, gently biting it with tender loving care.

Downstairs, Crystal can't get last night's experience out of her head, and as Sheena greedily drinks fresh milk from the bottle, Crystal holds her hand, preparing Sheena to walk on her own. As they walk from the kitchen into the living room, Crystal recalls a similar situation. At seven years old, she had awakened during the night and entered the bathroom, and while sitting on the toilet in the dark, she saw a shadow, in the form of a child, standing in the doorway. It, too, was as black as night. Resembling her younger brother Randall, and while it, too, sucked its thumb, it moved toward her. She said, "Randall, wait your turn. I'm on the toilet." As it moved closer, she saw a small black dog walking alongside it. The family didn't have a dog, so Crystal screamed, "Mama," as loud as she could, but it disappeared before Maylene came running, wearing only a white bra and panties. When she turned on the bathroom light, she was surprisingly calm. "What's wrong?" She had asked Crystal.

"I saw somebody coming toward me, and I was scared."

Maylene then looked around the bathroom. "There's nothing here." She turned and said before walking away, "Girl, go back to bed."

The thought of that shadow of a thing touching her abdomen is mentally disturbing. Back in the kitchen, now preparing breakfast, Crystal's mind is preoccupied with thinking, *What is it? Is it real? Where is it coming from? Where does it go?*

A second voice emerges and has taken Crystal under its full control, telling her specifically what she is to do—its purpose is to destroy. The other voice, which has been silent lately, tells her both what not to do and what to do, and it's protective. Yet, not knowing the difference between the two, she withdraws and becomes non-responsive to both voices.

Casually, as she moves through the living room, going up and down the stairs without saying a word, Travis, who is at home for a change, observes that her state of mind is absent—out of it. After a certain length of time passes and he doesn't see or hear her, he goes to investigate. Quietly, he slowly creeps up the stairs. Stopping short of the top three steps, he sees Crystal standing in the middle of the girls' bedroom and staring out of the open window.

He says softly, "Crystal." But she doesn't answer him. As though frozen, she can't speak or even turn to look at him.

The wicked voice in her head is commanding her, "Go ahead, jump."

Crystal is tempted to jump out the window but doesn't want to die.

Travis then enters his and Crystal's bedroom and calls Maylene on the phone. "Mama, I don't know what's wrong with Crystal. She won't talk. Maybe she'll talk to you."

He yells across the hallway, "Crystal, your mama wants to talk to you."

After numerous failed attempts to get Crystal to the phone, Travis comes and puts his arm around Crystal's shoulders, walking her to their bedroom, where she sits on the bed.

He says into the phone, "Here she is, Mama."

With the phone to her ear, Crystal falls backward onto the bed, listening as Maylene demands, "Crystal, what's wrong with you?"

The phone falls onto the bed, and in the girls' room, Crystal listens to Maylene's voice that's now in her head, repeatedly asking, "Crystal, what's wrong with you?" until her continued persistence pulls out of Crystal the bitter painful truth. *Mama, I don't want this baby.*

Later that evening, Crystal begins to talk again. Travis doesn't know about the voices because he doesn't ask.

Crystal figures, *What's the use of telling him? He doesn't care.*

25

At her OB-GYN appointment, Crystal lies supine on the examining table when Dr. Lizzy Trumpleton, a short, stocky older woman, enters the examination room and looks up from reading Crystal's medical chart.

"How are you doing, Mrs. Wallace? Is everything going OK?"

Smiling to put on a pretentious act, Crystal says, "I'm doing fine."

Dr. Trumpleton lifts Crystal's blouse, exposing her huge abdomen. She then removes the measuring tape from her white jacket pocket, placing one end of the tape below Crystal's rib cage and the other end just above her pelvic region.

"Mrs. Wallace, you're quite large at this stage of your pregnancy. I'm going to order an ultrasound to confirm that you're carrying twins."

Dr. Trumpleton writes in Crystal's medical chart,

talking as she writes. "Because your abdominal muscles aren't strong enough for you to give birth, I'll have to do a C-section."

Crystal struggles to sit up while silently repeating the doctor's words: *twins, ultrasound, C-section...*

Dr. Trumpleton isn't the only one with suspicions. Crystal, too, at times, feels multiple kicks on both sides of her midsection, near her ribs, her back, and her pelvic region—all occurring at the same time.

The prophecy that was spoken to her is now unfolding.

Wanting clarity about being pregnant with twins, the following week, Crystal is on time for her scheduled appointment.

Staring at the ultrasound monitor, she's frustrated because as she stares into the monitor screen, she can't figure out what she's looking at. The image is one big blob.

"Mrs. Wallace, I'm almost done," says the technician as she slowly slides the handheld device across Crystal's abdomen. She then pushes the button, capturing the final image. "There. We are all done," she concludes as she wipes the gel from Crystal's belly.

Crystal steps down from the examining table and goes into the cubicle and is getting dressed when the technician, showing excitement, abruptly opens the cubicle door without knocking and shouts, "It's twins. I don't know their sex, but I am sure you're having twins."

Crystal's maternity blouse slides down over her head, covering her extremely large belly, and while caught off-guard, she doesn't share in the enthusiasm but sternly stares into the technician's eyes as though she's crazy for having barged into the cubicle and startling her.

The thought of that technician expecting her to jump for joy when she has nothing to feel joyful about rattles Crystal's mind while she drives home from the hospital. Preoccupied with thoughts of that night seven months ago when the voice told her that she'd have twins, she then questions fate. *Why me? Why do I have to be the one to live through—no, suffer through this supernatural stuff?*

Losing all self-control, she screams, "God, how many times must I tell you. I don't want more children."

Holding back the tears, Crystal takes a long deep breath to calm herself down.

Arriving home, she walks through the kitchen and into the living room, where Travis sits, strumming his electric bass guitar. She says dully, "I'm carrying twins."

Travis said he didn't want any more children, either, but suddenly acts as though he hit the lottery. He immediately runs into the kitchen, snatches the telephone earpiece from the wall, dials the number, waits for his grandmother to answer, and then shouts, "Nana, guess what? Crystal is having twins."

Her response is disappointing.

"Nana, I'm for real." Travis then hands the phone to Crystal. "You, tell her. She doesn't believe me."

Crystal puts it to her ear, confirming what Travis just said. "Yes. It's true. I'm having twins."

Nana chuckles softly. "Child, I shouldn't be surprised; twins run in our family, you know?"

Crystal doesn't say it out loud but is thinking: *You don't know what I know, and if you did, you would agree that these twins didn't get inside of me because of genes.*

After talking briefly, she hangs up the phone and

waddles over to the open kitchen door, looking through the plexiglass storm door and watches Kimberly play outside with the next-door neighbor's seven-year-old daughter. She wants so badly for her life to be normal but dares not to tell anyone about the voices; people will automatically think she's mentally ill.

It's possible that she could be, but knowing herself well, her perception of reality is typical. The problem is that she's ignorant of the spiritual realm and doesn't clearly understand how it is operating within herself. Crystal walks away from the door. Still, yet, to figure it out.

26

In mid-October, it's not cold at all but slightly warm and delightful—a perfect Indian summer day to be outside.

Downtown, walking with Sheena in his arms, Travis, in a hurry to get to the traffic light to cross the busy downtown street, has left Crystal and Kimberly behind, who slowly poke along.

He has found a half-story, three-bedroom house that he must have regardless of whether Crystal wants it or not. She pokes along with Kimberly at her side, pondering: *He's the one who wants the house. I don't.*

With only a few steps away from the crosswalk, Travis turns and yells, "Crystal, ya'll hurry up! We're late already as it is."

Her midsection, larger than she is, is extremely heavy. Crystal expresses her discontent, "Travis, I'm walking as fast as I can. I would like to see you walking fast at seven months pregnant with twins."

Upon entering the third-floor conference room fifteen minutes late, Travis apologizes to those seated around the large and wide table that takes up most of the room. "I'm sorry for our tardiness," he says and then cracks a joke about Crystal's condition, causing everyone to laugh.

We're late not because of my condition, but because he was out running the streets when he should have been home so we could get here on time, thinks Crystal, smiling as she has a seat.

Again, Crystal visits Dr. Trumpleton's office. Sitting and flipping through the pages of a magazine, she looks up to see the doctor walk into the examination room, rehashing old news. "Well, Mrs. Wallace, you're definitely having twins."

Just as she did with the ultrasound technician, Crystal hides her true feelings. "Yeah, I know. The hospital tech told me."

"In my opinion, the twins are still too small. I don't want you up and around. I'm going to insist that you be on bed rest until you go into labor. I don't want you driving, either. Your abdomen is just too large for you to be behind the steering wheel."

The doctor pauses from writing in Crystal's medical chart and looks up from her notes. "Did your husband bring you?"

"No. I drove. Is there a reason why I have to stay in bed?"

"Taking you off your feet will allow the twins to put on extra pounds. After today, I don't want you to drive."

Crystal crosses her legs below the knee, thinking, *Hmm, that sucks.*

Leaving the doctor's office, and driving home, Crystal is very dissatisfied with the doctor's plan.

When she walks into the apartment, Travis, as always, sits strumming his electric bass guitar with the music on blast. Upon seeing her, he quickly lowers the volume.

"Well, what did the doctor tell you?"

"She put me on bed rest until I go into labor," Crystal grumbles.

With his voice raised, Travis asks, "She's putting you on bed rest?"

As Crystal nods, he points to the stairs. "Well, doctor's orders. Go get in bed."

Crystal stomps her feet up the steps. Upset at Travis laughing, she says sarcastically, "I don't think it's funny."

Sitting in bed and watching TV, she anxiously waits for Travis to leave for work. Then she'll have free rein to do what she darn well pleases, and with a bit of impatience, she glances over at the clock on the nightstand. One hour to go.

Then, at exactly two-thirty, Travis leaves the girls upstairs with her and goes to work. After waiting three hours, she waddles into the kitchen to cook dinner and grumbling, "Dr. Trumpleton must be out of her mind if she expects me to take care of my girls from a bed."

After washing dishes around nine, Crystal strolls into the living room and finds the girls nodding off. She takes them upstairs, and while they sleep, she has plenty of free time.

Stepping off the stairs and into the living room, the wicked voice suggests, "You must miscarry. Pack boxes so you will miscarry like Penny did."

That's stupid, she thinks. *Since when does packing boxes cause a miscarriage?* She then questions the idea and wonders, Maybe it is possible.

Crystal rushes to the closet underneath the staircase and removes one of the boxes that she and Travis have been collecting for when they move into their newly bought home. Besides, she's bored, and she has nothing else to do.

After looking around in the kitchen cabinets and drawers for items she seldom uses and packing them for two hours, with very little discomfort, Crystal picks up the unfinished box of small kitchen items and carries it into the living room, putting it down on the closet floor and pushing the box far beneath the stairs.

Having escaped being caught, she lies in bed from where she listens to Travis unlocking the kitchen door. She then hears another loud click, letting her know that he's inside and has relocked it.

The following night when he returns home, Travis opens the door, catching Crystal bent over the same box she started packing the night before.

"Crystal, didn't the doctor tell you to stay in bed?" he shouts.

As she's now made aware of the time, Crystal stares into Travis's eyes, which expresses his anger, and she replies, "The girls and I have to eat. If I don't pack, no one else will."

He slams the door shut. "It'll get done, so don't you worry about it."

Her excuse is legit and without remorse. No way can she tell him about the wicked voice telling her to do it so she'll miscarry.

"Keep packing," the voice says.

While in pain, Crystal continues to do so and outrightly ignores Travis.

His anger mounts. "Crystal, get your butt up

those stairs and lie down!"

Her response isn't fast enough, so he rushes over and grabs her by the arm, pulling her through the living room and up the stairs to their bedroom, where he stands guard until she's in bed.

In the morning, she awakes to the sound of footsteps on the stairs. She opens her eyes to see Travis walk into the room with a lit cigarette clenched between two fingers. "I got Felicia to come over to take care of the girls and to cook while I'm at work."

"Oh, you just take it upon yourself to talk to her without talking to me first?"

"Crystal, we don't have anyone else who can do it on this short notice."

Travis leaves the room for her to ponder that thought. Whenever they're in some kind of a predicament, Felicia is the only person he runs to, which prompts Crystal to wonder, *What's really going on?*

Although Felicia isn't her favorite person, Crystal can't ignore the fact that she does a good job at taking care of the girls, and the girls love her very much. Whether Crystal likes it or not, she needs Felicia, who later enters the apartment just before Travis is about to leave for work and says loud and clear, "At seven o'clock, I'm out of here."

Upstairs listening, Crystal silently mumbles, "I wish I could kick your butt out right now."

With a snobbish attitude, she reaches for the Bible on the nightstand and begins to read the Book of Psalms.

The smell of fried chicken cooking downstairs is disturbing her concentration. Crystal then begins to imagine Felicia as her personal maid, and when she finally enters the bedroom, handing Crystal the plate of food, Crystal is starving. Her snobby attitude quickly disappears, and she gladly takes the plate, saying humbly, "Thank you."

Felicia's stone expression softens and cheerfully answers, "You're welcome. I'll be back to get your plate when you're done eating."

At the time she said she would, Felicia brings the girls upstairs with Crystal and leaves. Later on while the girls are in their room, asleep, Crystal finally grows weary with reading and puts down the Bible. Instead of getting out of bed as planned, she sits there with her head tilted back against the wall, trying to relax and remain in bed as she has been instructed to do, but her thoughts are like a syringe that keeps injecting her heart with hate directed at the babies growing inside her.

Then, the hateful and persistent voice, which had been silent while she read the Bible, begins to tell her, now that she is no longer distracted, "You have to miscarry. The twins cannot be born. Go pack boxes."

Downstairs, Crystal removes the box that she started last night from the closet and then searches for things to place in it. Again, she loses track of time, and when Travis enters the apartment, finding her bent over a different box, he slams the door shut, furiously screaming, "Crystal, you just wait. First thing in the morning, I'm calling the doctor to have her put your butt in the hospital."

The weight of Crystal's abdomen doesn't allow her to straighten up easily. Holding the weight of her belly with both hands lightens the heavy load and relieves the pain. Crystal looks over at Travis and rolls her eyes before waddling out of the kitchen. "I don't care if you do or don't call the doctor."

He follows her upstairs.

"I don't see a problem with me being up and about. The doctor doesn't have to lie around in bed, putting on added weight, but she wants me to."

"Crystal, just do what the doctor wants you to do," Travis advises her.

"That's easy for you to say. You don't have to stay in bed all day, every day." Crystal pauses and turns to look at him with angry eyes. "I do, and I don't like it."

Travis keeps quiet as she rambles on and watches her get into bed.

First thing in the morning, as usual, Travis lights a cigarette, and just as he threatened that he would do, he sits on the edge of the bed, picks up the phone from the nightstand, exhales smoke, and calls the doctor's office.

When he says, "Good morning, Dr. Trumpleton," Crystal now believes he meant what he said. She then listens to him squealing on her. "Sorry to bother you, but I'm concerned about my wife. She isn't following your instructions. We just bought a house, and we'll be moving into it real soon. While I'm at work, she gets out of bed. I keep telling her to stay in it, but she won't listen to me. Is it possible for you to put her in the hospital?"

Dr. Trumpleton must have considered his concerns. He now appears relaxed.

Wearing only his underwear briefs, he walks over to the dresser and taps the cigarette ashes into the ashtray. While clinching the cigarette between his fingers, he points at Crystal, who attempts to read his lips that are saying, "You're going into the hospital."

He finally hangs up the phone and tells her, "The

doctor is making the arrangements, and as soon as she can get you a bed, your butt is going to be admitted."

"Who's going to take care of the girls while you're at work, Travis?"

"Don't you worry about the girls; they'll be fine. I'll work it out. I'll do whatever I have to do."

That remark makes Crystal wonder, *Will it be for the girl's best interest or his?* With Travis, she never knows.

At the bottom of the hill, Crystal sits in the car, waving goodbye to the girls standing alongside Felicia behind the storm door and waving back. Travis then starts the engine and drives her to the hospital, where she's transported up to the maternity floor.

In a wheelchair, she's pushed out of the third-floor elevator with Travis close behind, carrying her baggage to the end of the long corridor and straight into the large, spacious room occupied by other women who are up and moving about.

Travis glances around at them. Seeing that he's the only male, he sets the small suitcase on the only available bed in the room. Crystal also looks around the room and thinks, *I'm not going to like being around all these strange women.*

At the same time that she's thinking that, Travis says, "Well, since I don't fit in here, I'll be going now."

He quickly kisses Crystal on the mouth and walks toward the door. "I'll see you tomorrow."

Early the next morning while Crystal is still asleep, a nurse rushes into the room and shouts, "Mrs. Wallace, wake up, dear."

Crystal lifts her head, looking past the foot of the bed at the clock on the wall. It's seven o'clock. Her head then sinks into the pillow, and she groans. It's way too early—for her.

"Come on, Mrs. Wallace," the nurse says as she gathers Crystal's belongings onto a cart. "I need you to get out of bed. I'm moving you into a semi-private room at your husband's request. We checked his insurance, which will pay for the upgrade."

The women begin to chatter loudly. "I wish my husband would have done that for me," one says as Crystal is pushed out of the room, understanding their feelings but glad she doesn't have to stay in a room full of strange women coming and going for the next thirty days or more.

Three rooms down, the nurse pushes Crystal into the semiprivate room, announcing Crystal's arrival to the woman lying in bed near the window, "You have a roommate. This is Crystal. She's also having twins."

"Hi, Crystal."

"Hi."

"I'm Mendy. I've been alone in this room for months now, but it feels like forever. It's good to finally have someone to share it with. I'm in my second trimester. How far along are you?"

"In my third," says Crystal as she rises from the wheelchair and climbs into bed.

"I guess I'll go and let the two of you get acquainted," says the nurse as she passes the kitchen staff delivering breakfast trays on her way out the door.

27

A week before Thanksgiving, Travis is busy moving into their new house, and with the help of uncles and cousins, they carry boxes and furniture from the driveway and through the sliding doors. While at the same time they're unloading the U-Haul truck, the previous owners carry their furniture out the front.

Crystal, meanwhile, sits upright in bed watching TV when a nurse walks into the room. "Honey, I have a bed pad made of sheep's wool that the doctor ordered for you when she came earlier this morning."

Crystal stands at the foot of the bed, watching her remove the old padding and carefully position the sheep's wool, talking as she does it. "She is taking very good care of you. She left specific instructions about your care. You're getting the best of everything that your husband's insurance can afford to pay for, and the kitchen has been put on notice to send up two pieces of meat with each of your meals. She wants you to eat everything on your plate."

Weight-conscious, Crystal asks, "Eat everything? Why?"

"She's a very good doctor, and she knows what she's doing, dear," says the nurse as she affectionately touches Crystal's shoulder on the way out of the room.

Before lying down, Crystal runs her hand across the sheep wool, and by the feel of it, she doesn't understand the significance of it.

As she lies in bed, her mind begins to drift, recalling thoughts of yesterday when Travis came to visit and acted strangely. She had asked him, "What's wrong?"

And that's when he confessed, "Felicia is living with us, so she can be with the girls while I'm at work."

Very displeased to find out after the fact, Crystal yelled, "What! Travis, why didn't you ask someone in the family?"

"Because I knew they'll want me to pay them, and Felicia needed a place to go. She'll be calling you tomorrow."

"Yeah, and you tell her I'll be waiting for that call."

Crystal stared at him, tempted to smack his face, but he was seated too far away.

She reaches for the Bible on the adjustable bed table, needing to read Psalms 23 and has been memorizing it. While she is learning the verses, the phone rings and re-ignites her anger. With such strong emotions, Crystal answers, "Hello."

"Hi. Travis told me that you're upset."

"Yes, I am. I need to know, why are you living in my home without talking to me about it first?"

"Well, my cousin and I had a fight, and she put me out. Travis said I could stay here if I keep the girls while he works. I didn't have anywhere else to go."

Gifted with a sharp memory, Crystal recalls when she and Felicia were talking on the back porch of their townhome apartment; Felicia had mentioned that her parents have a room waiting for her if she ever wants to return home.

"Uh, uh. I don't think this is a coincidence," Crystal says. "This had to be planned."

"You don't believe me?"

Crystal raises her voice, "No. I don't believe you." Rapidly growing angrier, Crystal is about to scream, "Get the hell out of my house," but before the words could exit her lips, she remembers the girls. They are being well taken care of, which matters most to Crystal, who then sits with her jaw tight, struggling to keep quiet.

Felicia then says squeamishly after a long pause, "Well, I'll talk to you some other time." Crystal slams the phone down and mumbles, "You, just wait till I get out of here."

Crystal already feels like a stuffed turkey when Travis walks into the room on Thanksgiving Day with a large paper bag of cooked food, setting it on the adjustable bed table in front of her.

"I got a surprise for you, Crystal," he says as he begins to unpack the bag.

"What?"

Pulling it out, wrapped in tinfoil, he sets it down on the bed table.

She removes the foil, singing, "Ooh, a sweet potato pie. My favorite, thank you!"

"And I made it myself. The girls helped a little bit."

Travis sets the table, and they eat together for the first time in a long time. It's thoughtful moments like this that Crystal misses, which are now very few.

He then calls the girls on the phone so Crystal can spend time talking to them. Then, like in years past when they were newlyweds, he pulls out a board game, and before leaving, he beats her at playing Battle Ship.

Shortly after Thanksgiving, Mendy allows her frustration to get the best of her and begins to sneak out of bed to use the toilet, not once, but repeatedly. Then on the second day, in the middle of the night, while Crystal lies sleeping, several nurses scramble into the room. Awakened by the noise and commotion, Crystal opens her eyes and sees the nurses moving about, each having a different agenda.

Mendy is then rushed into the delivery room, and after two days, she's released from the hospital, leaving her twins in the ICU.

Now alone in the semi-private room, Crystal takes a chance and sneaks out of bed, walks over to the window, and stands there with her arms crossed and resting on her huge belly.

Absorbing the moment, she watches the beautiful cascading snow settle on the rooftops below, thinking, *It looks like it might be a white Christmas.*

The chilling December air seeps through the glass window seals. Feeling the coldness of it, Crystal quickly hurries to her side of the room, where she cuddles underneath the warm blankets and waits for Travis to come.

Due to his low seniority status, he keeps getting

bumped from one shift to another. Now, on second, he visits the hospital at noon, for an hour, instead of in the evenings before work.

In the past couple of days, he has been rubbing Crystal's belly and saying, "Today will be the day you'll go into labor."

When Travis walks into the room, Crystal is glued to the television.

"Hey, baby," he says, sitting in the chair beside the bed. He watches TV with as much intensity as she does and then complains during the commercial break, "Crystal, I can't believe you're getting me hooked on this doggone soap opera."

She's amused by him and giggles.

The soap opera ends. When Travis stands up to leave, he rubs her belly and says, "Today is the day that you'll go into labor."

"You said that yesterday."

He reaffirms himself as he walks toward the door, "I know, but watch and see." He then disappears around the corner.

After five hours, Crystal begins to experience pain and massages her abdomen as she reaches for the nurse call button. It's what the doctor told her to do when she feels the slightest contraction.

The nurse promptly enters the room. "What is it, dear?"

"I'm cramping."

"Well, we better get the doctor here right away," she says, turning around and walking back out.

Within thirty minutes, Dr. Thrumpleton stands at Crystal's bedside. "Mrs. Wallace, how are you feeling?"

"I feel fine."

The nurse reenters the delivery room. "Mrs. Wallace, did anyone contact your husband yet?"

"Not that I know of."

"I guess I better get him here, too."

Crystal monitors everyone coming and going, in and out of the operating room, preparing for the C-section when Travis walks through the door and over to where she's lying.

"How did you get here so fast?" Crystal asks in surprise.

He giggles. "I was speeding. I don't want to miss this. I told you today would be the day."

"You did say that, although, you were guessing."

Excited to know the sex of the twins, Travis waits by Crystal's bedside as the doctor warns, "I am now cutting you open, Mrs. Wallace. Let me know if you feel anything."

As they both anticipate the birth of the firstborn twin, Crystal does not take her eyes off Travis's unchanging expression.

"What's going on?" she asks.

"The doctor is cutting you open," he says without taking his eyes off the procedure.

Then, finally, Travis's head drops and he mumbles softly, "Another girl."

"Oh," says Crystal as Travis lifts his head and continues watching.

After a one-minute interval, his eyes broaden. Travis's face lights up with a joyous smile. He says, "A boy! About time."

"It sure is," says Crystal, smiling. "We now have our son, and he will be the last."

The doctor yells, "Mrs. Wallace, I am now tying and burning your fallopian tubes."

That's what she wants to hear and says, "OK."

Now that the girls are allowed to visit her at the

hospital but not allowed in her room, Crystal stands at the elevators across from the nursery, waiting anxiously for them. The elevator doors open, and Kimberly runs out into her arms, screaming, "Mommy! Hi, Mommy."

"Have you been a good girl?" Crystal asks, holding her tightly in her arms.

"Yeah. Me and Sheena been good."

Crystal reaches for Sheena now one years old and takes her from Travis, kissing her fat cheek. "Hi, Sheena. Did you miss Mommy?"

Shy, she quietly answers, "Hi."

"Can you give Mama a big hug?"

Sheena's arms circle around Crystal's neck as they cross the corridor, walking to the nursery. The twins, in separate incubators, are already near the window and are being treated for a slight case of yellow jaundice.

Acting as the very proud father, Travis brought his 35mm camera and is taking pictures as the girls stand at the nursery window, fascinated over the birth of their twin sister and brother.

Felicia makes a bold move, walking up to Crystal and getting all up in her face. Looking past her, Crystal continues to ignore her as though Felicia isn't there. To Crystal, she isn't.

Felicia takes the hint and walks away, joining the girls at the nursery window. Crystal eyes her, looking her up and down and thinking, *How dare you move into my home and disrespect me.*

Animosity stirs within her, and while she's staring at Felicia, resenting her for pretending she's not emotionally involved with her husband, Travis walks up to Crystal, kisses her, and says, "Well, baby, I have to be at work at three. I have to drop them off at home and be on my way."

Felicia, known for her jolly personality, stands in the elevator with an expression of sadness. The elevator door closes, and Crystal walks away with a slight grin and mumbling, "Little heifer."

Crystal goes to her room and comes back out, headed to the cafeteria, when she notices Leon and Penny outside the nursery. "Hi, I didn't know y'all were coming."

"We didn't either. It was a last-minute decision before Leon goes to work," says Penny, who then takes Leon's hand. "We're about to leave. We didn't want to bother you and thought we'll be coming over to the house after you are home."

"We should be home tomorrow."

The next day, it's nearly noon, and Crystal still hasn't been released from the hospital. An older nurse walks in and begins to strike up a conversation. She's someone Crystal hasn't seen before, and for some strange reason, Crystal sensed that the nurse had a motive for coming into her room. With it still on Crystal's mind as she's finally leaving the hospital, she leans over the side of the wheelchair, looking back at the two young nurses, each carrying a twin, and following Travis as he pushes her down the corridor and toward the exit doors. Crystal then faces forward and confronts the nurse's question, "Are you ready for twins?"

In her head, Crystal replays the answer she gave. "I'll just have to do the best that I can."

Actually, she's afraid—afraid that she can't be the loving mother the twins will need her to be.

The car, parked just on the other side of the automatic doors, awaits them with the engine idling. The doors slide open, and everyone braces themselves before stepping outside into the blistering cold.

The only thing on Crystal's mind as they drive away from the hospital is Felicia—she has to go and will not be sleeping another night in her house.

Arriving home, Travis slowly coasts the car into the driveway, and before he can put the gears into the park, Felicia comes rushing outside in the snow, wearing house shoes and without a coat. She reaches into the car and removes Candice, leaving Brandt for Travis, who warns as she steps onto the porch, "Crystal, watch your step. It's a little slippery up here."

Crystal takes precautions as she's warned, stamping the snow from her shoes and onto the doormat.

It's no secret that Crystal disapproves of Felicia being there, and as she walks toward the front door, Crystal isn't expecting her to say, before leaving, "Crystal, I'll be back at eight o'clock, and I'll put the girls to bed."

It's good she does leave because Crystal is not about to hide her true feelings. Travis and Felicia will not flaunt their undignified, innocent-like relationship that they're having in her face and think she will allow it—hell no!

Prepared to end their charade of pretending that nothing is going on between them, Crystal, sitting in the living room, bottle feeding Brandt, waits patiently to do what she has been anticipating to do for weeks when Felicia, later that evening, enters the living room.

"I put the girls to bed already. Do you want me to help you feed the twins now?"

Crystal coldly answers, "No. You can go. I got this. I don't need your help."

“Are you sure?” Felicia asks as if in shock. She stares into Crystal’s eyes and sees how serious she is.

“Well, before I pack my things, do you mind if I call my parents so they can come get me?”

“No. I don’t mind. Go right ahead.”

Crystal is seated in the same spot on the sofa when Travis arrives home from work and looks over her right shoulder to see him quickly open and close the entry door to prevent the cold air from coming indoors.

“Hey, baby,” he says, walking past her as Candice, already fed, sleeps on her lap.

"Hi," says Crystal. Her eyes follow him as he steps into the dining room and disappears behind the wall. She then listens to his footsteps as he walks off the carpet onto the tiled kitchen floor. From inside the kitchen, he opens and shuts the door leading to the family room and the basement. Knowing his every step, Crystal leans forward to see him in the hallway and peeping into the girls’ dark bedroom, which he never does.

"Where's Felicia?" he has the audacity to ask.

Crystal can’t believe what she just heard him say. She turns to look at him, and as if her words were a knife, says, "I told her that it was time for her to leave."

"You did what?!"

"You heard me!"

"Crystal, why did you do that?"

"I didn't want her here—that’s why.” Becoming angry, she asks, “Do you have a problem with that?"

Travis sits down, propping his fingers on his forehead, and shakes his head.

Feeling justified, Crystal watches him and thinks, *You’ve had all the fun you’re going to have at my expense. It's over.*

Travis comes home the next night from work and walks into the bedroom. He tosses the car keys on the dresser and surprises her, saying, "I bumped someone off third shift, so I can be here to help you with the kids."

She doesn't believe it for one second. "That's good," she answers, pulling the blanket back as she eases herself under the bed covers and continues, "Travis, you know darn well that when you get off work, you'll be too tired to do anything."

"I said I will help," he says, deepening his voice.

"Okay," she says, calming him down.

Arriving home from his first night on third, Crystal is sitting up in bed, feeding Candice. Travis enters the bedroom and looks down into the bassinet at Brandt and asks, "Has he been fed?"

"No. I left him for you."

Travis turns and walks toward the door. "I'll be back."

Crystal waits patiently for him to come out of the bathroom. "I want to see this," she softly mumbles.

Within the first few minutes of placing the bottle into Brandt's mouth, Travis's eyes begin to close. They continue to open and close until he finally nods off, and he sleeps.

"I told you that you couldn't do it," she says, shaking her head.

After placing Candice in the bassinette, Crystal removes Brandt from Travis's arms and watches as he slides beneath the covers, sleeping all day and each consecutive day thereafter, as Christmas quickly approaches.

28

Having volunteered to babysit so that Travis and Crystal can shop for the girls and buy new living room furniture, Penny and Leon arrive at the house on Christmas Eve. They sit in the living room while Crystal finishes getting dressed.

Upon first seeing Candice and Brandt at the hospital nursery, they marvel over how much they resemble the twins they lost due to miscarriage and as Crystal walks into the dining room, applying lotion to her arms and hands, she overhears Leon saying to Travis, “Hey, bro, we found that picture of our twins that we told y’all about. Man, they look just like Candice and Brandt.”

Leon stands and reaches into his back pocket. He pulls out his wallet and hands the picture to Travis, who screams, “You ain’t lying. They sure as hell do!”

“Let me see,” Crystal says, snatching the picture from Travis.

In the dining room, beneath the ceiling light, she looks at the twins' dead bodies lying side by side beneath a blanket while Brandt and Candice lie together in the bassinet near the fireplace just ten feet away.

Astounded by what she sees, Crystal is speechless, and upon further investigation, she discovers that the boy, like Brandt, is larger than the girl and has a head full of curly black hair. The girl, like Candice, is bald. All the facial features look the same, even the shape of their heads. It's evident that the picture she holds in her hand confirms what she heard prophesied that spring night when *something* told her that she would have the twins.

It happened just as it was spoken—call it a miracle. She calls it like she sees it—spooky!

Crystal is now truly convinced that the *something*, which she identifies as the whispering voice, is of a higher power. No one can ever know. She's keeping her lips sealed so that no one will form the impression that she's mentally ill.

In the basement, removing a load of laundry from the washing machine and placing an armful in the dryer, on New Year's Eve, Crystal converses with one of Mr. Ryder's sisters, who's saying, "I left church and came straight here to see the twins; and they're beautiful, Crystal."

Outwardly, Crystal acts as though she has everything under control but she doesn't and replies, "Talking about church, you just reminded me of a nurse who invited me to her church while I was in the hospital. I completely forgot."

Carrying another armful of laundry to the dryer, Crystal pouts, "Dog gone it, I spent yesterday watching my favorite pastor on the Christian channel, and I didn't have to."

With all the clothes now in the dryer, Crystal turns it on and begins to walk toward the stairs and their visitor, smiling as a cover to hide her madness. "Well, I'm done down here for now," she says.

Upstairs, music is playing, and after closing the basement door, Crystal follows her guest through the kitchen. Seeing Travis sitting in the living room and strumming his Bass guitar, she says, "Travis, I didn't know you played an instrument."

Tired of his negligence around the house, Crystal wishes he weren't there and insults him, "Yeah, that's about all he does."

Travis looks up at her. "Crystal, you're insulting me in front of guest?"

"If you don't like it, too bad," she tells him, but thinking, *What are you going to do, hit me?*

"But, Travis, I'm family first, and I do see her busy and you playing with that man toy," the relative then giggles.

"Ok. Two against one," is all Travis says, and he begins to pat his foot and rocks his head back and forth to the beat of the guitar as Crystal walks Mr. Ryder's sister to the front door.

After New Year's Day, when Travis returns to work, the late hours of the night are the only free time that Crystal has to herself.

Now alone in her own world, the voice that she hasn't heard from while in the hospital for a month, returns and begins to tell her, each time the twins cry, "Hate them."

Struggling to keep her sanity, Crystal sits on the living room floor, browsing through Travis's huge music collection, flipping through them, and then finally selecting one.

While the song plays on low volume, she goes into the kitchen and pours a glass of wine, hoping it will silence the voice. She isn't in the mood and doesn't want to hear it. Relaxing on the sofa, she allows the Christian lyrics of the song to soothe her soul and ease her fears. After refilling her glass twice, Crystal begins to feel tipsy. One of her favorite songs starts to play, and when it ends, she plays it repeatedly just so she can sing along with the female songstress, singing, "Child of the man who holds the master plan..."

She then begins to feel tired. After turning off the stereo and while on the floor, Crystal takes a moment before going to bed, speaking things into existence, *I will never stop believing, God, that in the midst of my troubled life, somehow you're going to work things out in my favor.*

A different night, after Travis has left for work, Crystal stands on top of the heating vent, just inside the kitchen door, keeping warm, and dreading the twins' early morning feeding. Since their birth, she has barely gotten any sleep.

The baby bottles, in a pot of boiling water on the stove, begin to rattle in the pot when the voice inside her head suddenly shouts, "Hate them."

Then the other voice whispers, "No, Crystal, love them."

Confusion rushes in and stirs up difficulties within her mind as though her thoughts are the petals of a flower being plucked—she loves them; she loves them not.

So that she doesn't have to listen to the voices as they compete to gain power over her thoughts and behavior, Crystal fills the sterilized bottles with formula, and after placing all four of them in the refrigerator, she switches off the kitchen light and gladly goes to bed not, yet, able to distinguish the distinct difference between the two voices.

Lying in bed beneath the blankets, Crystal moans as the slow motion of the warm king-size waterbed allows her to destress.

At 5:00 a.m., before Travis returns home from working the third shift, she's up again feeding the twins, and by the time he walks through the door, the twins are fed and sleeping; it becomes Crystal's morning routine.

Crystal's lack of sleep begins to wear her down, mentally, and over the months, her coping ability weakens.

Feeling as though she got up on the wrong side of the bed this morning, she finished feeding Sheena and the twins their lunch. Leaving Sheena sitting in the living room, watching cartoons, she puts the twins down for a nap in their room, and while they drink from their bottles, she passes through the hallway into her bedroom, moaning as she lies across the bed and says, "I just need this time alone."

Candace empties her bottle of milk and cries.

"I know you can't still be hungry," Crystal mutters as she turns to lie on her side, ignoring Candace and hoping she'll stop and fall asleep, but the crying persists.

"Girl, you better take a nap. I'm not in the mood to be bothered by you right now," Crystal yells.

Deprived daily of Crystal's love and affection, the twins' world consists of the two of them behind their closed bedroom door, which does not quiet their cries that want so badly to be heard.

As Candice's obnoxiously loud crying intrudes on

Crystal's peace of mind, she can't stand to listen to it anymore and covers her ears with both hands. She begins to roll from side to side. "Shut up!" she shouts.

The evil voice then screams, "Don't you just hate her? Shut her up. Suffocate her."

As though hypnotized, Crystal, unable to think, leaves the bedroom carrying a pillow. The sound of Candice's cry is agonizing, and it hurts her eardrums. Crystal quickly lunges forward, placing the pillow over Candice's face and violently pressing down, drowning out her cry. Candice wiggles, fighting wildly for air.

Suddenly, she hears a voice of authority shouting, "Crystal, no! Love her."

In obedience, as if awakened from hypnosis, she lifts the pillow from Candice's slightly blue face as Candice, four months old, desperately gasps for air.

Crystal turns to walk out of the room and sees Sheena standing in the doorway. Regretting that Sheena saw everything, she takes her into the living room and with Sheena on her lap, Crystal's conscience begins to scold her for attempting to take Candice's life, and she feels the painful welts of its reproof. She wraps her arms around Sheena, and while Kimberly attends kindergarten and Travis is out on the streets somewhere, she rocks back and forth, praying silently, *God, help me.*

29

With two years under his belt as a GM employee, Travis is laid off. In the meantime, he receives severance pay and accepts a job offer from an uncle to paint houses. The jobs are few and come between rainy days.

And now that Travis is home at night, they occasionally have houseguests throughout the week, and it's not just on the weekends, which takes away from Crystal's time that she has for herself.

Usually, the evil force within her doesn't appear around others, but tonight, a weeknight, while she and Travis are entertaining Leon and Penny in a card game of spades, it reveals itself as Candice's constant whining begins to get on Crystal's nerves. Her whining, like drumsticks, beat upon Crystal's eardrums until she can't take the pounding anymore, and the thought, "Ugh! I hate to hear that girl cry," escapes the inside of her head and slips out of her mouth without realizing it.

While all eyes are on her, Crystal sorts her cards into suits. Feeling so ashamed, she avoids their gaze.

"Why? What's wrong with her crying?" Penny asks and then gets up from the table and goes into the twins' room.

Returning to the dining room with Candice resting on her hip and no longer crying, Penny wipes Candice's tears and says, "See, Crystal, she's all right."

Penny, on occasions, ever since she and Leon babysat Christmas Eve, has obsessed about the twins being her deceased twins reincarnated.

Angry that Penny overstepped her boundaries, Leon yells, "Penny, put her back in the crib. If Crystal and Travis want her out of bed, they'll take her out themselves."

"OK, Leon. I just wanted to help."

Crystal leaves her cards, faced down, on the table and rushes into the kitchen, where she quickly pours milk into a bottle. She goes into the twins' room and tosses it into the crib as she turns and walks out.

Sitting across from Travis, she picks up her cards off the table, noticing how quiet he is. There's no noise—except for Crystal's conscience badgering her for what she said.

The following morning, as Crystal is laying the twins down for a late morning nap, the phone rings. She goes into the dining room and picks it up. "Hello."

"Crystal, I've been so worried about you and the kids. I can't focus on doing my housework." Penny giggles. "I keep picking up the phone to call, but then I'll hang up."

"Why?" ask Crystal.

"Girl, I guess I don't want you thinking I'm intruding or anything like that. I just want to see if you are feeling better."

"No different than any other day," says Crystal, frowning as she glances into the kitchen at the sink of dishes that's more work to be done, and she still hasn't thought about what's for dinner.

"With four kids, all under six, you have to be dealing with a lot."

Crystal pulls out a chair while Penny is talking, and with her back facing the kitchen, she proceeds to sit down at the table and then says, "I am dealing with a lot, and I apologize about last night. My nerves got the best of me."

"It was just a slip of the tongue. If it were me, I would be out of my mind. A lunatic."

She and Crystal laugh it off. Crystal hasn't laughed in a long time.

"We think it's funny, but for real, Crystal, raising kids is not easy. I know because I had to help my mother with my three siblings."

"I do feel like I'm over my head in responsibilities. Travis doesn't help. He's always gone, and when he is home, he's useless."

"I'm here, Crystal. You know I love those kids, and I'd love to babysit them so you can have some time for yourself. And while we're talking about the kids, why don't we have the twins dedicated to God because, Crystal, you and I know how the devil is. We can't let that evil spirit come and destroy them. What do you think about it? Are you with me?"

In response, Crystal bows her head, resting her forehead against her open palm. "Yeah, you're right. I never thought to do that. I'm with you."

"Good. I'll call Bethel and set it up for this coming

Sunday, and I'll call you right back."

Crystal hangs up the phone, trusting that the twins will be better off in God's hands than in her own. Just as she's walking into the kitchen, Penny calls right back. Crystal grabs the phone and hears her laughing.

"What's so funny?"

"Girl, they must have been waiting for my call."

"Why do you think that?" asks Crystal, pacing alongside the wall where the phone hangs.

"Because she answered the phone on the first ring."

Now standing at the dining room window, Crystal asks, "What did she say?"

"The woman I talked to said the pastor can perform the dedication at Sunday service. Leon will be working, so I'll have him drop me off at your place and ride there with y'all."

Looking outside, Crystal agrees, "That'll work."

Ending the conversation, Crystal walks into the kitchen where she begins to fill the sink with soapy water. It then becomes apparent in her thinking that *Penny still believes the twins are hers.*

Sunday morning at the set time, Crystal and Penny, each holding a twin, walk side by side up the aisle and stand at the front of the church. Travis and the two girls, seated in the congregation, watch attentively as the pastor places both his hands on the heads of the twins, praying over their lives. He then asks Crystal, "Do you promise to love and raise these children for the kingdom of God?"

Crystal and Penny both answer, "I promise."

Sadly, viewing Travis as being in the children's lives but not taking his rightful place as their father, Crystal returns to her seat next to him, and with Penny to her right, Crystal repositions herself, giving

Penny more room for comfort. Slightly brushing against Travis, Crystal thinks, *You should have been the one at my side instead of Penny.*

With every intention of keeping her promise, Crystal wakes up each morning over the next two months with a positive attitude that has improved the atmosphere within the home.

Entering the twins' room on a Saturday afternoon, Crystal stands over them and changes their soiled diaper. Smiling, she acknowledges, *I can be a good mommy, uh?* She then tickles them, making them giggle.

Feeling better than she has felt in a long time, Crystal says a silent prayer: "Thank you, God, for giving me more grace."

Leaving them in bed, Crystal enters the kitchen, where she begins to prepare a snack for all four children. Deciding to bring the twins out of their room, she stops what she's doing and, one by one, they are carried into the living room and placed on the floor to play with toys. After returning to the kitchen, she hears a loud, abrupt cry.

Crystal rushes into the living room. Candice, displaying the hateful behavior she learned from her mother, is beating Brandt on the head with a hard plastic toy as he lies helpless and screaming in pain.

Driven by her defense mechanism to protect her child from danger, Crystal, without thinking, slaps Candice very forcefully across the face, leaving her left cheek swollen and red. Crystal picks Brandt up and comforts him. While rubbing his head, she looks down and yells at Candice sitting on the floor, "Why did you do that with your mean self?"

The voice whispers, "No, Crystal, pick her up.

Love her."

Ignoring it, Crystal gives Candice an evil look. Her efforts to bond with the twins end miserably. It has now gone from being a good day to a bad one.

Still out of work, Travis returns home hours later and enters the dining room, walking past Crystal at the table typing and then passing Candice sitting at the entrance of the hallway, sucking her two middle fingers before going into the hallway bathroom, closing the door.

He comes out minutes later, looking down at Candice on the floor, shouting over the clacking sound of the electric typewriter,

"Crystal, what happened to her face?"

Fascinated with the typewriter and aspiring to be a typist some day, she's working on increasing her speed. She stops typing. Crystal turns to look at Travis and says remorsefully, "I hit her."

"Crystal, don't you ever hit this girl again. I will beat your ass," Travis threatens.

Crystal resumes typing and thinks, *If you care so much, where were you when she needed you? Just wait. One of these days, mister, you are going to get what you deserve.*

30

The need to have solitude and confinement forces Crystal to withdraw to one part of the house—the master bedroom, where she lies down, staring up at the ceiling. Travis lies at her side as though he has nothing better to do.

Resting on his right elbow, Travis silently watches her as she watches him with her peripheral vision, and thinking as she stares at the ceiling, *Any other time, you wouldn't be hanging around here as though you care about my well-being. You have failed me miserably so why now?* She then rolls over with her back to him, screaming inwardly, *Go away! Be a father to your children. Leave me alone.*

Occasionally, Crystal defers from her thoughts to listen to Kimberly and Sheena talking and laughing while watching TV in the living room.

The twins are in their room and whining. Intermittently, they stop to play with crib toys, being loud and noisy.

Then it gets very quiet. Travis, curious, leaves Crystal lying in bed as he tiptoes out of the room to the opposite end of the hall and slowly opens the twins' bedroom door.

He then yells, "Crystal! Come look at this."

Hoping he would get the hint that she does not want to be bothered, she doesn't respond, but he says it a second time.

Now irritated, she yells, "What? I don't want to."

"No. You need to see this."

Begrudgingly, she rolls out of bed, passes Travis at the twins' bedroom door, and enters the stinky room that smells of feces. Feces cover their bodies. Candice, diaperless, drops down onto the mattress and hurries to the opposite side of the crib, where she begins to cry in fear as Crystal approaches her.

Travis rushes past Crystal, slightly pushing her out of his way, and grabs Candice. Holding Candice at arm's length, he carries her into the bathroom. He leaves Candice there and then walks into the twins' room, eyeing Crystal as she angrily jerks the crib sheet off the mattress. Without taking his eyes off her, Travis grabs Brandt and quickly leaves the room. After bathing and dressing them, he stands in the door to ask, "Crystal, what do you want me to do with the twins?"

Now, sanitizing the crib, Crystal sneers. "Don't ask me. You figure it out."

Gathering the twins in each arm, Travis carries them into the living room and sets them both down on the floor next to Kimberly and Sheena.

Crystal finishes disinfecting the crib and returns to the master bedroom. Again, she lies down but begins to feel annoyed by Travis's loud music and the strumming of his electric bass guitar. The bedroom walls soon begin to rattle. Crystal can't hear herself think. She gets out of bed and goes searching for peace.

Passing through the dining room, and the narrow kitchen, she steps down into the unfinished family room, where she goes to stand at the glass storm door, looking out as the sun shines bright. Even though it's chilly, for whatever reason, nature seems to tarry, withholding the lively colors of spring.

Desiring to feel the sun's warmth, Crystal steps outside and sits down on the pile of firewood outlining the patio. Now feeling the heat of the sun rays streaming down on her, she sits observing the straw-colored grass covering the fenced-in backyard; she wishes it was green. So disappointed with life, her thoughts quickly shift to setting the wood on fire and burning to death in the flames.

Having been through so much rejection, being molested, which led to becoming pregnant at the age of sixteen, and spousal abuse, she cannot bear the sorrow, the pain, and the heartache any longer.

The evil voice in her head then suggests, "In death, you shall find peace."

Crystal's desire is not to die, but it seems to be the only way to end her affliction. She begins to talk to the Creator, "God, I know you're real. I've been seeking you, but I haven't found you. I try my best to be a better person, but what has it gotten me? My life hasn't gotten any better. I don't know what else to do. I am miserable."

Rising to her feet, Crystal leaves the backyard and goes into the house, where she lies down on the bed.

Day after day, the thought of death is on her mind, as she continuously hears the words, *In death you shall find peace.*

Not finding peace in living, she begins to believe it,

and on a cold wintery day, while Travis is away from home, participating in a bowling league, Crystal obeys the evil voice and goes into the bathroom, where she withdraws a bottle of Travis's little blue pills from the medicine cabinet and swallows a handful of them.

While the twins, who are now one year old and Sheena, two years old, nap in their room, Crystal escapes to her bedroom and lies down to die. Within minutes, it hurts even to breathe. She quickly leaps out of bed and runs into the bathroom, where she induces herself to vomit. Her reality is that she doesn't want to suffer in death; she just wants to die in peace.

Experiencing feelings of heaviness, tears begin to swell up in her eyes and spill out as she goes back to her bedroom and flops down on the bed.

The whispering voice brings to mind the verse Deuteronomy 30:19: "I have set before you life and death, blessing and cursing; therefore, choose life that both thou and thy seed may live."

Magically awakened to this wisdom, Crystal realizes how stupid she really is. She then allows what she's been praying for—wisdom—to do its work. She thinks, *Just because things aren't going my way, it isn't cause for me to give up on life.* Crystal wipes her tears. Instantly, she stops choosing death and chooses life.

Suddenly, overpowered by a supreme presence, Crystal, for the first time, realizes that the presence, the one she had felt as a child, is the Holy Spirit, and at the age of twenty-four, she has a "wow" moment. Seated on the edge of the bed, she leaps forward with joy and falls back down, expressing,

"God, you came. It's you! I know it's you. I feel your presence. I didn't know it was you before, but now I know—it's you."

Crystal begins to rock back and forth. She then calms down and just like when she was a child, she begins to pour out her heart to God. "I don't want to live with hate in my heart. I don't want to hate my babies. Please, help me. Teach me how to love them and not to hate them."

While Crystal asks God to intervene, the power of the Holy Spirit instantly moves on her behalf as it has never done before. The verse, Matthew 7:7, "Ask, and it shall be given unto you; seek, and ye shall find; knock, and it shall be opened unto you," to her, it did not make sense but it has now become life-like and real to her. With a clearer understanding, Crystal stands to her feet and dashes out of the bedroom and into the living area, where she removes the phonebook from the coat closet. In desperation, she sets the book on the dining table and flips the pages. Scanning with her index finger, she comes across a business ad sponsored by United Way. Crystal dials the number, and makes an appointment for next week.

She then looks in on the three little ones napping and softly says as she watches them, "Our lives, now, are going to get better. I promise."

Arriving on time at her appointment not far from the house, a female therapist leads Crystal into her office and instructs her, "Have a seat, Mrs. Wallace. I'll be right back."

Facing the large, wide view window, Crystal sits overlooking the parking lot across the street, observing the huge horizontal pile of shoveled snow, dividing the rows of parked cars, and dislikes how messy the scenery looks from the windows' view when the therapist reenters the office.

Crystal watches her close the door, and then sits at her desk, asking, "OK, Mrs. Wallace, what brings you here today?"

With an outpouring of tears, Crystal confesses her child abuse and suicide attempt, and while the therapist responds very warmly, she withdraws some tissue from the box on her desk, hands them to Crystal, and says, "From what you are telling me, it sounds like you have a great deal of responsibility. You just need some time for yourself, and with that said, I do have to report it to Children Protective Services."

Crystal becomes alarmed but relaxes when hearing the therapist's reassuring words, "The children will not be removed from the home since you are seeking help. It would be beneficial, however, for you and the children if we place them in the children's services' day-care program, twice a week for two weeks. Would you agree to that?"

Crystal nods in agreement even though she isn't sure if two weeks would be enough time to make a difference.

In the second week of therapy, Crystal's assumption is correct; she decides that it's a waste of her time discussing irrelevant concerns and having to answer the questions, "How did your day go yesterday?" or "Do you feel that the counseling and placing the children in daycare are helping?"

No! They aren't helping. Nothing has changed for the better. Feeling worse after her fourth session, Crystal stopped going. She's not a talker. She's a doer.

Sensing that doomsday is inevitable, Crystal

begins seeking a miracle because, without it, she knows she will not survive.

Down the street from the United Way building, Crystal and the female head director of the mental ward unit at Good Samaritan Hospital sit opposite each other in the middle of a private room. Again, Crystal confesses the cruelty that she inflicted on herself and Candice.

Abruptly the director interrupts Crystal's confession to ask, "Who's helping you with the children? That must be overwhelming."

"No one is helping me, but I was talking to a counselor. It wasn't helping, so I quit going."

"How long were you in counseling?"

"I had four sessions over two weeks."

"Well, that isn't enough time to resolve your issues."

Facing the director, Crystal's crippled, pain-riddled spirit becomes camouflaged by her outward, calm exterior, which misguides the director into believing that Crystal's life is improving.

Lacking an understanding of the severity of Crystal's predicament, the director looks straight into her eyes and says, "I'm sorry, Mrs. Wallace, that you're dealing with some issues, but it appears to me that you're coping with them, and are seeking help outside the home. I don't see what we can do for you. We can't help you here."

The director then proceeds to stand and walks to the door. With her hand on the doorknob, she turns to see Crystal still sitting and trembling uncontrollably.

Responding quickly, the director sprints over and kneels, grabbing Crystal's hands, which are clasped and resting in her lap, shaking profusely as tears stream down her face. Crystal tries to speak, but her words are incoherent and run together as she grapples to talk about the horror that awaits her if she doesn't get the help she deserves.

"Just relax. It's going to be OK, dear. We're going to help you. Come back tomorrow, and we'll have you committed."

Crystal and Travis arrive at the hospital around noon and are given a tour of the mental ward.

While standing in her assigned room, along with the director and the male nurse, who is giving the tour, Crystal notices the director staring hard at Travis with a very displeased look, and when they are motioned to move out of the room, the director rolls her eyes at him. Crystal interprets those actions to convey that the director understands her pain, and it expresses that she cares.

Never having looked her in the eyes, Travis avoids the director's look of derision.

Now, at the elevator, Travis and Crystal stand silently awaiting its arrival. He tries to appear normal, but it's obvious when the elevator doors slide open, and he steps inside it that he's preoccupied with worry and should be. It is now apparent that Travis hasn't been there for her or the kids.

"I'll call you later, around five," he says, pressing the elevator down button.

Crystal nods as the doors slide shut.

Inside her assigned room, lying down, she's absorbing the five minutes of quietness and confinement before the male nurse barges in. "Mrs. Wallace, it is our policy that no one stays in their room during the day. You are expected to be sociable. You may come back to your room after dinner if you wish to."

Crystal silently grunts and gets out of bed. She

then crosses the corridor and enters the break room, where she sits watching TV when Travis calls, and because he is lousy at verbalizing his true feelings, it's easier for him to talk about mediocre things. It's a brief conversation, and at around seven, Crystal enters her room, reclaiming a relaxed position in bed, uninterrupted, listening to the stillness of the night. Wow! Peace and quiet—it's such a beautiful sound. "Mmmm, it feels good," she mumbles, appreciating the soothing vibration as she soaks it all in. She hasn't felt this relaxed without a glass of wine in years.

On the second day, after eating breakfast, Crystal begins to participate in different group therapy sessions, which is a requirement during the length of her seven days on the mental ward.

Stretched out on a floor mat inside the activity room, Crystal lies on her back with her arms stretched alongside her, eyes closed, listening as the instructor eases her and the group into a state of relaxation. "Try and picture yourself at the beach..." she tells them, but Crystal is not participating. Her mind is too busy thinking about going back to her room just to absorb the stillness while she reads the Bible.

The one session that Crystal doesn't expect is when she enters the psychologist's office and sees Travis sitting there. Her eyebrows rise. "I didn't know you would be here," she says, sitting next to him across from the psychologist, who then says, "I thought it would help your situation more, Mrs. Wallace, by having your husband be a part of this last session I have with you, and Mr. Wallace, thank you for coming at such a short notice."

Travis nods.

"Your wife has expressed to me that she doesn't get out very often. This is concerning because, as you may or may not know, it is very difficult for anyone to wake up every day and live their life with nothing to look forward to. Would you agree, Mr. Wallace?"

Travis answers, "Yeah."

"We all need to have things we enjoy outside the home. It is an integral part of life if we are to grow and develop intellectually. I believe that your wife's problems will resolve themselves once she is given the freedom to do so. You can understand that, can't you?"

Travis's eyes widen as though he hadn't thought about it before now. Nervously, he slightly raises a finger of the hand resting on his leg and says, "I guess it could help."

Seeing how nervous Travis is and the hard stare that he's showing everyone in the room, he isn't happy about being put on the spot. Crystal secretly shouts for joy.

Returning home a day later, Crystal is overburdened by feelings of condemnation, guilt, and sorrow whenever she sees her image in the full-length mirror that faces her each time she walks into the hallway. Resentful toward the mirror for reflecting her inner turmoil, Crystal goes into the tool room off the family room. Finding the screwdriver, she returns to the mirror, mumbling to it as she removes the four screws, "You're coming down. I'm not going to deal with you any longer."

She then carries it upstairs and leaves it leaning against a wall. Crystal steps down into the dining room, thinking as she closes the shutter doors, *Out of sight, out of mind.*

The days are much more bearable with it out of the way—until one day, as she leaves the bathroom, she hears the voice of *Something* whispering, "Crystal, go look in the mirror."

Curious, she turns around and goes back into the bathroom. Looking at herself, she mumbles while looking into it, "What's the big deal? Look at what?"

Crystal walks away, and again, she hears another whisper. "The eyes; look into your eyes."

Recalling the old saying, "The eyes are the window to the soul," Crystal now stares into the mirror, looking deep into her soul. Instead of seeing, as she has in the past, a reflection of her loving spirit being reflected at her, Crystal sees cold, callous eyes suspended in darkness. Love has gone out of her.

Baffled by this hideous and hateful entity staring at her, Crystal, incapable of identifying it, mutters, "Who are you?"

Every day, she is obsessed with looking in the mirror—only to find herself staring into spiritual darkness and thinking as she walks away, *I know I see it, but what am I looking at?*

Her trying to identify what it is, over time, becomes a thing of the past, and staying closely connected to God through Bible reading, prayer, and fellowship, Crystal effectively keeps the wicked entity at bay and bound as it goes undetected by anyone—not even she knows of it lurking within her.

31

As usual, Travis is out in the streets somewhere. Kimberly is at school, and Sheena and the twins are napping. The house is still and quiet.

Sitting at the dining room table with her chin resting in her hand, Crystal gazes out the window at the dead grass and the leafless crabapple tree in the front yard. Feeling thankful that February is coming to an end, and with spring on its way, the skyrocketing cost of heating the house will soon decrease, lessening her worries. And ever since Travis lost his job, living on welfare has been very difficult, especially during the winter.

As Crystal blankly stares out the window, spiritually alert, she feels as though she's in a very dark place. Then, the leafless crabapple tree disappears and is replaced by a vision of her standing in darkness. As though she's in a tunnel; there's light at the end of it and in the far distance.

Then the vision disappears as quickly as it appears, and she, again, becomes aware of the bare crabapple tree. Understanding the meaning of the vision, Crystal begins to believe that there's hope for her and that the light will lead her out of spiritual darkness.

Crystal then hears the voice of *something* saying, gently yet urgently, "On Sunday, Crystal, go to church. Go to the front of the church for prayer and ask for spiritual strength."

Feeling the seriousness of the situation, she reacts in complete obedience, and on Saturday night, Crystal begins to prepare the children ahead of time.

While she's corn-rowing Candice's hair, Travis enters the house. It was morning when she and the children last saw him.

"Hi, Daddy," the four of them yell.

"Travis, will you take me and the kids to worship service in the morning?" Crystal asks as he passes her and walks past the children scattered about on the floor.

"Yeah," he says reluctantly.

Travis still doesn't know of Crystal's plight—the spiritual battle occurring within her as she is led to the battleground, where good and evil will fight it out for the possession of her soul.

Normally, when they're at church, the choir will sing, and then the pastor stands to speak, but this particular morning, he doesn't get out of his seat. A visiting evangelist stands and walks to the pulpit. The congregation rises on their feet, clapping to welcome him.

Crystal's mind wanders from his sermon and focuses on going to the front for prayer—the reason that she's there.

Sitting next to Travis, she becomes anxious and begins to convince herself not to obey the instructions given to her by *something* with a whispering voice.

The evangelist moves from behind the pulpit and walks down three steps covered with red carpet, saying, “If there be anyone who needs prayer—or whatever the need or the request may be—come. If you would like to join and become a member, please come also.”

People stand, one after another. Crystal doesn’t know what to expect and hesitates. Then it’s as if someone has taken her by the hand and leads her to the front—although she went on her own free will.

Standing at the end of the line, waiting her turn, the other voice that speaks evil and controls her begins to demand, “Go sit down.”

Intercepting to keep her on a righteous path, *Something* whispers, “No, Crystal. Stay.”

She’s afraid to go and afraid to stay but chooses to listen to the whispering voice that she has come to trust.

Finally, the evangelist moves to the end of the line, and with the microphone in hand, he asks, “What is your prayer request, young lady?”

In a frightened and timid voice, Crystal softly answers, “I need prayer for spiritual strength.”

He stares into her eyes as a look of surprise disfigures his face. Does he, too, see those cold, callous eyes suspended in darkness and looking at him, causing him to jump backward?

After collecting his thoughts, the evangelist boldly places his right hand on the top of Crystal’s head, and as he’s praying, Crystal suddenly becomes light on her feet—weightless. She falls backward in a trance-like state, floats into the arms of those waiting to catch her, and they lower her slowly to the floor.

Although Crystal lies there with her eyes closed, she sees the inside of the building as everyone stands very quietly at their seats.

The evangelist's loud, deep, and authoritative voice then penetrates the silence as he demands, "By God's mighty power that's bestowed unto me, I command you to come out of this woman in the name of Jesus."

Crystal's body begins to wiggle wildly. Those gathered around her tightly hold her legs and arms to the floor. Her mouth opens, and a scream erupts as the evil entity resists.

The evangelist shouts, "In the name of Jesus, I command you to come out!" Shouting it repeatedly and after his every command, the demon cries out until finally, without resisting, it departs from Crystal's motionless body on the floor, encircled by those coaching her to speak in tongues.

The words flowing from her mouth are a fast repetitive "Lalalalalalalalalala", overpowering their chatter.

Then without speaking-in-tongue, and now released from the heavy burden of hate that had her bound, Crystal rises to her feet—literally, she cannot feel the ground beneath her as tears stream from her eyes.

Travis, who, without words, looks to be in a state of shock as he watches her come stand at his side.

While clapping and rejoicing to the music, Crystal, at twenty-six, becomes suddenly overtaken by a strong sense of peace.

She then sits down between Travis and the twins, who are now three, and giggles when she overhears Brandt saying to Candice, "Mommy was scared."

"Sh-she not scared," Candice stutters in Crystal's defense.

"Yes, she was. That's why she was crying."

"W-what sh-she scared of then?"

"I don't know."

Crystal is just as mystified about what has just happened as they are. She smiles and looks straight ahead, thinking, *I never thought that this type of thing happens in real life but only in the Bible.* Crystal then wonders, *Did I unintentionally and unknowingly summon a demon?*

The feeling she's left with is unexplainable. Tuning in to the choir singing, Crystal redirects her attention and begins to clap her hands with the congregation praising God, and so thankful that it's over.

On the way home, squeezed between his three sisters in the backseat of the car, Brandt takes advantage of the opportunity and asks, "Mommy wasn't you screaming because you were scared?"

"No, Brandt, I wasn't scared."

"Why were you screaming then?" Sheena, four years old, blurts.

Crystal understands their concern and begins to reason that they're too young to comprehend what she just experienced. She says, "I can't tell y'all why."

Seven-year-old Kimberly persistently asks, "Why can't you tell us, Mommy?"

Being that they're getting on his last nerve, Travis intervenes. He yells, "Didn't your mother just tell y'all that she can't tell you?"

After he shuts down their curiosity and questions, the remainder of the ride home is in complete silence; and as Crystal stares out of the window baffled, she thinks, *Is it possible that the shadow resembling a man, which stood in the bedroom doorway, and the evil entity that possessed me are the same? Were those cold, callous eyes suspended in darkness, the eyes I couldn't see that night when it touched my belly when I was four months pregnant with the twins*? She then concludes—*it had to be.*

32

Eight months have passed, and Crystal still feels the peacefulness within. It's a peace she has never known. And as she continues to be spiritually alert, her mind is clear. The only voice in her head, now, is her own.

But although Crystal can naturally see the world with twenty-twenty vision, she struggles with inner darkness. Having a look about her, that's a blank stare that causes others' heads to turn and look her way, and now that she's getting out of the house more often than she had previously, she feels out of touch.

To get back into the swing of doing things outside of home for the first time since Kimberly became of school-age, Crystal attends a parent-and-teacher conference held within a different school district.

Having received a good report on Kimberly's second-grade performance, Crystal leaves the classroom in a good mood.

Driving the long travel home, Crystal decides, *I need to go buy a few things from the grocery store.*

While stopped at a red light, a speeding vehicle suddenly comes from behind and crashes into the Cougar XR-7, ramming it into the vehicle in front of her.

Stunned, Crystal's thoughts twirl around in her head. Not knowing what happened, she mutters, "What the..."

She then focuses on the huge city utility truck that she crashed into. When Crystal turns to look behind her, she sees that a vehicle has rammed into the back of the car. She now realizes what has happened.

It's not until that evening that the whiplash she sustained begins to cause her pain. Seated in the living room, Crystal massages her neck and shoulder, frowning.

Travis, who has been waiting for her to feel any signs of an injury, looks at her and asks, "You in pain?"

"Yeah. My neck hurts."

He lays the guitar on the floor. "Time to go to the emergency room and then find us a lawyer," he says, almost smiling.

Crystal walks into the emergency room, looking around, "Thank God, it's not busy," she says.

After X-rays, a nurse enters the room. "Mrs. Wallace, we're going to begin physical therapy as soon as possible. Is tomorrow afternoon a good time?"

Crystal looks over at Travis, who nods and says, "Sure."

The nurse hands her a piece of paper. "Here's your Tylenol prescription for pain."

Experiencing occasional stiffness from the injury she sustained in September, Crystal takes a break from doing laundry. Climbing the basement stairs, she switches off the light and closes the basement door to quiet the washing machine's pulsating and the dryer's tumbling noise. She then goes outside and stands on the front porch. Feeling the chill of the day and neck stiffness, she crosses her arms and looks in the direction of the elementary school that Kimberly no longer attends. The huge maple trees line the winding street and block her view of it.

Crystal then admires the giant trees' beautiful red and reddish-orange leaves as she glances about the vicinity, noticing the three trees with yellow leaves interspersed among the others. What was once strange for her to look at—the beautiful colors of autumn—she now loves.

While the October wind blows slightly, Crystal watches the leaves fall to the ground, creating piles in the neighboring yards and the street. Observantly, she listens to the noise the leaves are making as they roll across the ground, mimicking the sound of crackling paper when being crumpled into a ball.

She then opens the glass storm door, intentionally leaving the entry door open, and while she's in the basement, Travis, unemployed for two years, drives the used Lincoln Town car that was purchased with the insurance settlement money into the driveway.

Just as Travis strolls through the front door, returning home from an interview at a printing company, he walks into the dining room, and upon seeing her with a load of clothes folded in her arms, walking through the kitchen, he instantly begins to complain. "Damn. That welfare department sent me to a job that pays minimum wage. How in the hell do they expect us to live off that? They're crazy if they think I'm going to work at that place."

With the dining table between them, Crystal proceeds to the open shutter doors that close off the upstairs bedroom, and before climbing the steps, she pauses to say, "Well, Travis, I don't think we have a choice. If you turn down this job, welfare will think you don't want to work, which means they'll take us off welfare."

"Crystal, why should I take a job that ain't going to pay enough to pay the bills? And we do have to eat!"

"I know, but we can't afford not to."

For the first time in their marriage, he listens to her and takes the job, grumbling and complaining, but quickly adjusts to being back to work.

Mid-January, Travis has been on the job for three months. Next year, he's expecting quarterly pay raises—thanks to the union.

Arriving home after his third shift, Travis surprises Crystal, who, putting on socks and ankle boots, looks up to see him walk into the house. "Oh, you're home early," she says.

"We didn't have much work last night. Is Kim ready for school?"

"She's brushing her teeth."

"You don't have to go outside in the cold. I'll walk with her to the bus stop."

"I'm already dressed. I'll go."

The corners of his mouth become lopsided as he expresses his frustration and says, "Well, you can get undressed. I said I'll walk with her."

"OK. Thank you," she says, yanking off the one ankle boot she had put on, and without verbalizing it, she's thinking, *It's about time you help around here.*

"Hi, Daddy," says Kimberly, a second grader who's usually gone to school by the time he gets home.

After a puff from his cigarette, he answers, "Morning, baby girl. Are you ready to go?"

"Yeah. I'm ready."

The door closes, and Crystal rushes to the window to the left of the fireplace, looking out as they carefully cross the icy road and walk the width of the city park across the street from the house.

At each end of the sidewalk, the lampposts illuminate their path, and in the below-freezing temperature, they cross over to another street alongside the nursing home and fade away in the distance. Crystal loves what she observes: a father making time for his daughter and a daughter who loves her father.

By the time Travis returns, Crystal is comfy and warm in bed. She can't get used to this cold—no, not cold—but freezing weather.

She had drifted off to sleep when Sheena descends the steps coming from the upstairs bedroom that she and Kimberly share and then enters the twins' room. Before Crystal finally insists that Sheena play with her sister and brother, she played alone, not wanting to be associated with them until recently.

Lately, Crystal has made every effort possible to be a good mother to Candice and Brandt and has opened her heart unconditionally; she accepts them with all the love she can bestow upon them and labors daily to undo the damage she has done to their development, but their loud bickering and fighting over toys and about who is not playing fair eventually disturbs Crystal's rest. Annoyed, she gets out of the warm, comfortable waterbed and rushes across the hallway, bursting into the twins' room, saying with a low voice, "Be quiet. Your father is sleeping."

She then goes into the kitchen to begin breakfast but cannot ignore how loud they are, so she goes back into the room, takes away their toys, points at the door, and says softly but firmly, "Go into the living room and sit down."

Crystal leaves them watching a children's program and then serves them breakfast. After eating, Candice stands in the kitchen doorway, where Crystal is busy washing dishes. Nervous and with tears in her eyes, Candice begins to stutter fragmented and indecipherable words.

Crystal has no idea why Candice is upset or what she's trying to say, so she turns away from the sink, asking out of frustration, "Girl, what's wrong with you, and what are you talking about?"

Candice wipes her tears and tries again.

So, not to make Candice more nervous than she already is, Crystal does her best to remain calm but still can't understand a word Candice is saying, and that's when Brandt comes and stands beside his twin and begins to speak for her. "She says, can she go in the room and play? And that she won't make no noise."

Still confused by Candice's nervousness, Crystal asks without expecting an answer, "You have to act like that just because you want to play in your room?"

The twins are speechless.

"Go ahead, but you better be quiet, or you'll have to sit back down."

It irritates the heck out of Crystal that Candice isn't communicating as well as she should be. As she washes each dish and rinses it one by one, she holds a frown. Shaking her head, she asks, *How can I help her? If I don't, she'll be teased by others, and it will only make things worse for her.*

Crystal then questions herself, *What type of programs are there in Dayton that she can benefit from?*

Now done in the kitchen, Crystal enters the living room and takes the phone book from the closet. At the dining room table, she flips through the yellow pages until her eyes fall upon an ad listed by United Way offering speech therapy. Excited to find the listing, Crystal yanks the phone from the wall and calls them.

Within days, Travis drives her and the three younger children to the appointment, and for a small fee, both twins are evaluated. The assigned speech therapist walks into the waiting area with the twins. Carrying a lollipop, she hands it to Sheena, who, sitting between Crystal and Travis, says softly, "Thank you."

The therapist informs them, "Brandt's speak isn't as underdeveloped as Candice's is, but I do recommend that he be enrolled as well."

Nodding, Crystal watches the twins lick their lollipops and asks, "So, when can they start?"

Crystal reaches for the schedule the therapist hands her and then looks in the direction that the therapist points. "The receptionist will set up the appointments with you. Due to family size and income, your weekly payment will be five-dollars. Do you have any questions?"

Crystal reviews the schedule. Satisfied, she answers, "Not at all."

"Well, Candice and Brandt, I'll see you next week," she says, smiling and waving as she walks away.

During the spring, at one of the twins' afternoon speech therapy sessions, Crystal and Sheena sit behind the two-way mirror, observing them when Crystal becomes riled up as she witnesses the therapist hold up a large picture card, asking Candice to pronounce with her, the two-syllable word, wagon. But Candice is preoccupied with making faces in the mirror and completely ignores the therapist.

Brandt then gets out of his seat and goes to the other side of the room to play with toys.

"I don't believe this," Crystal mumbles.

"Brandt," the therapist says. "We have work to do. Come sit down, please."

Candice then leaves her seat to join Brandt.

Feeling the therapist's frustration, Crystal is fuming when she says out load and unheard by the twins, "Y'all know better. Just wait. I'm going to spank your butts."

Finally, the therapist says, "If you don't come have a seat, we'll have to stop our work for today."

The session, which is supposed to be thirty minutes, ends fifteen minutes early.

Standing outside by the Lincoln Town car, Crystal repeatedly slaps the twins' backside before allowing them in the car and then strapping on their seatbelt.

Now in the driver's seat, she starts the car, shouting over the roaring engine, "The next time Miss Glassy tells you to do your assignments, you better do it." Turning toward the back seat, looking into their teary eyes, she demands, "Do you hear me?

The twins' behavior improved, over the summer months, and so did their speech. Then, unexpectedly, as she's about to pay the receptionist for the twins' end of the week section, the receptionist hands her a new schedule. "If you want to continue therapy, the pay increase begins next week. Would you like the same schedule?"

Crystal looks at her. "Pay increase?"

"Yes. Sorry, but it can't be helped. Your payment will now be ten dollars a week."

Crystal's eyes fall from the receptionist and onto the sheet of paper that she's holding, and she says with uncertainty, "I'll call to schedule if we can continue."

At the dining room table, days later, Crystal sat feeling frustrated as she strategized ways to keep the twins in speech therapy. While tapping her fingers on the table surface, she hunches her shoulders. *There is no way I can do it. With a mortgage, the high cost of heat, and the need to buy school clothes and supplies, I have to discontinue therapy no matter how small the increase.* Crystal then gets up from the table. "The only thing I can do is to pray and have faith."

Outside, walking up the winding street from the house toward the elementary school, where she's going to register Sheena for Kindergarten and hopefully get the twins involved in an educational program, Crystal ponders at how quickly the last five years have gone by.

Strolling up the sidewalk, she becomes emotional and tries her best not to cry, muttering, "My Sheena is growing up."

Just when Crystal returns home, Travis's aunt Fran calls the house phone. Crystal trots up the porch steps to answer it and immediately recognizes her.

"Hi, Fran."

"How are you and the family?"

"We're doing fine. How's yours?"

"We have a problem as of now. I have all these grandchildren here with me, and LeAnn starts kindergarten this year, you know? That's why I'm calling, to see if you'll be able to help me get her in school. If you can, I sure would appreciate it."

"Sure, Fran, I can do that tomorrow."

"Thank you so much, Crystal. You are the best thing that ever happened to that nephew of mine, and y'all have such well-behaved children. Are they all in school this year?"

"No. I've been looking for a school program for the twins, but every school I go to, they're all full."

"Have you tried over here by me?"

"No, but when I register LeAnn, I'll see if they have openings, and if they do, I'll pick her up for school in the afternoons and drop her off at home when it lets out. That way, you won't have to worry about her."

Crystal's prayer manifests and the twins are enrolled in the school close to where Fran lives.

While they attend their first day in the afternoon Head Start program, Sheena, already dismissed from morning kindergarten, plays at her friend's house down the street.

In the kitchen, washing the morning dishes, Crystal looks up from the sink to stare out the window, admiring the two large maple trees in the neighbor's yard across the street, full of reddish-orange leaves. Her thoughts are meditative as she searches for a solution to Candice's stuttering problem.

Then, suddenly, she recognizes the voice that has been speaking to her in whispers, saying, "Tell

Candice that she doesn't have to stutter if she doesn't want to. Tell her to take her time, think about what she wants to say, and then say it."

Rinsing the dishes, Crystal mumbles, "That makes plenty of sense. I can't wait to see if it works—plus, it's a good opportunity to practice using my faith."

She then takes a break from housework, goes into the living room, and rests her buttocks on the arm of the loveseat. Overlooking the front yard from the side of the house, the scenery outside the window is nature, and she begins to take it all in—the colors of autumn, the cloudless blue sky, and flying birds. Crystal now feels thankful to be alive.

Functioning in life behind the veil that has concealed her ability to see with her spiritual eyes, Crystal's inner spirit then knocks on the door—that is her darkness. Pounding loud and hard, she begs from the very depths of her soul, *God, the creator of heaven and earth, where are you? If you love me, why can't I feel your love?* But to her dismay, no answer ever comes.

Looking away from the window, Crystal glances over her shoulder at the TV. City events and other announcements scroll up the blue screen. There's one announcement that captures her interest, and as it slowly scrolls upward, she reads: "The Roosevelt Recreation Center is hosting an exercise class during the winter. Classes are held Mondays, Wednesdays, and Thursdays from 6:00 p.m. to 7:00 p.m."

"Good. It's Wednesday," she mumbles. "That's just what I need to get out of this house."

Taking a glance behind her at the wall clock and seeing the time, she quickly dashes across the room and turns off the TV. Running to the door, she stops at the closet and grabs her purse and coat, putting it on as she runs out the house, driving three miles to Stonedale Elementary School and arriving just before the two-thirty bell rings.

By five, the aroma of ground beef and onions simmering on the stove arouses Travis out of his sleep. Crystal stirs the mixture in the skillet, listens for the bedroom door to open, and as usual, smoking a cigarette, he strolls past the kitchen and stands gazing out of the dining room window overlooking the front yard.

"Travis, I learned the rec center has an exercise class today, and after I finish with dinner, I'll be leaving to join it."

"Go ahead. What time is it over?"

"I'll be home before you leave for work."

Now dressed in warm workout clothes, Crystal approaches the front door, yelling loud enough so that Travis can hear her from the living room to wherever he is in the house, "I'm gone."

"Bye, Mommy," the children say as she walks out the door, leaving them sitting at the dining room table and eating spaghetti.

Now coping and adjusting well to being out and about, the anxiety Crystal had felt from other people's reaction to her blank stare no longer bothers her, and with Travis on third shift, it has freed up more time for her to be alone at night, which has made a big difference in her mental health.

Strolling up the long sidewalk in front of the newly renovated recreation center constructed of red bricks, Crystal admires its massiveness and speculates that it must stand at least four stories high. As she begins to mount the many steps, it feels like climbing a mountain.

Entering the building, Crystal gets directions and is the first to enter the small gym where the exercise class is held. Sitting on the floor beneath the open window, she watches as other women enter.

When the exercise instructor finally walks in, scans the gym, and then sets the boom box down on the floor against the wall, Crystal is wired up and ready to get started.

She glances up at the wall clock. It's 5:55. The instructor walks towards her, grinning and smiling. Briefly, he stops to chat with other females before passing them by. His radiant confidence is alluring. Crystal silently moans, *uh uh uh,* and as he stands chatting with the women, she studies his physique, low-key. The white T-shirt he's wearing perfectly defines his not-too-large bicep and tricep muscles, which are just right for his body size. Her eyes scrutinize his sculptured, firm buttocks. Crystal can't resist thinking, *He got it going on.*

Tilting his head upward to view the large clock above him, he then says, "OK, ladies, let's get started."

Crystal stands on her feet, and with the boom box blasting, he leads the class into warm-up exercise routines, stretching to a slow beat that gradually changes to a faster tempo and then into a thirty minute intense aerobic workout.

While jogging in place, he encourages the all-female class, "Pace yourselves, ladies. You'll need your energy to run laps around the racetrack."

Yes, for the other women, but for Crystal, the workout only energized her, and as she climbs the stairs to the second floor along with a few complaining women struggling to make it to the track, she has plenty of energy to spare. When entering the racetrack, more women, paired in twos and threes, walk and run around the track with their feet, loudly pounding the hard wooden floor. For someone who has not been active for a long time, Crystal takes off running, passing the women in front of her. It seems like she runs for an hour, burning off nervous energy accumulated over the years, before she finally quits and realizes as she looks around that all the women have left.

Now alone, she walks around the track, looking down through an opening in the center of the floor, watching and listening to the men below as they hustle the basketball back and forth on the court, and she's not even tired.

Enjoying a moment to herself, she's looking forward to coming back every week.

Crystal then walks around the track one last time, wondering about what Travis has up his sleeves. Last weekend, he walked into the family room and sat next to her saying, "Crystal, I want to get re-baptized, but I want us to do it together."

He has made it difficult for her to trust him. "If you want to, do it. I don't need to."

"I know I can," he begs and snorts. "Crystal, please."

She shouts, "OK," but thinks, *This time, I will do it with true intentions of becoming the best version of me and for no other reason.*

Crystal is closer now to obtaining her breakthrough than ever before.

After returning home from the baptisms on

Sunday, she steps down into the family room where Travis plays his electric bass guitar and yells, "Travis, it's too loud."

Turning down the amplifier, he says, "Crystal, I did it for us."

"You did it for us? What are you talking about,

Travis?"

"I love you, and I want us to stay together. That's why I got baptized."

"Oh, you think that because we got baptized together, God will save our marriage?"

"Yeah."

Staring into his lying eyes, Crystal is thinking, *You will never change.* Angry, she stomps up the two steps. Allowing his intentions to fester in her mind, Crystal mumbles, "Be satisfied with what I am able to give you."

33

At the Roosevelt Recreation Center, the children follow Crystal's lead, climbing the massive steps sprinkled with snow salt. Without counting all the wide steps, she instinctively guesses that there are nine in all before reaching the top landing.

Stepping inside the rec center, they walk past young boys playing table tennis and goes into the small gym, where Crystal exercises. It's occupied by teenage boys shooting basketball hoops.

"Well, let's go upstairs and see what's up there," Crystal says, leading them to the stairwell just outside the gym door. They are halfway up the stairs when Brandt begins to complain, "Dang. It's too many steps. My legs hurt."

Crystal laughs. "Stop crying, boy, and keep going." That's what his father would have told him.

Now standing in the open doorway of the larger gym and watching older men dribble the basketball up and down the court, Crystal is saying as she walks away from the gym to the opposite side, "There has to be more than basketball and table tennis to do around here."

Together, they pull the handles on a row of locked steel doors when a potbellied, six-foot-tall black man approaches them. He yells, "The auditorium is behind those doors.

What are you all looking for?"

Crystal has seen him around and knows that he's the big man in charge.

"I'm looking for some activities that my children can get involved in. What do you offer that's in their age group?"

The children gather around her. "Are all of these yours?" he asks.

"Yep. They're mine."

"Well, we have swimming. Can they swim?"

"No."

"We also have swimming lessons if they want to learn, and there's karate. They're having class now. Would you like to go check it out?"

"Yeah. I sure would."

Inside a small temporary room, the karate instructor, teaching a class of three, looks toward the door and sees them, nodding when told, "I have a lady and her kids here who want to observe the class."

Crystal walks inside and is surprised to see that he's also the exercise instructor.

After five minutes of observing the participants walk up and down the middle of the floor, kicking and punching the air, Crystal looks at each child and asks, "Who wants to learn karate?"

Individually, two answer, "I don't."

"Not me."

"Me either."

"Well, let's go," says Crystal as she helps herself off the floor.

Down in the basement pool area, the strong chlorine scent saturates the air. A radio is on, and they walk toward it. At the counter, Crystal taps the little bell. "Hello," she yells.

No one answers.

A loud noise of a door slamming behind them causes their heads to turn, and they see an average-height, young black male asking, "Can I help you?"

Crystal hasn't seen him before and questions him. "Who are you?"

"I work here. I'm the pool attendant."

"I was told that the center offers swimming lessons. Are the pools open during winter?"

"Yeah. They sure are. Are y'all here to swim?"

"No. Not today." Crystal then asks the children,

"Y'all want to learn how to swim?"

There's a unanimous "Yes."

Crystal looks at them in surprise. "Y'all are scared of the pool?"

"That's because we can't swim, Mommy," says Kimberly.

"Well, I will be the one teaching them, so whenever they're ready, I'll be here," he says as he walks away.

Crystal follows him out the door. "Expect us tomorrow after they get out of school."

Walking the long wide corridor, Crystal begins to foresee a challenge in the horizon and envisions Travis swearing up and down, "You're seeing other men behind my back, Crystal?"

Already imagining the trouble she's going to be in when he finds out, she thinks, *I hope he doesn't start anything, and if he does, all hell is going to break loose.* She then turns and says to the children walking behind her, “Come on, let’s go back home.”

Due to exercising three days a week, Crystal has lost eleven pounds and is getting a lot of attention from strange men who come around the pool area, lusting after her body. Travis has already told her that she possesses the kind of body that a man wants to make love to. She doesn’t like the attention but men have always treated her that way.

At home, in the master bedroom, she stands in the mirror, wearing a red bathing suit. Arousing Travis’s sexual appetite, Crystal turns from side to side, caressing her curves while Travis, bumped from third shift to second, watches as she behaves like the bad girl she’s not. Crystal then begins to taunt him.

“I don’t see what men are looking at or why they’re whistling at me for,” she says, admiring how stunning she fits into the bathing suit she’s wearing to the pool today after the kids get home from school.

Then there’s a loud, intrusive horn from outside, blowing twice.

“There’s my ride. See you tonight when I get home,” says Travis before kissing her and then rushing out of the house.

“The trouble begins,” she mutters.

Nine hours later, Travis walks through the front door, and as Crystal sits watching the late news, he walks toward her and begins to explain, “Tomorrow, Friday, I’m off. I start working the day shift on Monday.”

Her face tenses up as she asks, “Why? You don’t like to work the first shift.”

He sits next to her on the sofa, and while acting like he loves his family so much, he says, “I will if it allows me more time to spend with you and the kids.”

Crystal stares into his eyes, having the thought, *Yeah, that’s what you want me to believe* and then says, “No. You don’t trust me. What? You think I’ll have an affair?”

“If I can prevent it, why not be there?”

“Travis, I’m doing it for the kids. Do you think I’ll be having an affair around them?”

“I hope not. Anyway, it can become a weekly family thing.”

Crystal rolls her eyes and looks at the TV, seeing right through his controlling ways, and thinks, *here, we go again. He is still the same. So jealous and possessive.*

Saturday afternoon, while she’s busy cleaning the house, Travis secretly goes shopping and then returns home carrying a small shopping bag.

Crystal spies him out as he walks into the living room. “Where did you run off to?” she asks.

“I went to the mall.” He reaches into the bag and shows off the swimming trunks.

“Yellow.” Crystal laughs. “You’re going to be clowning.”

“No, I won’t. You’ll see.”

“Put them on, and let me see, now. I don’t want you embarrassing me in public.”

“Sorry, but you’ll have to wait until Tuesday when we go swimming,” he teases, knowing good and well that he barely knows how to swim. The only difference between him and all four children, he isn't afraid to put his head underwater.

Standing in the swimming pool, clinging onto the side of it, Crystal watches as Travis finally leaves the men's dressing room, walking in her direction.

"Oh, my God," she softly mumbles and then yells, "Travis, this is so embarrassing. You might as well be naked. Those swim trunks are too small."

He dips his toes into the pool, testing the water temperature, and says, "It's the new style for men. It's supposed to fit tight. You know you like this bikini cut."

"What I would like is for you to take it back where you got it from."

"Anyway, where's that swimming coach?" He says, changing the subject. "I don't want to be here too long. Tonight, I'm joining the karate class."

Crystal looks around. "I don't know where he's at. Maybe he feels threatened by you being here."

"Oh well. We might as well have some fun." Travis then dives into the heated pool and does a belly flop.

During the next two weeks, he is fixated on Crystal learning karate, and as Travis climbs the stairs behind her, coming from the pool, he's telling her, "I think you'll enjoy karate, Crystal."

Stomping up the stairs, she yells in frustration, "No, Travis, and I wish you would stop talking to me about it."

Then, three days later, Crystal gets up from watching the karate class from the sidelines, and while no one is watching, she attempts to perform a punching technique along with the class. Master Masterson turns around unexpectedly and catches her.

He shouts, "Come join us, Mrs. Wallace."

"Yeah. Come on, Mommy!" says Kimberly.

Then Travis yells, "Crystal, come on."

But her shyness prevails. Crystal sits back down and then quickly changes her mind. Kicking off her shoes, she bows before walking onto the training floor, and she, too, joins the class.

Because all four children fear drowning, swimming lessons cease and quickly become a thing of the past.

Twice a week, Crystal struggles to learn the techniques correctly in class. Travis intervenes. Getting her attention, he lowers his voice and says softly, "Crystal."

Looking in his direction, she watches how he demonstrates how to do it behind Master Masterson's back, who catches them.

Walking up to her, he says, "Mrs. Wallace, raise your hand whenever you need my help. That is what I am here for." He then teaches her to execute the technique.

Her unique style soon elevates her to be one of Master Masterson's top students. One should think Travis would be happy because he was right, Crystal enjoys the sport. However, seeing Crystal infatuated with another man disturbs Travis, and his bitching about it only escalates the situation, causing Master Masterson to become more appealing, which has pushed Crystal to fall for another man right before Travis's eyes. No longer having control over her, Travis stoops back to his abusive ways.

During Tuesday night's class, he attempts to regain that control. Paired together, Travis and Crystal practice their round-house kick and blocking techniques. Within minutes, as one kicks and the other one blocks it, a fight breaks out, which Travis started, inflicting a lot of pain on Crystal, and she on him.

The sound of their bones, forcefully hitting one another, is that of two baseball bats clashing and is heard throughout the gym.

Master Masterson charges over to where they are. “What are you two trying to do, kill one another?”

Travis and Crystal stand silently, staring at each other with a look of anger in their eyes.

They’re married. There is nothing Master Masterson can do but insist before walking away, “Line up,” and he then yells it across the gym to the rest of the class.

A Wednesday, after a good aerobic workout, Crystal leaves the exercise class, pushing open the double steel door, and as she walks down the long corridor with a hand towel dangling, she sees far ahead, at the end of her path, Master Masterson and one of the women from the exercise class, standing around and talking. With his back to Crystal, Master Masterson keeps turning to look in her direction.

What is he looking at? she wonders, turning to see what’s behind her, but there’s nothing there but a wall of yellow closed, steel doors. And while she’s observing him observing her, he’s curious as to why his newfound friend, who’s also his student, acts the way she does—as though her head is in the clouds—spaced out.

From observing Travis’s jealous behavior in karate class, Master Masterson suspects that Crystal is being abused, and he wants to be a friend. She needs a friend.

Reaching the end of the corridor, Crystal turns right, hoping she doesn’t get nervous and reveal to him that she likes him beyond friendship—yes, Travis’s observation was right again; she, at the age of twenty-seven, is smitten.

When Crystal passes him without making direct eye contact, he initiates to her, "Good night, Mrs. Wallace." She then waves.

With a glimmer of daylight savings remaining, Crystal slowly coasts the Lincoln Town car into the driveway behind the wrecked and totaled silver Cougar XR-7.

She ascends the porch steps, stopping all of a sudden before opening the door and glances around at the neighboring houses, unable to remember the drive home. It's as if she drove on autopilot. Finally, she opens the door and inside, she walks past Travis in the living room, strumming his guitar as though he isn't there, only aware of the darkness that occupies her from within.

The next day, Crystal attends to the same everyday chore of dusting. Without having any thought processes of what she's doing, and seeing only darkness, her actions are those of a blind person, aware of her surroundings as she skillfully swipes the cloth over the top of each living room lamp table.

As though robotically programmed, Crystal then moves from room to room, in her search for God, and upon entering, she cries out, inwardly, *God, I can't feel your presence. Where are you?* But to her dismay, there's no answer.

Friday, at the start of karate class, Crystal stands in the front row. As she and the class observe Master Masterson pace the training floor, she thinks, *What's bothering him?*

He then stops, lifting his head from staring at the floor. His facial expression shows that he's bothered, and Crystal tells herself, *Here comes one of his lectures.* She watches as his eyes move over the class and then remain focused on her. Looking her in the eyes and she into his, there's a mysteriousness about him that intrigues her. Crystal doesn't know why, that is, but what she does know is that while in his presence, he's captivating; his smile charming; how he struts his self-confidence; and the masculine tone of his voice commands respect and arouses her femininity.

With his eyes still focused on her, Master Masterson waves his hand over his head and says, "Whatever it is you're looking for, it's not out there in space somewhere."

He places his hand over his heart, patting his chest. "It's on the inside." Nodding, he continues, "Look inside of you; it's there."

At that very moment, Crystal reflects inward, connecting with the love she feels for him, and when she does, a light automatically switches on, and the darkness within her is literally gone. Spiritually, she has finally stepped out of the dark tunnel and into the light. With her eyes now sparkling with joy, she and Master Masterson share the biggest smile.

He then claps his hands. Stepping backward, he moves out of the way and commands with authority, "Now, let's get started, class. Chumbie."

Adorned in her white uniform and orange belt, she chumbies, and now stand with her legs slightly apart, arms in front, and fists touching.

The gym echoes Master Masterson's loud masculine voice as he commands the class to begin, making a loud thrusting sound from his throat—"Huh."

Now feeling love again, Crystal's joy is about to explode outwardly as she plunges forward like a mighty warrior, punching with power.

This is the message which we have heard of Him, and declare unto you, that God is light, and in Him is no darkness at all, (1 John 1:5).

34

Just days before Mother's Day, Crystal and Travis sit at a distance from one another in the family room and watch TV. Ever since the fight they had in karate class, they have barely spoken.

Having had the courage to stand up to him and fight back, Crystal's level of confidence begins to soar to new heights, and as she watches Travis leaving the family room, she's in pursuit of him. Boldly testing her wings to see how much higher she can go, she stomps up the two steps behind him and into the kitchen.

Finally speaking her truth, she says, "I don't love you, Travis, and I don't want to be married to you any longer. I want a divorce."

As they walk through the dining room and into the living room, Travis suddenly swirls around with his arm in motion, and she feels a powerful blow across her face. Stumbling backward, she falls hard onto the dining room floor. Having begun her monthly cycle, blood gushed out of her. Slapped senseless, Crystal sits there dazed until she regains her thoughts. She then realizes, *He hit me!*

Unprepared for what he has done, Crystal quickly stands to her feet and sprints past him, thinking as she passes, *This is the last time you will ever hit me. I'm going to kill your ass.*

Stepping out of the house and onto the front porch, she runs into the street with a busted lip and blood splattered all over the front of her long, silky, pink lounging dress.

From behind her, Travis bursts out the front door, shouting, "Crystal, come back here!"

Ignoring him, she mumbles, "No. You haven't changed one bit."

Trotting farther up the street, she turns left at the corner and walks two blocks to Uncle Joel's house. There, Lilly, Joel's wife, attends to her menstrual needs, and while Crystal sits pressing the ice pack against her swollen lip in tears, Joel insists on knowing what happened, but then he answers his own question with a question. "You and that nephew of mine are over there fighting?"

Sitting in a wooden chair with her back against the wall, Crystal only nods.

"He busted your lip. Did you bust his?" Joel then laughs.

Across from Crystal, crunching on a piece of ice, Lilly turns to him and says with a frown of disapproval, "Joel, stop it."

A very loving man to his wife, Joel changes his tone to a more serious one. "I don't mean any harm by it, sweetie. Don't pay me any mind," Joel apologizes to Crystal. Seated at the dining room table, he raises his voice and demands from his four children in different areas of the house, "One of you bring me the phone!"

Now using his normal tone, he then says, "Let me call that nephew of mine and get on him. He shouldn't be hitting on you."

Crystal silently plots, thinking, *Travis, your controlling days are over. I'm taking full control of my own life and taking my freedom back.*

Joel quickly captures her attention. "You want to talk to her, yourself?"

Making eye contact, Crystal responds by shaking her head.

Joel hangs up the phone and begins to convince her to take her home. Promising that it's safe, he drives her there.

A week after Mother's Day, on a Sunday, and in the kitchen preparing pot roast for dinner, Crystal can not shake off that powerful blow to the face she received unjustly. After placing the foil-wrapped roast, potatoes, and carrots into the oven, she leaves the kitchen with an outlandish look in her eyes and begins to mope around the house.

Travis follows her, watching her every move as she is unable to avoid him.

Travis, beware! In Crystal's head, there's nothing good going on.

Before it all happened, she and Travis swapped bedrooms with the three girls. In their now upstairs bedroom, Crystal stands looking out the window as Travis lies stretched out across the bed behind her, unaware that she's premeditating how to kill him. *If I don't stop him, he'll continue to intimidate me, hoping I'll fear him and not divorce him,* she thinks. *But the devil is a lair. Fear ran out the door the day he hit me. I'm not afraid anymore, and it's time that he finds out.*

Crystal's mind wanders, and she admires the tall, huge, silver pine tree outside the window. She's thinking how beautiful it would look, decorated with lights this coming Christmas.

Her mind again drifts back to her original thoughts of killing Travis, but because she has a conscience, to do so isn't worth it, and what about the children? Crystal quickly chooses another route and decides to give Travis a taste of his own medicine—the power of fear—and without turning away from the window, she warns him, "Travis, if you ever hit me again, you better kill me or I will kill you."

She then turns to look him in the eyes with an ice-cold mixture of anger and revenge.

Travis's eyes widen and dart away from her stare as if to ponder over the thought of what she just said.

Feeling triumphant, she stands with her back to him, looking out of the window and thinking, *You better believe me.* She then prays, *God, please give me strength. I don't want to do what I'm threatening to do.*

Now feeling a glimmer of hope breaking through, she releases the thoughts of doom from her mind and looks ahead to the future. No longer wanting to be a typist, she now wants to pursue a career as a hairstylist and really enjoys styling hair. It's what she had thought about becoming after high school, but then it was only a thought.

As Crystal now looks to the future, she calculates that in four months, which will be September, the twins will begin Kindergarten; *therefore, I will no longer be needed at home as much. So, tomorrow, I'll go and enroll in Cosmetology.*

Crystal then walks away from the window, and as she does, she glances at Travis, who, looking pitiful, has nothing to say. Crystal rolls her eyes and proceeds to walk down the stairs, breathing in the aroma of the pot roast cooking in the oven and thinking, *He looks sad, like I should care.*

After meeting with the beauty school administrator and obtaining grant applications from him, Crystal rode the city bus home from downtown.

Stepping off it, she crosses over to the opposite side of the street. Turning the corner, she observes Travis outside at a neighbor's house and then crosses over to the opposite side of the street from where he glances at her walking by.

Crystal comes to their corner lot and then enters the house. Overtaken by the hot, humid air circulating through the box fan in the living-room window, she drops both financial aid applications onto the dining room table and goes into the kitchen, where she pours a tall glass of an ice-cold drink.

Outside, on the front porch, she sits, quenching her thirst while watching Travis and the neighbor, an older man, talking. She politely waves to him.

Travis then begins his way home, and when he steps onto the porch, Crystal says, with a moody undertone, "I'm still filing for a divorce."

As if he could care less, Travis walks into the house, yelling back at her, "If that's what you want, go right ahead. The Legal Aid office is downtown at the Reibold Building."

Now knowing exactly where she needs to go, the next day, Crystal dashes out of the house, ahead of the approaching city bus, and with the completed grant applications in her hand, she quickly drops them into the corner mailbox before claiming a seat on the bus.

While riding past the long block of houses on both sides of the street, the bus approaches the street Joel lives on, and as it passes, Crystal looks at his house, thinking, *Joel is the kind of man I wished I had married. Unfortunately, Travis is nothing like any of his uncles.*

While admiring the well-kept homes that the bus passes, Crystal begins to question her decision to divorce Travis. *He doesn't give me good cause not to. He's always in the streets and spending money, leaving me at home with the children to clean house, doing yard work, and nearly everything else.*

In her mind, Crystal can't find a good reason to call off the divorce, not even for the children. *When he's home, he's asleep, and since I sleep alone, I'm used to being without him.*

Arriving downtown, Crystal braces herself and stands on her feet, gripping the side railing. The bus comes to a halting stop, and she gets off, walking around the corner to where she needs to go to end this one-sided marriage arrangement.

Usually, Travis is home from work and is in bed snoring when the children leave for school in the mornings, but for whatever reason, he doesn't come home until much later.

"What brings you home so late?" asks Crystal as he walks into the kitchen where she is and stands in the doorway. Wearily, he answers, "I've been to see my attorney. He advises me that I can continue to live in the house while we're going through the divorce."

Crystal looks away from the sink. "When did you get an attorney?"

"Today, so I'll understand what my rights are."

Feeling as though Travis is making her out to be the bad guy, Crystal asks, "What is it? Are you afraid that I'll leave you out to dry?"

Tired and frustrated, he answers, "Crystal, nowadays, I don't know what you'll do, but I don't think you'll do that. I want you and the kids to live in the house. All I want is the Lincoln Town Car to get me to work, the waterbed, the stereo, my music collection, and my personal things."

"Thanks. I appreciate that you're looking out for the kids and me. I think it's best that their lives remain as much the same as possible, and it's all right if you stay here with us so you can save enough money for the day when you do move out, which will be in a few months. You think?" she hints as he raises his cigarette to his mouth and, while his elbow rests on his other arm that's crossed in front of him, he takes a puff from the cigarette, silently staring into space.

I know that look. He's plotting, thinks Crystal, expecting him to fight with her.

Travis then says, as if to tell her to stop the divorce, "Or not at all."

Crystal releases the water from the kitchen sink down the drain and assures him as she looks his way, "It will happen."

Travis, leaning with his back against the countertop has a look of sadness in his eyes. Curving the corner of his upper lip, he says in a low tone, "Well, you can't blame me for trying, but as for now, I'm going to get some rest before I go in to work tonight."

At Beauty College, Crystal sits in the break room and looks up at the door when someone enters carrying an arrangement of flowers, yelling cheerfully, "Crystal, this came for you."

Removing the note that says, "I love you," Crystal now knows what Travis has been plotting. She tears it up and places it in the trash. Frowning in disgust, Crystal sets the flowers on the break room countertop and says to the other women in the room, "Whoever wants flowers is welcome to take them."

Then leaving the building, dressed in all white, she hurries up the street to catch the bus, deciding as she goes, *I'm not coming back the rest of the week. I need a short break. The stress and pressure of going through the divorce, and with Travis now involving my classmates, is more than I am willing to deal with.*

While home, there's a knock at the door. Having lost weight due to stress and not eating, Crystal stands up from sitting on the sofa, and the black jeans she's wearing fall from her waist. Crystal quickly pulls them up and opens the door. On the other side are two Jehovah's Witnesses. "Hi, we're in the neighborhood handing out our Watchtower pamphlets."

One woman points out a chapter about family and marriage. Crystal's mind drifts. I know t*his can't be God sending me a sign to stay in this hell of a marriage.*

The woman then asks, "Would you like one?"

Crystal shakes her head, turning up her nose. "No, not today."

Glad that it wasn't one of Travis's family members coming to talk on his behalf and to encourage her not to divorce him, she walks back to the living room sofa, and while sitting there, she mumbles, "No one can stop me from doing what I should have done thirteen years ago. They have no clue what Travis has put me through. No more. I've had enough."

Late one Saturday night, while watching TV, Crystal sits rolling her hair for church the next morning and looks away from the TV at Travis walking through the front door, carrying a small paper bag.

In the kitchen, he unpacks it, setting the bottle of dark rum on the countertop and saying, "Crystal, have a drink with me."

"I don't want one," she says, snapping a roller into place.

Travis refuses to take no for an answer and fills two tumblers with rum. "Come on. Have a drink."

"I said, no, Travis."

Carrying both glasses into the living room, he sets them on the coffee table in front of her and leaves the room.

Something whispers to her, "Don't trust him. Hurry up. Switch glasses," and before he comes out of the bathroom, Crystal switches them. Acting normal as he hands her the glass she switched, Crystal sets it down on the coffee table, and repeats herself, "I don't want it."

"Crystal, I just want us to spend some time together talking. Can we at least do that?" he says, as he has a seat at the other end of the sofa.

"Talk about what?" she sneers, watching as he sips his drink of rum and Coke. She thinks, *If he did put some witch potion in my drink, it would affect him and not me.*

Done rolling her hair, and by her own choice, Crystal reaches for the tumbler and takes a sip from it. The rum bottle soon becomes half empty as they bicker about the failed marriage.

35

Underneath November's bright blue sky, Crystal keeps warm by the sun's heat, and as the sun combats the chill of fall, she's busy raking the dry leaves in the front yard when a yellow truck, with Travis in the passenger seat, backs up into the driveway.

Crystal stops raking and asks as he exits the truck, "Travis, what's going on?"

"You want me gone, so I'm moving out," he says, stepping onto the porch, mad because Crystal discovered his deceitfulness and forced him to leave.

Having a rapturous burst of energy, she continues to rake the leaves into a massive pile. Her joyfulness then switches to feelings of sadness as she begins to think about the children growing up without their father in the home and the hardship it will have on her, *I can do this,* she tells herself. *I've been doing it with him here, and I have trusted God this far. I'm going to continue walking by faith for the rest of the journey.*

Yesterday, she quit beauty school so she could be home when the children get there.

Crystal then looks up from raking and watches as Travis removes his belongings from the house and loads them on the back of the truck. She continues to rake while contemplating: *Giving up my hairstyling career is what I had to do. The kids are my number one priority. I don't want them returning home from school and I'm not here. Plus, I don't want to put my responsibilities on Kimberly. At eleven, she shouldn't have to miss out on her childhood, babysitting, because I chose to divorce their father.*

Hearing the truck engine roar, Crystal looks up from raking and watches Travis ride away. She mumbles, "I'm glad he moved out before the kids came home."

That night, having never suspected their parents' marriage was doomed because Crystal concealed it very well, they sat around the dinner table asking questions. "Mama, what happened to the stereo, daddy's bass guitar and his speakers are gone, too?"

Eating in the living room because there's no seat for her at the table, she answers, "Your father and I are not together anymore. He moved out and left us the house."

With sadness in her tone, Kimberly asks, "Y'all getting a divorce, Mommy?"

Crystal stirs her mashed potatoes and reluctantly answers after a minute of silence, "Yes, Kim, we are."

All four heads drop, and they begin to eat in silence. Their drooping faces express their pain.

Crystal tells them, "Just because your dad isn't here with us, doesn't mean you won't see him. You will. So don't be sad. He loves you."

A daddy's girl, Kimberly asks, "Where is he?"

"He has his own apartment. You all will be going there and will stay the weekends with him, sometimes."

Crystal then witnesses their sad disposition change to one of an approving smile. Kimberly begins to tease as always, taking after her father for laughs. "I can't wait so I can tell Daddy what you did, Brandt. You're going to get the belt."

Everyone, but him, begin to laugh.

Feeling very much in control of her life and her destiny, since taking a leap of faith, two months ago, to raise the children without Travis hanging around, Crystal stands over the kitchen sink washing dishes. Occasionally looking out of the window while in deep thought, she sees the mailman walk across the snow-covered yard and onto the porch.

Turning off the water, she rushes through the living room and out the front door, yanking the one piece of mail from it before grabbing hold of the storm door as it's closing, and quickly goes back inside before her body senses the coldness outside.

Ripping open the one piece of mail, Crystal withdraws the divorce decree from the envelope. Her one-sided, loveless marriage is over—finally!

After reviewing the decree for content and clarity, she then drops it onto the dining-room table, and as she resumes washing the dishes, Crystal thinks, *It's difficult, bringing up these four children alone.* She wipes a plate clean and rinses it. She then begins to talk to God. "I am thankful that Travis pays child support, and even though welfare takes it, I'd rather receive welfare so the children can benefit from the healthcare and dental care it provides."

Interrupting, the phone rings, and she answers it.

"Hi, girl," says Penny.

"Hi."

"What are you doing?"

Now standing in the dining room window, Crystal answers, "I'm cleaning the kitchen and thinking about my life without Travis being here."

"Girl, I was shocked when Leon told me. I didn't know y'all were having problems."

"He wasn't having any problems, but I was," Crystal giggles as she kneels down in front of the window, looking out. "I know welfare is going to bother me about getting a job but I am going to refuse to leave these children home alone to get into things God only knows about."

On her knees and watching cars pass by, Crystal jokes, "If they insist I work, I bet if I show up at their office all the time because I keep losing my job, they'll get tired of seeing me and then tell me to just stay home."

They laugh a good laugh.

After ending the conversation, Crystal returns to the kitchen to finish the dishes. She then remembers karate and mumbles, "I haven't been to class lately. I miss karate. Two more tests and I'll be a black belt."

Crystal leaves the kitchen. Passing through the dining room and into the hallway, she realizes, thinking, *it's Tuesday*. Crystal decides and tells herself, "I'm going to class tonight."

Master Masterson stands with his back to the door when Crystal walks into the gym. The sound of it closing gets his attention. Turning to look, he sees her and smiles. Rushing towards her, he says, "Hi.

It's been a while since I've seen you. How's everything, and the kids?"

Crystal, also smiling, glances around the gym and answers, "Everything is going good, and the kids are doing fine."

"Great! I'm glad that you came to join us tonight," he says, punching into the air.

"You always do that." She giggles, tying her red belt around her waist. "I hoped you would be here. It's not the same when you're away at other recreational centers."

"I do be here. You're the one who doesn't come."

Crystal then bows and walks onto the training floor. Moving up and down it, kicking and punching. She then roll her eyes when Master Masterson shouts, "Ms. Wallace, those punches are weak. I want to see power coming from those punches."

In motion to execute a punch, Crystal gives it her all, punching so hard she feels her shoulder socket jerk, and then cringes in pain. But no matter how hard she tries, the love, the passion, and the fight that were in her are no more.

Now sitting on the sideline, watching other students perform katas, and waiting her turn, Crystal's mind wanders. *The mood in here sure has changed,* she thinks.

Reflecting, she begins to feel the noticeable difference in the gym's atmosphere, which was once filled with animosity.

"Next," yells Master Masterson.

Crystal stands, bows, and runs onto the training floor, where she stands before him. He gives the command, and she begins to perform her katas.

After everyone had had a turn, the class was then dismissed.

Crystal goes and stands near the door, removing her red belt. She feels dismayed, thinking, *I did so poorly tonight.*

She turns and faces the training floor, curious as to why karate class isn't the same anymore. She hears laughter and glances over at Master Masterson across the gym, chatting with someone.

He's here, so it's not his presence that I've been missing. So what is it? she concludes her thinking.

Folding the long red belt, being careful not to let it touch the floor, Crystal then removes the white uniform top she's wearing and starts to neatly wrap it around the belt as she continues to question herself about the lack of interest in karate and is hit hard by reality, screaming inside her head, *It's Travis!*

He had harassed her so badly about joining that she must have joined out of frustration. Unknowingly, using karate as the arena in which every punch and kick that she executed was aimed at Travis. Imaginarily, he was her punching bag, and while releasing years of pent-up anger, it worked to her advantage, defeating Travis and regaining her freedom.

Satisfied with her analysis, Crystal then yells across the gym at Master Masterson, "Bye-bye," and waves. Walking toward the door, she softly mumbles, *"If I don't see you again, I will always cherish our friendship."*

Trotting down the many steps outside, in the dark, she rushes to catch the bus. On it, Crystal stares out of the window at the streetlights passing in the night, while embracing motherhood and thinking, *My children are home waiting for me. They're my love and my focus now.*

Along with the children, and now taking in alteration work, it keeps her busy, which helps financially. Seated in the living room, altering the hem on a pair of women's pants, Crystal glances away from her work and observes Candice and Brandt, now first graders, sitting in front of the TV, ignoring the program. Crystal listens curiously as they express certain things that happened earlier in the day at school. Candice laughs so hard she can't complete her sentences.

Watching, Crystal realizes that Candice very seldom stutters these days and while stitching the pants hem, Crystal confronts the issue that arises within her: *What if Candice feels nervous and anxious again, causing her to stutter?*

The words the voice instructed her to say, "Candice, take your time, think about what you want to say, and then say it," came to mind, reassuring Crystal that the technique worked so well, she shouldn't worry.

While watching Candice's bright personality shine forth and her wall of defense tumble and shatter into dissipating, itty-bitty pieces, Crystal smiles, amazed at how well they have grown.

Once again, she hears the voice whisper, "Love them. They belong to me."

Instantly, for the first time, Crystal realizes, *I do love them.* She then silently prays, T*hank you, God, for teaching me to love and not hate and for restoring me to my normal self.*

He that loveth not knoweth not God; for God is love, (1 John 4:8).

36

Travis suddenly takes ill and is in the hospital's ICU. Lying on his back, unable to speak and with a tracheostomy tube down his throat, he looks towards the door and sees Crystal walk into the room.

Smiling, he watches her walk up to the bed and greets her with a nod.

So the day has come, and finally you're getting what you deserve, she thinks. Instead, she says, "Hi, I started classes at the community college while the kids are in school. I'm on my way now. I just wanted to stop by to see you."

He nods and tries to speak. Crystal reads his lips, "Thank you."

To see him like this and in such a vulnerable state, there is nothing that would be more pleasing than to tell him what she's thinking, but she's not that person. Crystal only feels sympathy.

"Are you comfortable?" she asks, brushing aside her sadness.

Travis nods.

A nurse then walks into the room. Instantly feeling relieved, Crystal silently expresses to herself, *Time to make my escape.* She leans over the side of the bed railing, "I have to go, but I'll be back when I can."

Within days, Travis is moved out of the ICU and into his own room. Every day, Crystal and the children wait to hear that he will be released. Seated around the dining table, Crystal and Kimberly sort his medical bills. "At least, when Daddy gets out, most of his bills will be paid."

"And there's a lot of them," says Crystal, as she decides to pay the least amount of what he can afford, stacking them into a pile.

It's months later when he's released.

On the phone with Kimberly, now eighteen, Crystal is told, "Mommy, this morning, they transported Daddy to a nursing home facility outside of Dayton, where he'll have to be on a ventilator."

"This morning?" asks Crystal in shock.

"They said there was nothing more that they could do for him, and they had to arrange for him to be placed into a nursing home."

"He was there a long time," says Crystal. "But we hoped he would get better."

"Grandma and grandpa will be driving there on Saturday to visit him. I can't go because I have to work."

"You can't take off?"

"No, I'm still on probation."

"Well, your sisters, brother, and I will go with your grandparents on Saturday."

While at the facility, weeks later, Crystal and Grace walk from the parking lot with one of Travis's doctors, asking, "What is wrong with him?"

The perplexed female doctor, walking with a fast pace, then tells them, "We're not sure if it's an autoimmune disease. We've done many tests and we can't figure out what it is."

Not knowing is very frustrating for Crystal as she finally walks into Travis's room. As always, he is happy to see her and smiles. At least until she tells him, "I'm selling the house."

His eyes widen as he stares into hers. He didn't expect it as tears begin to appear.

"With a mortgage and four teenagers, I can't afford to keep it any longer."

She then bends forward and reads what Travis writes on the device in front of him, *Do what you have to do,* and t*ry to get as much as you can for it.*

Crystal nods. "I will."

On the highway, riding in the back of Travis's father's van with the three younger children, Crystal listens to the conversation Travis's paternal parents are having in the front seat. She begins to drift away, drowning out everyone's voices and the noises from the road until she's preoccupied with thinking of Travis's reaction to her decision to put the house up for sale, *I wonder if he was sad because he thought he would return to the house and live?*

Turning her head to now look out the side window, Crystal's thinking becomes fixed on what the doctor said, and she tells herself, *It's strange that the doctors don't know what's wrong with Travis. If it was cancer due to many years of smoking, they could determine that, but it's been months now, and still nothing.*

At home, Crystal can't stop thinking about it. Sitting on the living room sofa with the TV on, gazing out of the picture window from a distance, Crystal questions herself, *Why can't I stop thinking that it was food or drink that made him sick. He was drinking a diet drink to lose weight. I told him that he shouldn't drink that stuff. Could it be that?!*

"This is strange," she mumbles, and as she continues to sit looking out the front picture window and into the past, the puzzle pieces begin coming together in her head, showing that night when Travis insisted that she have a drink with him.

As though to haunt her, Crystal then hears the words she spoke years ago, *Travis, if you ever hit me again, you better kill me or I will kill you.*

Shocked at what the Holy Spirit is revealing, Crystal stands to her feet. As though to get a closer look at what she's observing, she walks over to the window beside the fireplace. Gazing out, she mutters, "If that drink was meant to harm me, then I am thankful that I listened to the voice and switched the glasses."

Feeling agitated while looking out past the pine tree that stands at the side of the house and partially blocks the view of the park, Crystal rests both hands on the window frame for support. As she bows her head, she asks silently, *God,* is *it really true*? W*as it an attempt to take my life?*

That, she will never know for sure.

Two weeks after the house is put on the market, a sign that reads, 'sold', now stands in the front yard.

Fortunately, before she and the three younger children move out, Crystal locates a new three-bedroom apartment not far from the house, and they move in weeks before Thanksgiving.

Receiving survivors' benefits, Crystal comes off welfare and now works. Employed at a factory, working third shift—the hardest shift to work—she's paired with a young man five years younger than she. At thirty-nine, Crystal strikes up a conversation as he reaches into the laundry bin and pulls out a tan colored hospital blanket.

"I see you moving all over this building. What is your position here?"

He hands her one corner of the blanket, explaining, "I'm the shift lead worker. I basically keep the work flowing and help out wherever I'm needed."

Poorly keeping up with his pace, Crystal rushes to place the blanket onto the pressing machine, saying, "Well, I need you to slow it down. You're working a little too fast, and it's making me tired."

There's giggling from male coworkers nearby.

"We're not allowed to," he says, quickly grabbing another blanket from the cart. "The machines are set to run fast. You have to keep up."

As Crystal finally adapts to his rhythm and starts to keep up, he entertains her with his naturally comical word usage that makes her giggle.

Before the night is complete, she enters into a new relationship.

While held in his arms, two months later, she looks into his dark pupils, and interrupts the words his eyes are saying, "I love you." And as he looks into hers, her eyes express to him, "I love you."

Detecting his gentle spirit, and giggling, Crystal verbalizes before kissing him, "You have spiritual qualities about you. I laugh because you don't know it yet."

They're sitting and eating carry-out in the kitchen of her new apartment home before work, when Sheena, now seventeen, answers the ringing phone. In the living room that's adjacent to the kitchen, she begins to cry.

"What is it, Sheena?" Crystal asks.

Almost breathless, her words stumble from her lips, "My daddy. He died."

"Sheena, no," says Crystal as she goes and wraps her arms around her daughter, holding her until she stops crying.

When Crystal can no longer subdue the anguish that she feels, she unleashes it while in the arms of her new love, bursting into tears—not for Travis, but for her children. All that she has gone through with him, she did it for them while learning that God is real.

Author Notes

I now understand that marriage is ordained by God and should not be rushed into, nor should it be taken lightly. If you are contemplating marriage and having children, just know that it is a lifelong commitment that one should consider wisely and with a clear conscience—with no ulterior motives and without being influenced by persuasion.

I now understand and believe that marriage should be a union woven in and built on love—the greater the love, the stronger the marriage will be.

When marriage involves children, love must be the center focus—leaving no place for selfishness, which is an enemy to any relationship. If love is not the center focus, the family will without a doubt suffer and be outside the will of God (John 15:12).

In 1 John, chapter 4, the Bible teaches that God is love, and without love, there is no hope for a better you, a better marriage, a better family, or a better tomorrow.

About the Author

Ms. Bellamy attended Sinclair Community College in Dayton, Ohio. While there studying to pursue a career in medical office administration, she decided instead to answer the call in which she had been spiritually led to begin the intensive work of writing her first book, *Spirit Led, Conscience Guided,* Something is Real, a true story.

It wasn't easy to relive the horror she suffered, but Ms. Bellamy's hope is that by telling her story, she would enlighten and empower the lives of people experiencing similar life-changing challenges.

As a grandmother and great-grandmother, Ms. Bellamy looks forward to the future as she instills in her grandchildren that God is not just real, but God's spirit dwells within. God's power does not depend solely on the name of Jesus as its source; it will manifest and operate regardless.

www.ingramcontent.com/pod-product-compliance
Lightning Source LLC
LaVergne TN
LVHW010601100826
845148LV00014B/2801

* 9 7 9 8 2 3 4 0 6 2 4 3 7 *